THE ONE IN THE MANY

D1115859

THE ONE IN THE MANY

A Contemporary Reconstruction
of the God-World Relationship

JOSEPH A. BRACKEN, S.J.

William B. Eerdmans Publishing Company
Grand Rapids, Michigan / Cambridge, U.K.

© 2001 Wm. B. Eerdmans Publishing Co.
All rights reserved

Wm. B. Eerdmans Publishing Co.
255 Jefferson Ave. S.E., Grand Rapids, Michigan 49503 /
P.O. Box 163, Cambridge CB3 9PU U.K.

Printed in the United States of America

06 05 04 03 02 01   7 6 5 4 3 2 1

Library of Congress Cataloging-in-Publication Data

Bracken, Joseph A.
    The one in the many: a contemporary reconstruction of the God-world
relationship / Joseph A. Bracken
        p.   cm.
    Includes bibliographical references.
    ISBN 0-8028-4892-3 (pbk.: alk. paper)
        1. Philosophical theology.   2. Intersubjectivity — Religious aspects —
Christianity.   3. Process theology.   4. Trinity   I. Title.

BT55.B73   2001
231.7 — dc21

                                                            2001040272

www.eerdmans.com

To the memory of my brother Ed,
whose courage while dying of cancer
impressed us all so deeply,
this book is fondly dedicated

Contents

Foreword

It's not only within philosophy. Also in discussions within the sciences, the humanities, and theology one finds these days a renewed interest in metaphysical reflection. Thus one cannot help but welcome a perceptive and well-informed book that attempts a "reconstruction" of metaphysics in response to some of its most vocal critics.

Metaphysics, Professor Bracken argues, is inescapable; even its biggest opponents find themselves committing it. As much as we may labor under the influence of our social conditioning and historical location, still something there is within us that is able to transcend such boundaries. The very language that locks us in also holds the key: "language, properly used, liberates human beings from sociocultural constraint so as to enable them to imagine and conceive the new and unexpected." Thus for Bracken even the *infant terrible*, Jacques Derrida, is still "inadvertently" writing a new metaphysics of becoming. Perhaps one or another reader will complain that the links between Derrida and Whitehead are not quite so tight. Still, the comparison is revealing, for it shows deconstruction is less free from metaphysics, and Whiteheadian metaphysics less foreign to the *Zeitgeist* (including the French one), than is often claimed.

The book makes two important contributions and should thus be of interest to two separate audiences. It is a contribution to the ongoing task of formulating an adequate doctrine of God in the face of modern skeptical critiques. Some scholars continue to work mostly within a medieval or early modern conceptual framework; others employ traditional Christian concepts without stopping to worry much about their interpretation or adequacy; and still others hook their theologies completely to the cart of this or that contemporary philosopher. Although he draws from biblical, medieval, and modern traditions, Joseph Bracken's research program fits under none of these categories. In a series of essays and books over the last years, Bracken has developed a distinctive position; *The One in the Many* represents his most sophisticated effort to date. It will be appreciated by scholars and students in systematic theology, the history of metaphysics, and philosophical theology.

The book has a second audience, however: those interested in the fate of religion in general, and belief in God in particular, in what many are now calling a "postmodern" age. Bracken wisely writes the book against the backdrop of this debate, giving ground where important modern assumptions have become questionable and yet maintaining the viability of metaphysical reflection in a postmodern (or, as he prefers, "late modern") guise. To my mind, the book sets precisely the right balance in this debate: it does not become imprisoned within the epistemology and methodology disputes, as many authors do, nor does Bracken merely nod his head in passing at the challenges and then lose himself in old-style metaphysics. Instead he asks the reader to engage in systematic reflection with him and shows, *in the midst of such reflection,* how the late modern context affects our very approach to the question of God. There are very few books on the market that detail for the postmodern skeptic how she can still engage in constructive theology in light of the contemporary challenges. Reading the book, I was repeatedly struck to see a sophisticated metaphysical thinker granting at the same time "the inevitably tentative character of all metaphysical schemes," including his own.

Because of its breadth and clarity, the text offers an excellent (if not uncritical) introduction to many of the key thinkers and movements in contemporary philosophical theology. One learns about Whitehead's thought, of course, but also about more recent process or "neo-Whiteheadian" thinkers; about American pragmatism; about French deconstruction; about the systems philosophy of Erwin Laszlo; about traditional metaphysics, Roman Catholic theology, and neo-Thomist thought; and — most rare among books in this field — about the resources of non-Western thought for conceiving God in a postmodern context. I particularly single out the chapter on the vertical dimension of the metaphysics of intersubjectivity, which draws on the great founder of the Kyoto School of Zen Buddhism, Nishida Kitaro (chapter 4).

What is remarkable about this book is that the constructive thesis it contains *actually does* in theoretical terms what it advocates in methodological terms. Bracken urges the reader away from pure theory and toward acknowledging the situatedness and contingency of all reflection; his methodology thus focuses on communities, dialogue, and interrelationship. What is fascinating is that his theoretical position does precisely the same thing. Bracken offers a metaphysics of community or what he calls "intersubjectivity." This allows him to correct for the overemphasis on substance, Being, and other static categories in the history of Western thought (I will not repeat his various criticisms here). But it also allows him to criticize thinkers who claim to offer community without preserving conceptually the very subjects who are supposed to be engaged in intersubjective dialogue. Thus he argues against Derrida, Elizabeth Johnson, and purely ethical post-theologies (e.g., Jean-Luc Marion). Part II presents his constructive response in detail — a metaphysical position that is meant to be the outworking in theoretical terms of the practice of communities in dialogue! The impact of this startling thesis runs all the way through the book: from Bracken's modification of Whitehead to his resistance to the French radicals; from his appropriation of St. Thomas to his critique of Habermas; from his refinements to feminist theology to his appreciation of Japanese Buddhist thought.

"My starting point is Christian theology," Bracken notes at one point. If so, it is not a theology that isolates. The subsequent journey is motivated by "the need for common ground." One may not agree with all Bracken's moves along the way, or with all of his criticisms of his fellow travelers (thus, for example, I do not agree that my own view leaves "no philosophical common ground with nonbelievers" [p. 171]). Still, one must admire his attempt to give an account of the God-world relationship that is responsive to postmodern criticisms, to non-Western philosophies, and to science. With regard to the science-theology debate, I particularly endorse Bracken's attempt to work the widely used concepts of supervenience, emergence, and panentheism together within a broader metaphysical framework.

What is sketched here represents the most sophisticated defense yet of what I have called the Panentheistic Analogy — the view that the relationship of God to the world is in some important senses analogous to the relationship of our mind to our bodies.

Of course, one would not expect completeness in an essay that takes on some of the most difficult dilemmas in philosophy and theology. Is metaphysics still possible after Derrida (or after Kant, for that matter)? Can the intersubjective rationality of Jürgen Habermas be extended to this sort of reflection? What tensions arise when one tries to fuse the "Absolute Nothingness" of the Buddhist traditions with the concept of God? And has Bracken really succeeded in solving philosophical theology's most difficult task: to conceive God as "a non-dual reality," both "universal ground of being and a personal being at the same time"? But perhaps the strength of a scholar should be judged less by the finality of his or her words than by the importance of the fields in which he or she labors.

One thing metaphysics tends to share with its predecessor discipline, physics: both can quickly become so technical that they become completely opaque to the outsider. Bracken has produced a book that (largely) avoids that danger: the arguments are accessible to the non-professional while still making contributions to the academic discussion. Indeed, isn't this what one would expect from a position that calls itself a *relational* philosophy, a *social* ontology, an *intersubjective* logic?

PHILIP CLAYTON

Acknowledgments

Abbreviated and adapted versions of Chapters 1 and 6 have already appeared in print as articles in *Theological Studies* 59 (1998): 703-19 ("Toward a New Philosophical Theology Based on Intersubjectivity") and in *Zygon* 36 (2001): 137-52 ("Supervenience and Basic Christian Beliefs"). Likewise, in a new electronic journal, *The International Journal for Field-Being* 1 (2001), a somewhat revised version of Chapter 4 has appeared, titled "Absolute Nothingness and the Divine Matrix." Finally, a similarly revised version of Chapter 3 will appear next year as one of a series of essays comparing the philosophies of Alfred North Whitehead and Jacques Derrida. Titled *Process and Difference,* the book will be published by State University of New York Press with Catherine Keller and Anne Daniell as co-editors. My thanks to all who thus helped to make my work more widely accessible.

Introduction

In the later years of his life, the German philosopher Martin Heidegger proclaimed "the end of philosophy" as an academic discipline even as he asserted the ongoing need for philosophical reflection on contemporary issues.[1] In similar fashion, contemporary philosophers like Richard Rorty and Jacques Derrida have spurned systematic philosophical reflection in favor of a more fluid style of thinking which refuses to assign fixed meanings to philosophical concepts. Derrida, in particular, has proposed as the task of contemporary philosophy to "deconstruct" the work of the great classical philosophers and theologians and thereby to lay bare their implicit presuppositions, above all, the "logocentrism" (cf. Glossary) implicit in their thinking.[2] The indirect result of this line of thought, how-

1. Martin Heidegger, *The End of Philosophy*, trans. Joan Stambaugh (New York: Harper & Row, 1973); cf. also Stambaugh's introduction, p. xi: "The end of philosophy does not mean for Heidegger that philosophy as such has become a thing of the past, a pursuit which has outlived its meaningfulness for human nature. Nor does Heidegger mean that philosophy in its essential sense has fulfilled its telos, that the 'hard labor of the concept' [Hegel] has accomplished its task. Rather, he means that philosophy as *metaphysics* has come to a completion which now offers the possibility of a more original way of thinking."

2. Cf., e.g., Jacques Derrida, *Of Grammatology*, trans. G. C. Spivak (Baltimore: Johns Hopkins University Press, 1976), 10: "All the metaphysical determinations of truth, and even the one beyond metaphysical ontotheology that Heidegger reminds us of, are more or less immediately inseparable from the instance of the logos, or of a reason thought within the lineage of the logos, in whatever sense it is understood."

1

ever, has been for many a loss of any sense of objectivity in the publications of scholars engaged in the humanities and, to some extent, even in the natural and social sciences.

My project in writing this book, on the contrary, will be to attempt a "reconstruction" of the metaphysical tradition of the West, albeit on a new basis and with allowance being made for the justifiable critique of that tradition by Heidegger, Rorty, Derrida, and others. For, as I see it, a new social ontology (cf. Glossary) is in many respects already at work in much contemporary philosophy and theology as well as in the natural and social sciences. What is needed by way of a "reconstruction" of metaphysics, therefore, is to call attention to this largely implicit but still recognizable new way of looking at reality and to give it further elaboration in terms of a specific conceptual scheme. The metaphysical scheme which I have in mind for this book will be a somewhat modified version of the process-relational philosophy of Alfred North Whitehead. For, as I shall indicate later, while "systems philosophy" as elaborated by Ervin Laszlo and others could certainly be counted as a new social ontology in that it gives ontological priority to corporate or social realities over individual entities as their constituent members, the metaphysics of Whitehead is in my judgment even better qualified to serve as the starting-point for such a specifically social ontology because of its insistence on "actual occasions" or momentary subjects of experience (cf. Glossary) as "the final real things of which the world is made up."[3]

Thereby Whitehead retains the classical emphasis on the individ-

---

3. Alfred North Whitehead, *Process and Reality: An Essay in Cosmology,* corrected edition, ed. David Ray Griffin and Donald W. Sherburne (New York: The Free Press, 1978), 18. N.B.: It is in my reliance on a suitably modified version of Whitehead's metaphysics that I differ most significantly from the viewpoint expressed by Donald L. Gelpi, S.J., in his recently published book *Varieties of Transcendental Experience: A Study in Constructive Postmodernism* (Collegeville, Minn.: Liturgical Press, 2000). For, while we share the concern for a constructive postmodern metaphysics grounded in the North American philosophical tradition, he favors the metaphysical vision of Charles Sanders Peirce and Josiah Royce rather than that of Whitehead and his followers. In any case, it is a pity that Gelpi's book came to my attention so late in the writing of my own text since I could have included references to it in various places, above all in the Appendix where I overview the thought of other authors offering a constructive response to postmodernism.

ual entity as the agent of its own self-constitution even as he likewise maintains that these momentary subjects of experience are rarely found except in combination as members of temporally and spatially organized "societies" (cf. Glossary). These "societies," moreover, are hierarchically ordered vis-à-vis one another so as to constitute the unity of the world around us. Finally, Whitehead also claims that each actual occasion in its self-constitution "repeats in microcosm what the universe is in macrocosm";[4] for, only in this way, does it have an inbuilt tendency to aggregate with other similarly constituted actual occasions so as to constitute the various hierarchically ordered societies to which it belongs.

Over and above these basic tenets of Whitehead's metaphysics, however, I believe that Whitehead's thought can serve as a foundation of a new social ontology only if one allows for the virtual equiprimordiality of Whiteheadian "societies" with Whiteheadian "actual occasions" within his metaphysical scheme.[5] For, as I indicated above with respect to systems philosophy, within a *bona fide* social ontology one would expect corporate realities to enjoy an ontological priority over individual entities as their constituent members. Put otherwise, the *raison d'être* of actual occasions as individual entities must be to exist not in themselves but as members of various corporate realities or "societies." Hence, what needs further elaboration within Whitehead's scheme is the precise ontological status of a "society" over and above the dynamic interrelatedness of its constituent actual occasions. Societies, in other words, represent the broader social dimension of Whitehead's thought which he seems not to have thought through in all its complexity. In his own words, societies are the "layers of social order"[6] which inevitably coexist along with the individual actual occasions present in the universe at any given mo-

---

4. Whitehead, *Process and Reality*, 215.

5. Whitehead himself appears to classify "societies" as one of the "derivative notions" within his philosophical scheme (cf. chapter three of *Process and Reality*, pp. 31-36). On the other hand, he counts nexuses, namely, aggregates of actual occasions with or without the serial order characteristic of "societies," as one of the eight Categories of Existence along with actual entities or actual occasions (cf. *Process and Reality*, 22). There is, accordingly, an ambivalence in Whitehead's thought on the nature of societies.

6. Whitehead, *Process and Reality*, 90.

ment, but what precisely are we to understand by the term "layers of social order"?

Contemporary deconstructionism, as noted above, harbors a deep suspicion of the claims of classical metaphysics to an objective understanding of the world in which we live. My plan in this book, as already indicated, is to offer a new process-oriented metaphysics based on what I call a logic of intersubjectivity. Within this metaphysics of intersubjectivity, objectivity will be assessed not with reference to an external world presumed to exist apart from the individual human subject but rather with respect to the "layers of social order" which individual subjects of experience set up over time as part of their ongoing exchange with one another. Objectivity and intersubjectivity will thus be consciously aligned with one another within this metaphysical scheme. Subjects of experience inevitably presuppose a given state of affairs as the objective context for their dynamic interrelation but then subtly alter that same objective state of affairs by their sustained interaction.[7]

Moreover, as I will make clear in a subsequent chapter, if one likewise conceives of God in line with the Christian doctrine of the Trinity as a community of divine persons in dynamic interrelation, then the world of creation can be seen as a hierarchically-ordered set of communities, each with its own "layer [or layers] of social order," which is ultimately integrated into the communitarian life of the divine persons. Reality, accordingly, is on this view composed primarily not of individuals as such but, as noted above, of social totalities or systems of which the individuals are integral parts or members. Just as the three divine persons of the Christian Trinity are one God in virtue of their dynamic interrelation, so all created entities have their identity not in terms of their individual being but rather in terms of their participation in various social groupings or functioning systems of which they are members.

Much work, to be sure, has already been done along the lines of a positive response to contemporary deconstructionism. Yet no author,

7. Cf. my article "Authentic Subjectivity and Genuine Objectivity," *Horizons* 11 (1984): 290-303, where I compare Josiah Royce's ideal of a universal "community of interpretation" with Whitehead's metaphysics, in which each actual occasion is successively "interpreter" of a previous state of affairs and "sign" of a new state of affairs.

to my knowledge, has addressed the notion of a reconstructive postmodern metaphysics in precisely the same way that I plan to do. The English theologian Colin Gunton, for example, in his book *The One, the Three and the Many: God, Creation and the Culture of Modernity* proposes that a paradigm shift in the classical understanding of the One and the Many is underway in contemporary Western culture along much the same lines as I have suggested above.[8] That is, he suggests that the older understanding whereby the One was seen as a higher-order entity which gave unity and order to the empirical Many is no longer suitable to describe, in the first place, the God-world relationship and, in the second place, the multifarious relations of created entities and institutions to one another within contemporary life. What is needed, he argues, is a new communitarian understanding of the Christian doctrine of the Trinity whereby the divine persons in their dynamic interrelations provide a model of mutual coexistence and relatedness for their creatures in which the particular (as represented by the individual entity) is not sacrificed to the universal (as represented by the overarching structures of society) or vice versa.[9]

With these goals I am in complete sympathy and will seek to perpetuate them in my own work. My own project, however, will consist in giving a more systematic framework to Gunton's three "transcendentals": namely, *perichoresis,* substantiality, and relationality. My argument would be that these transcendentals are best understood within the broad lines of Alfred North Whitehead's process-relational metaphysics provided that within the latter, as noted above, the category of society be given equiprimordial status with that of actual entity or actual occasion. In this way, as I have indicated in previous publications,[10] allowance can be made for a trinitarian understanding of God within Whitehead's metaphysical scheme and, even more fundamentally, a genuinely social ontology can be developed in which the basic units of reality are not individual entities as such but social groupings or societies of such entities.

8. Colin E. Gunton, *The One, the Three and the Many: God, Creation and the Culture of Modernity* (Cambridge: Cambridge University Press, 1993), 11-125.

9. Gunton, *The One, the Three and the Many,* 129-231.

10. Cf. especially *Society and Spirit: A Trinitarian Cosmology* (Cranbury, N.J.: Associated University Presses, 1991).

Nancey Murphy in a recent book likewise claims that there is a shift taking place in the Anglo-American intellectual world from a focus on individuals as such to individuals as dynamically interrelated members of various social totalities or ontological wholes.[11] As she indicates in her introduction, this is not simply a new focus on the whole rather than the parts. Rather, it is a new recognition of the "complex mutual conditioning between part and whole."[12] In effect, she too, like Colin Gunton, is arguing for a new paradigm to govern our human understanding of the relationship between the One and the Many. Their differences lie in his giving more attention to strictly metaphysical issues (e.g., the God-world relationship) and her devoting more time to epistemological issues (e.g., truth and objectivity both in the research programs of the natural sciences and in the interpretation of Scripture). Where I myself differ from both of them, as already noted above, is in the advocacy of a single metaphysical scheme, basically the philosophy of Alfred North Whitehead, to give greater consistency, in effect to "systematize," these otherwise very insightful reflections on the paradigm shift taking place in the Western world at present.

Somewhat akin to Nancey Murphy, Calvin Schrag in his book *The Self after Postmodernity* focuses on the ways in which human beings are heavily conditioned (though not fully determined) by the historico-cultural tradition in which they find themselves even as they partially reshape that same tradition in the act of receiving it and transmitting it to others.[13] The paradigm shift for Schrag, accordingly, consists in moving from the question "What is a self?" to "Who is a self?"[14] Instead of following Descartes in thinking of the human self as a thinking substance in distinction from its body as a material sub-

11. Nancey Murphy, *Anglo-American Postmodernity: Philosophical Perspectives on Science, Religion and Ethics* (Boulder, Colo.: Westview Press, 1997).

12. Murphy, *Anglo-American Postmodernity*, 34.

13. Calvin O. Schrag, *The Self after Postmodernity* (New Haven, Conn.: Yale University Press, 1997).

14. Schrag, *The Self after Postmodernity*, 11-41. Schrag has reference to a distinction originally made by Paul Ricoeur in his Gifford Lectures between "*idem*-identity" and "*ipse*-identity" (35). *Idem*-identity corresponds to the essence or nature of a self, equivalently, the answer to what it is. *Ipse*-identity corresponds to the historical character of a self, equivalently, the answer to who it is.

stance, one should think of the self as a socio-historical reality, namely, "a who of discourse, engaged in action, communally situated, and tempered by transcendence."[15] As I shall indicate below, the human self for Schrag could readily be explained in terms of Whitehead's metaphysical scheme, in which actual occasions as momentary subjects of experience are strictly historical and social realities which nevertheless possess an element of spontaneity and originality so as not to be totally governed by that same social and historical context out of which they arise and to which they contribute in passing out of existence.

David Griffin, of the Center for Process Studies in Claremont, California, is the editor of an academic series published by the State University of New York which is explicitly dedicated to "Constructive Postmodern Thought" as a response to the negative tendencies present within "deconstructive postmodernism."[16] He himself is committed to the process-relational metaphysics of Alfred North Whitehead and his principal disciple, Charles Hartshorne, even though Griffin recognizes that other modern philosophers like Charles Sanders Peirce, William James, Henri Bergson, and others should be considered as co-contributers to the same task of a rejuvenated metaphysics for the modern era. As I have indicated above, I too am a student of Whitehead and thus share with Griffin the basic presuppositions of Whitehead's worldview. Where I differ from Griffin, at least in terms of content, is in a much stronger emphasis on the importance of "societies" within Whitehead's metaphysical scheme. In this way, I believe that I can set forth an explicitly social ontology beyond what Whitehead himself envisioned. That is, where Whitehead (and Griffin) would see the interconnectedness of everything with everything else to be grounded in the way in which each individual actual entity "mirrors" the universe in and through its internal self-constitution, I propose that these actual entities are for the most part heavily conditioned by their membership in societies or specifically social realities. Not individual entities, therefore, not even God understood as a tran-

---

15. Schrag, *The Self after Postmodernity,* 148.

16. David Ray Griffin, William A. Beardslee, and Joe Holland, *Varieties of Postmodern Theology* (Albany, N.Y.: State University of New York Press, 1989), xi-xiv.

scendent individual entity, but the societies into which they aggregate (first and foremost, the society or community of divine persons) are, if not the *final* real things of which the world is made up, at least, the *ordinary* real things of which the world is made up.

A fifth philosopher/theologian with whose thought I find myself engaged in undertaking this research project is Robert Neville of Boston University. In his book *The Highroad Around Modernism,* Neville argues that postmodernism is not so much a reaction against "modernity," i.e, the modern era of Western civilization from the Renaissance onwards, as against "modernism," a school of thought initially prominent among playwrights, architects, composers, etc., which spurned traditional cultural values in the interests of a new ahistorical approach to meaning and value.[17] In rejecting modernism, postmodernists have effectively ignored the efforts both of American pragmatists like Peirce, John Dewey, George Herbert Mead, etc., and of Whitehead and his followers to create an experientially-based metaphysics with an admittedly hypothetical starting-point but with aspirations to genuine knowledege of what is real and true.

Both Neville and I greatly admire the philosophical achievements of Alfred North Whitehead but nevertheless retain a certain reserve with respect to specific details of his system. Both of us, for example, believe that the relationship between God and creativity, the principle of process within Whitehead's system (cf. Glossary), is insufficiently clarified. Yet, where I propose that creativity is the principle or ground, first, for the existence and activity of the three divine persons of the Christian doctrine of the Trinity and then for the existence and activity of all created entities, Neville prefers to think of creativity as an underlying activity for the cosmic process which transcends the created order and is thus divine but cannot be ascribed to God as a personal (or tripersonal) being.[18] Likewise, Neville does not make use of my notion of Whiteheadian societies as structured fields of activity for their constituent actual occasions (cf. Glossary) to account for the continuity of human self-consciousness. Part of my task

17. Cf. Robert C. Neville, *The Highroad Around Modernism* (Albany, N.Y.: State University of New York Press, 1992), 1-11.

18. Cf., e.g., Robert C. Neville, *Creativity and God: A Challenge to Process Theology* (New York: Seabury, 1980), 36-47; *Eternity and Time's Flow* (Albany, N.Y.: State University of New York Press, 1993), 153-58.

in reviewing Neville's work in an appendix to this book will be to sort out more carefully both the similarities and the differences between him and myself in the matter of a constructive metaphysics for the contemporary world.

A final contemporary philosopher with whose thought I plan to engage in this volume is William Desmond, the author of *Being and the Between*.[19] Like the others mentioned above, Desmond seeks to counteract the negative influences of contemporary postmodernism by setting forth his own version of a reconstructive postmodern metaphysics. He begins by distinguishing four senses of the word "being": univocal, equivocal, dialectical, and metaxological.[20] Above all, in his understanding of the metaxological meaning of being,[21] I find him touching on themes which I propose to consider in this book. For here he analyzes the elusive middle-ground between entities existing in dynamic interrelation, what Desmond calls "the between," which serves both to join and to separate them from one another. In any event, in thus working through these different definitions of being with Desmond, I hope to come to terms with his philosophical vision as a whole and to show its affinity with the neo-Whiteheadian scheme which I have in mind to set forth as part of this book. For both of us, as I see it, are working at a genuinely social ontology as the basis for a reconstructive postmodern metaphysics.

This book, accordingly, will be divided into two parts. In the first part, after an initial chapter in which I document what I believe to be a shift toward intersubjectivity as the implicit frame of reference for thinking of the God-world relationship within contemporary Roman Catholic systematic theology, I will respond in chapter two to one of the standard objections currently being raised against the use of

19. Cf. William Desmond, *Being and the Between* (Albany, N.Y.: State University of New York Press, 1995).

20. Desmond, *Being and the Between*, 3-46.

21. Desmond describes as follows the metaxological meaning of being: "Being is given as the happening of the between; but this between is *immediately given as mediated* between a plurality of centers of existence, each marked by its own energy of self-transcendence" (*Being and the Between*, 178). Cf. also below, Appendix, pp. 207-12, where I analyze further Desmond's notion of "the between" and its relation to my own understanding of the "vertical" dimension of a metaphysics of intersubjectivity in chapter four.

metaphysics in theology and other academic disciplines. That is, in terms of Whitehead's understanding of symbolism in general and language in particular, I will make clear how human beings can use language to transcend their "social location" and thus to set forth an understanding of reality with claims to truth and objectivity that are admittedly conditioned by that same social location but not fully determined by it. In this way, drawing up a metaphysical conceptuality for the illumination of certain features of reality is not an exercise in futility, doomed to failure from the start, as many academics influenced by contemporary deconstructionism at present seem to contend. Along the same lines, in chapter three I will examine the thought of Jacques Derrida, above all his understanding of the notion of *différance* within his philosophy, and point out its remarkable similarity to the category of creativity in Whitehead's metaphysical scheme. I will not thereby be suggesting, of course, that Derrida is a "closet" Whiteheadian but only that he may be more of a metaphysician than he himself realizes. That is, in my judgment, he appears to be implicitly involved in working out a new metaphysics of becoming even as he tries consciously to "deconstruct" the classical metaphysics of being.

Then in the second part of my project I will, in successive chapters, set forth the basic outline of a process-oriented metaphysics based on what I call the logic of intersubjectivity. That is, with help from the writings of the Japanese philosopher, Kitaro Nishida, I will first lay out what I believe is the inevitable "vertical" dimension of a metaphysics of intersubjectivity, that is, its grounding in what Nishida calls "the place of nothingness" and what Jorge Nobo of Washburn University in Topeka, Kansas, and I refer to as the necessary ontological matrix or ground for all entities, even for the triune God as Creator of heaven and earth. Afterwards, in chapter five, I will set forth the "horizontal" dimension of this metaphysics of intersubjectivity, that is, how within this all-encompassing context or "place," entities or, more precisely, subjects of experience exist in dynamic interrelation to one another as members of hierarchically-organized "societies" or social totalities up to and including the "community" of the three divine persons of orthodox Christian belief. In working out this metaphysical scheme, I will try to make clear how my adaptation of Whitehead's ontology is both akin to and yet distinct from the systems philosophy of Ervin Laszlo. Along the same line, I will also draw on the reflections of Jürgen Habermas and of Bernard Lonergan, S.J., on the nature of human intersubjectivity and the ways in which human beings can reach agreement on common points of interest and concern.

In chapter six I will apply this metaphysical scheme to one of the major problem-areas in contemporary systematic theology, namely, the ongoing debate between theologians and natural scientists about divine and human agency in a world governed by deterministic laws of nature. As I judge it, the field-oriented understanding of White-headian societies which I will have set forth in chapters four and five can contribute significantly to a satisfactory solution to the mind-brain problem as well as to a contemporary God-world relationship. In brief, I will be arguing that the mind is an ongoing intentional field of activity which overlaps and includes the interrelated fields of activity within the human brain as a result of neuronal interaction. Successive moments of consciousness thereby integrate data from the brain as well as from previous moments of experience before making their own self-constituting "decision" to be transmitted through the brain to the body as a whole. Similarly, the reality of the God-world relationship is to be seen as that of an all-comprehensive field of activity constituted, in the first place, by the three divine persons of Christian belief in their dynamic interrelations, but in the second place by the world of created entities in their ongoing relations both with one another and with the divine persons.[22] In this way, the classical dualism between mind and brain, God and the world, can be avoided even as one affirms the necessary distinctive differences between "spirit" and "matter."

Finally, in an extended appendix to this work, I will return to the authors surveyed above and indicate more in detail how my own scheme

---

22. There is, of course, considerable discussion among physicists about the reality and function of fields, above all, in quantum electrodynamics (cf. here Lawrence W. Fagg, *Electromagnetism and the Sacred: At the Frontier of Spirit and Matter* [New York: Continuum, 1999], 37-58). My purpose in this book, however, will be to propose the notion of field as a philosophical rather than a strictly scientific term. That is, as I will make clear in Part Two of this book, "field," properly understood, in many ways corresponds to the classical notion of substance as the underlying principle of continuity or endurance within a philosophical cosmology.

affirms many of their insights into the way that truth and objectivity can be vindicated even in the face of contemporary deconstructionism. At the same time, I will try to make clear the advantages of presenting these same insights within a more comprehensive metaphysical scheme such as I will have presented in this book.

PART ONE

1 The Shift to Intersubjectivity within Catholic Theology

There is, as I see it, a paradigm shift taking place in contemporary Roman Catholic theology away from the classical worldview of Thomas Aquinas and other scholastic thinkers in which the philosophy of Aristotle plays such an important role to a more interpersonal approach to the God-world relationship in which God is thought to be constantly interacting with creatures in the establishment of the Kingdom of God on earth. In most quarters, this shift in methodology has been warmly welcomed. Karl Rahner's book *The Trinity*, for example, has had such an enormous influence on contemporary trinitarian theology largely because he distanced himself from the classical treatment of the doctrine of the Trinity with its focus on the "immanent Trinity" or the inner life of God apart from creation and instead directed attention to the "economic Trinity" understood as God's self-communication to creatures, above all, to human beings.[1]

---

1. Cf. Karl Rahner, *The Trinity*, trans. Joseph Donceel (New York: Herder & Herder, 1970), 36: "God's self-communication is truly a *self*-communication. He does not merely indirectly give his creature some share of himself by creating and giving created and finite realities through his omnipotent *efficient* causality. In a *quasi-formal* causality he really and in the strictest sense bestows *himself*." "Quasi-formal causality," as I see it, represents an attempt by Rahner and other contemporary scholastic thinkers to stay within the general framework of classical metaphysics and yet introduce an interpersonal dimension into the Thomistic scheme of formal, material, efficient, and final causality as explanation for the God-world relationship.

What is not so clear in Rahner's presentation, however, is the theoretical framework for this new interpersonal approach to the God-world relationship. His "formal exposition of the concept of God's self-communication" in terms of four pairs of interrelated concepts, that is, (a) Origin-Future; (b) History-Transcendence; (c) Invitation-Acceptance; (d) Knowledge-Love, by his own admission is more a brief sketch than a full-scale presentation of a new interpersonal understanding of the God-world relationship.[2]

Furthermore, in my view, Rahner never fully resolved the inevitable tension between this new interpersonal approach to the God-world (or God-human) relation and the classical Thomistic understanding of that same relation. The model of God as interpersonally involved with human beings, for example, calls into question the classical understanding of divine immutability.[3] But, when Rahner alternately pictures God as *Ipsum Esse Subsistens* or the unchanging ground of being for all creation, then God's relation to creatures is no longer strictly interpersonal. That is, precisely as the unchanging ground of being for creation, God is more the impersonal "horizon" for the drive to self-transcendence on the part of human beings rather than the Personal Other with whom one is in ongoing dialogue. As I have pointed out elsewhere,[4] there is a way to resolve this tension in the understanding of God's relation to human beings, if one distinguishes properly between *person* and *nature* within God. That is, human beings have an interpersonal relation with each of the divine persons, but they are empowered to relate thus to the divine persons only in and through their created participation in the divine nature, the unchanging divine act of being. The divine nature, in other words, is first the enabling principle of existence and activity for the three divine persons in their mutual interrelation; then, by the free choice of those same divine persons, it is likewise the en-

2. Rahner, *The Trinity*, 82-99, esp. 83: "This attempt may be questionable but there is no way of avoiding it."

3. Cf., e.g., Mark Lloyd Taylor, *God Is Love: A Study in the Theology of Karl Rahner* (Missoula, Mont.: Scholars Press, 1986); see also, however, Howard Ebert, "Immutability of God: Metaphysical Inconsistency or Essential Grounding for Human Transcendence," *Philosophy and Theology* 8 (1993): 41-61.

4. Cf. my book, *The Divine Matrix: Creativity as Link between East and West* (Maryknoll, N.Y.: Orbis Books, 1995), 25-37, 52-69.

abling principle or ground of being for all creatures in their relationships to one another and to the divine persons. But this model is
somewhat removed from Rahner's own conception of the God-world
relationship. Hence, the tension in his thought between the classical
Thomistic understanding of the God-world relationship and the new
interpersonal approach to that same relationship which he himself
evidently favors appears to be unresolved.

In any event, my purpose in the present chapter will be to argue
that only a consciously conceived metaphysics of intersubjectivity
such as I have hinted at above, with its starting-point in the coexistence of subjects of experience in dynamic interrelation at different
levels of reality, will in the end prove to be a worthy successor to the
all-embracing metaphysics of being worked out by Thomas Aquinas
and his successors. Neo-Thomism as represented by Karl Rahner,
Bernard Lonergan, and others, on the contrary, seems to be more a
form of philosophical/theological anthropology than a cosmology or
metaphysics as with Thomas Aquinas. That is, its starting-point is
the individual human being in his or her drive toward transcendence
through dynamic relationship with the Other, both divine and human.[5] While this is from the perspective of Roman Catholic ortho-
doxy an enormous improvement over the methodological starting-
point of Immanuel Kant and his followers, it still indirectly reflects
the individualistic substance-oriented metaphysics of Aquinas and
Aristotle. As we shall see below, the late Catherine LaCugna argued
passionately for the substitution of "person" for "substance" as the

5. Cf. here Andrew Tallon, *Personal Becoming* (Milwaukee: Marquette University Press, 1982), esp. 161-77. Tallon's thesis is that in terms of Rahner's scheme
one becomes oneself through others: "One becomes a knower both through the
other who is God (the non-objectively co-known supporting horizon) and
through the other who or which is the objectively known. One becomes a lover,
in like manner, through the other, as when, in loving the concrete other, the
source and support of all being and goodness is co-loved" (173-74). The focus,
however, is still on the individual entity in his or her "personal becoming," albeit
through the mediation of the other, both divine and human. It is not on the
group or the community as such which I maintain is the necessary starting-point
for a genuine social ontology. I would have basically the same comments with respect to the otherwise very insightful essay of Kevin Hogan, "Entering into Otherness: The Postmodern Critique of the Subject and Karl Rahner's Theological
Anthropology," *Horizons* 25 (1998): 181-202.

first category of Being.[6] But, in my judgment, a fully-developed social ontology or metaphysics of intersubjectivity should begin not with an individual person even when it is consciously conceived as in ongoing relation with others, but with multiple persons who are corporately one even before they think of themselves as separate individuals. The group or social totality rather than the individual entity, in other words, should be the starting-point for a *bona fide* social ontology or metaphysics of intersubjectivity.[7]

In the following pages, accordingly, I will first offer some generalized remarks on the basic differences in orientation between a Thomistic and a Whiteheadian worldview and briefly review what I view as the advantages of the Whiteheadian scheme for a more interpersonal understanding of the God-world relationship. Then I will make clear how the objections of two prominent French Roman Catholic philosopher/theologians to the use of metaphysics in analyzing our human relationship to God can be satisfactorily met if one shifts to a Whiteheadian understanding of that relationship. Finally, I will review the much-acclaimed work of Catherine LaCugna and Elizabeth Johnson in recent years on the God-world relationship and indicate what seem to be shortcomings in their respective theories because they have not completely endorsed the implications of a social ontology or metaphysics of intersubjectivity. Their respective worldviews, in other words, are evidently no longer Thomistic in the strict sense; but basic presuppositions of that same metaphysical system still persist in their thinking about the God-world relationship which, if revised, would make their work far more consistent and for that reason much more persuasive.

---

6. Cf. below, pp. 40-41. Likewise, cf. Catherine Mowry LaCugna, *God for Us: The Trinity and Christian Life* (San Francisco: Harper, 1991), 243-317, esp. 248: "Personhood is the meaning of being."

7. One might describe the relation between the community and its person-members as non-dual. That is, the community is more than the sum of its members here and now and yet not separable from them as a reality unto itself. Cf. here my book *The Divine Matrix*, 5 and 76, where I use this term out of Hindu and Buddhist philosophy to explain with reference to the God-world relationship how the One can be immanent within the Many and yet transcendent of them at the same time.

A. Thomistic and Whiteheadian
Worldviews in Contrast

To the best of my knowledge, no one disputes the notion that Thomas Aquinas heavily relied upon the philosophy of Aristotle in constructing his own philosophical theology as expressed in the *Summa Theologiae*. Such a philosophical understanding of reality lends itself to clearly defined objective relationships in which causes and effects are carefully distinguished from one another. Nothing, in other words, can be its own cause, can bring itself into existence: *Quidquid movetur movetur ab alio* (whatever is moved is moved by another). Even within individual things which are said to move themselves, one part of the entity does the moving and the other part is moved.[8] Moreover, the part which does the moving is moved by an outside agent to perform that action and thus to pass from potency to act.[9] Admittedly, within the philosophy of Aristotle and the theology of Aquinas, there is apparently one exception: namely, the Unmoved Mover for Aristotle and God for Aquinas. But the exception is only apparent since the Aristotelian Unmoved Mover and the Thomistic God are pure actuality and thus never pass from potency to act. Accordingly, they have no need for an outside agent to move them from potency to act; they are always in act. But at the same time they are not in the strict sense self-actualizing realities. They do not experience ongoing self-realization since there is literally nothing more to actualize.

Given the rigor of this causal scheme for the God-world relationship, one may safely conclude that the Unmoved Mover for Aristotle and God for Aquinas are formally conceived not so much as dynamic subjects of experience but rather as fixed objects of thought, ultimate terms within a comprehensive set of cause-effect relationships which governs all the entities in the material world. For that matter, neither are the individual entities of this world genuinely conceived as subjects of experience since they too are theoretically related to one another as objective terms of various cause-effect relationships rather than as self-creative or self-actualizing realities vis-à-vis one another. Here one might well object that within the theology of Aquinas there

8. Aristotle *Physics* 257b13.
9. Aristotle *Physics* 202a4ff.

is explicit mention of entities that move themselves and thus are in some sense self-creative. As Elizabeth Johnson points out, for Aquinas "it is a measure of the creative power of God to raise up creatures who participate in divine being to such a degree that they are also creative and sustaining in their own right."[10] Thus God through the exercise of primary causality sustains in being entities which exercise their own secondary causality in order to attain the end for which they were created. In the case of human beings, this means that God sustains them in the exercise of their intellect and free will.[11] Even when human beings misuse their intellect and free will to commit sin, God sustains them in that physical activity and, more importantly for our purposes, orders even that objectively evil action to the universal good of the world order. Nothing, therefore, escapes the plan of divine providence.[12]

This last remark alerts us, however, to what I perceive as one of the basic flaws in Thomas's understanding of the God-world relationship. For Aquinas stipulates that the end to which creation is directed in virtue of divine providence is extrinsic to creation itself; the end of creation is the divine goodness as the universal good to which all particular goods chosen by creatures are necessarily ordered.[13] Furthermore, this universal good of divine goodness is further specified in terms of an order for the world known and willed by God in

10. Elizabeth Johnson, "Does God Play Dice?" *Theological Studies* 57 (1996): 11. Cf. also Thomas Aquinas *Summa Theologiae* I, Q. 103, a. 6 resp.

11. Thomas Aquinas *Summa Theologiae* I, Q. 105, aa. 3 & 4 resp.

12. Thomas Aquinas *Summa Theologiae* Q. 103, a. 7 resp. et ad 1. Cf., e.g., John H. Wright, S.J., "Divine Knowledge and Human Freedom: The God Who Dialogues," *Theological Studies* 38 (1977): 473: "God intends to realize in the universe the order of His wisdom — an intention which ultimately cannot be frustrated. He moves the human will in accordance with the plan of divine reason, but the human will can resist this motion and withdraw itself from this detail of the divine plan. The withdrawal goes contrary to the divine intention of a particular good but does not escape the universal order of God's will. For this divine order is manifold; and when the creature withdraws from one order by sinning, he enters into order again in another way — for example, through repentance or punishment." What Wright fails to mention, of course, is that this final order of things is already fixed and immutable since it is one with God's willing of the divine being itself, as will be noted below.

13. Thomas Aquinas *Summa Theologiae* I, Q. 103, a. 2 resp.

its entirety from all eternity.[14] Since there is only one eternal act of knowing and willing within God which both constitutes the divine being and at the same time sets the pattern for the order of creation,[15] the order of creation is fully actualized just as God's own being is fully actualized. As Aquinas himself notes, the plan for the order of creation preexists in the mind of God.

The logical consequence of this line of thought, however, is implicitly what may be called theological determinism. Every action taking place within creation is known and willed by God as part of a comprehensive scheme for the order and direction of creation as a whole. There can be no changes or alterations in this scheme with the passage of time since, as Aquinas sees it, God knows and wills every action of creatures precisely as it is taking place within the cosmic process.[16] Thus, even though God knows and wills the individual free actions of human beings, these same free actions fit into a plan of creation which is known and willed in its entirety from all eternity as part of God's own divine act of being. Hence, contrary to Aquinas's own intentions with respect to human free choice, his scheme for divine providence over creation as a whole would seem to be a type of theological determinism, since nothing is left to chance in terms of the overall divine plan for creation.[17]

I turn now to the Whiteheadian scheme for the God-world relationship in which causality, to be sure, still plays a role but in which "the final real things of which the world is made up"[18] are conceived not as objects of thought, that is, as terms in an objective causal scheme, but as momentary subjects of experience in dynamic interrelation within a social context which is itself in process of evolution. In contrast to the above-mentioned worldview of Aristotle and Aquinas, therefore, everything ultimately exists in terms of self-causation: *Quidquid movetur movetur a se, non ab alio* (whatever is

14. Thomas Aquinas *Summa Theologiae* Q. 22, a. 1 resp.
15. Thomas Aquinas *Summa Theologiae* Q. 14, aa. 4 & 8 resp.; Q. 19, aa. 1 & 4 resp.
16. Thomas Aquinas *Summa Theologiae* Q. 14, a. 13 resp.
17. Thomas Aquinas *Summa Theologiae* Q. 22, a. 2 resp.
18. Alfred North Whitehead, *Process and Reality: An Essay in Cosmology*, corrected edition, ed. David Ray Griffin and Donald W. Sherburne (New York: The Free Press, 1978), 18.

moved is moved by itself, not by another). Naturally, as we will see more at length in chapter five, Whitehead also postulates that this self-causation of the individual subject of experience is heavily conditioned by its social context or past world; here is where traditional notions of efficient causality play their limited role within Whitehead's scheme. But, since it ultimately is responsible for the way in which it exists in virtue of a self-constituting "decision" (cf. Glossary), Whitehead's actual occasion or momentary subject of experience cannot be fitted into a comprehensive scheme of cause-effect relationships governing the whole of creation after the manner of Aristotle and Aquinas. It is not, in other words, simply the effect of the causal activity of another entity; it is rather in the first place the agent of its own self-constitution.

Thus chance or, more precisely, spontaneity is in principle present at every moment and at every level of creation even though these spontaneous self-creations of actual occasions have in most cases a way of "averaging out" to produce the continuities in persons and things which we have come to expect in ordinary experience. Furthermore, moral evil or sin on the part of human beings is within this scheme clearly the result of the individual's own decision even though God according to Whitehead is likewise at work through the provision of divine "initial aims" (cf. Glossary): in the first place to counsel against the evil decision in question and then, after the fact, to assist in "damage control," that is, in helping the individual human being and others affected by the evil decision to cope with the inevitable negative consequences of that same decision.[19]

Another way to make the same point is to reflect upon the different ways in which primary and secondary causality are understood first in Thomistic metaphysics and then equivalently in Whitehead's scheme. Within Thomistic metaphysics the primary cause uses the secondary cause as an instrument for the execution of its purposes. For example, a carpenter uses a hammer to drive a nail into a wooden board. Even when the secondary cause is itself a cause with respect to still other effects, as a secondary cause it is still instrumental to the intention and activity of the primary cause. St. Thomas, for example, at one place in the *Summa Theologiae* describes

19. Whitehead, *Process and Reality*, 244-45.

the humanity of Jesus as the "conjoined instrument" of Jesus in his divinity or as a divine person.[20] But this means that the free actions of Jesus fit into a plan or order of creation willed by Jesus as a divine person together with the Father and the Spirit from all eternity as part of their unchanging divine being. The same, of course, would be true of all other human beings insofar as they are understood to be secondary causes empowered to exist by God as the primary cause of their existence and activity.

Within the Whiteheadian scheme, on the other hand, the primary causality is exercised by the creature, the actual occasion in process of concrescence (cf. Glossary), not by God as supplying divine initial aims to enable the creature to make its decision. Contrary to the Thomistic scheme, therefore, in the Whiteheadian scheme divine causality is instrumental to the exercise of primary causality by the finite actual occasion in its self-constituting decision. Moreover, God cannot know the decision of the creature until the creature actually makes the decision. So there is no way that the creature's decision can fit into an unchanging divine plan for the order of creation. God's "plan" for creation within Whitehead's metaphysics is totally contingent upon the self-constituting decisions of creatures from moment to moment. All that God can envision for the future of creation is the realization of various key values such as truth, goodness, beauty, harmony, or peace. But the way in which these values will be realized is left up to the creature, not up to God.

Once again, therefore, we are confronted with the logical consequences of two quite different worldviews. In the end, therefore, one seems driven to choose between these two competing worldviews and their corresponding value-systems. Keeping this in mind, I turn now to a brief overview of the thought of several contemporary Roman Catholic philosopher/theologians who, like Rahner, seem to be "midstream" between a classical Thomistic understanding of the God-world relationship and a new more heavily interpersonal approach to the same issue.

20. Thomas Aquinas *Summa Theologiae* III, Q. 62, a. 5 resp.

B. God Without Being in the Philosophy of Jean-Luc Marion

Jean-Luc Marion is a noted French Roman Catholic philosopher who regularly lectures at the Divinity School of the University of Chicago in the United States. Some years ago he published a book *L'Être sans Dieu* which caused a sensation in both France and the United States because of its basic thesis, namely, that the existence and reality of God should no longer be interpreted in terms of the classical metaphysics of Being. Rather, God is to be understood as transcendent of Being, manifest in this world only as pure Gift or other-directed Love. While he subsequently made clear that his critique of classical metaphysics was directed not so much at Thomas Aquinas himself but rather at his successors in the tradition of scholastic metaphysics, beginning with Duns Scotus,[21] Marion himself in my judgment is still an ambivalent figure. For, while he is clearly more interested in a purely phenomenological approach to the human condition, nevertheless his more systematic reflections are still largely couched in the categories of scholastic metaphysics. Even the assertion that God is pure Gift is explained in terms of the conflict between Aquinas and Bonaventure in the Middle Ages about the divine motive for the Incarnation.[22] My proposal to him and his disciples in this subsection, therefore, would be not to abandon metaphysical ways of thinking altogether but to change metaphysical worldviews: that is, to adopt the metaphysics of Whitehead as a philosophical conceptuality which is much more congenial to a naturally interpersonal approach to the God-world relationship.

As he states in the preface to the English edition of *God Without Being,* Marion is in no way denying the existence of God: "God is, exists, and that is the least of things. At issue here is not the possibility of God's attaining Being, but, quite the opposite, the possibility of Being's attaining to God."[23] With this laconic statement, Marion makes clear his refusal to think of the God-world relation in terms of

21. Cf. Jean-Luc Marion, "Saint Thomas d'Aquin et l'onto-théo-logie," *Revue Thomiste* 95 (1995): 31-66.

22. Jean-Luc Marion, *God Without Being,* trans. Thomas A. Carlson (Chicago: University of Chicago Press, 1995), 74-75.

23. Marion, *God Without Being,* xix-xx.

a rational a priori scheme in which God as the Supreme Being is the transcendent First Cause of all creatures as finite beings. This is in his mind to subject the God of biblical revelation to the logical requirements of a humanly constructed cosmology with Being as its principal concept and with the four Aristotelian causes (material, formal, efficient, and final) as its basic principles of explanation. Rather, one should begin with revelation, namely, the biblical statement that "God is love" (1 John 4:8), and proceed from there to an understanding of God's relation to the world, above all, to human beings.

What becomes clear, then, is "the absolute freedom of God with regard to all determinations, including, first of all, the basic condition that renders all other conditions possible and even necessary — for us, humans — the fact of Being."[24] We human beings must first be before we can act and eventually love. But "God loves before being, He only is as He embodies himself — in order to love more closely that which and those who, themselves, have first to be."[25] My question to Marion, however, is whether he has thought deeply enough about the nature of subjectivity, both divine and human. Perhaps not only God as the divine subject of being or existence but likewise all finite subjects of being only exist insofar as they objectify or embody themselves. They must, in other words, give objective expression or actuality to their underlying potentiality as subjects of existence in order simply to be.

Admittedly, this runs counter to the common sense axiom in scholastic metaphysics, *agere sequitur esse* (activity follows upon being). But perhaps this is the key point in dealing with the nature of subjectivity which Marion only realized with respect to God, namely, that *esse sequitur agere* (being follows upon activity). Contrary to common sense, subjectivity or potentiality is ontologically prior to objectivity or actuality. Alfred North Whitehead's understanding of "actual entities," for example, is grounded in this insight. That is, for Whitehead actual entities are the end-result of their individual processes of becoming.[26] Once their process of becoming is completed,

24. Marion, *God Without Being,* xx.
25. Marion, *God Without Being,* xx.
26. Whitehead, *Process and Reality,* 29, 245.

they are finished actualities ("superjects," in Whitehead's terms) but they thereby cease to be active subjects of experience. Their potentiality is used up in becoming this or that actuality; a new potentiality, a new subject of experience, has to come into being as successor to the antecedent actual entity if the "society" of which the two actual entities are members is to continue in existence.[27]

Thus Marion's polemic against metaphysical modes of thought may be misplaced. In my judgment, he is eminently correct in calling attention to the deficiencies of classical metaphysics in subordinating the biblical understanding of God to the philosophical categories of Aristotelian/Thomistic metaphysics. But the response to that critique, as I see it, is not to abandon metaphysical modes of thought altogether but to set forth a new metaphysics in which God and creatures can be understood as subjects of experience in dynamic interrelation rather than as inert objects of thought within an a priori causal scheme. In what follows, therefore, I will cite passages out of Marion's *God Without Being* and indicate how God's enigmatic presence and absence to human beings in the works of creation can be readily explained in terms of a philosophy of intersubjectivity in which by definition the subject always "transcends" its objective manifestations and thus is never fully available to the gaze or scrutiny of another subject (divine or human).

Marion, for example, makes a careful distinction between *idol* and *icon*. His argument, in brief, is that the classical identification of God with Being has become an idol which impedes our human communication with God; it is no longer an icon which facilitates that communication. As he notes, "the icon and the idol are not at all determined as beings against other beings, since the same beings (statues, names, etc.) can pass from one rank to the other. The icon and the idol determine two manners of being for beings, not two classes of beings."[28] An idol, in other words, in the eyes of the beholder ultimately substitutes for the reality which it signifies; an icon, on the other hand, is transparent to that same reality. Put in other terms,

---

27. Cf. below, chapter five, however, where I evaluate the recent hypothesis of Judith Jones on the enduring actuality of actual entities even after their process of self-constitution is completed.

28. Marion, *God Without Being*, 8.

within the divine-human exchange the idol refers back to the human being in his or her vain search for an adequate understanding of the divine Other. As Marion remarks, "the idol consigns the divine to the measure of a human gaze."[29] The icon, on the other hand, refers principally to the divine subjectivity in its quest for communication with the human subject through some sensible medium. "Whereas the idol results from the gaze that aims at it, the icon summons sight in letting the visible [the icon] be saturated little by little with the invisible [God as the divine subjectivity]."[30] God as "the unenvisageable" becomes partially manifest in a sensible object which radiates divinity to the believer much as the face of the human other imperfectly manifests the subjectivity of that person to one beholding it.[31]

Here I would maintain that not just divine subjectivity but in principle all subjectivity is necessarily impervious to what Marion refers as the "gaze." Hence, when Marion says that "the icon is defined by an origin without original: an origin itself infinite, which pours itself out or gives itself throughout the infinite depth of the icon,"[32] this can also be said with qualifications about human beings in their intersubjective encounters, even about animals and other living creatures insofar as they manifest a form of subjectivity. Naturally, the divine subjectivity is more difficult to discern since it is presumably more complex and certainly more variegated in its self-expression than the subjectivity of a human being or some other living creature. But in principle every subjectivity, however lowly, is "infinite" in that it cannot be fully objectified even in the eyes of an all-seeing God. Otherwise, it would cease to be a subject of experience and become instead simply an object of thought, even for God.

Marion seems to recognize this distinction between subjectivity and its objective expression in human concepts when he notes: "It is not a question of using a concept to determine an essence but of using it to determine an intention — that of the invisible advancing into the visible and inscribing itself therein by the very reference it imposes from this visible to the invisible."[33] Marion is contrasting

29. Marion, *God Without Being*, 14.
30. Marion, *God Without Being*, 17.
31. Marion, *God Without Being*, 17-20.
32. Marion, *God Without Being*, 20.
33. Marion, *God Without Being*, 23.

here the language of objectivity and subjectivity. Used objectively, a concept delimits an essence or fixed object of thought. Used inter-subjectively, a concept mediates an intentional presence, the presence of the Other to the self. No fixed object of thought "advances" from the invisible to visibility. But a subject of experience is constantly "advancing" from the depths of subjectivity into the clear light of objectivity (even for itself), thence to "retreat" into subjectivity before "advancing" one more time into still another form of self-expression.

In subsequent chapters of *God Without Being,* Marion distinguishes between "God" and G[⊠]D. "God" is for Marion a legitimate understanding of God for a given historical epoch but one which has become an idol insofar as it is mistakenly identified as the full reality of God. "It ["God"] clearly exposes what *Dasein,* at the moment of a particular epoch, experiences of the divine and approves as the definition of its 'God.' Only such an experience of the divine is not founded so much in God as in man."[34] As an example of this procedure, Marion singles out the implicit equation of God with moral goodness. "Of all the attributes which the understanding assigns to God, that which in religion, and especially the Christian religion, has the pre-eminence, is moral perfection. But God as a morally perfect being is nothing else than the realized idea, the fulfilled law of morality. . . . The moral God requires man to be as he himself is."[35] There is, of course, nothing wrong with attributing moral perfection to God, provided that one does not thereby confuse the divine subjectivity with one of its objective manifestations or characteristics. When this identification is made, however, inevitably someone like Friedrich Nietzsche will arise to denounce that particular ideal of moral goodness and by implication proclaim the "death of God." Paradoxically, as Marion points out, critics like Nietzsche perform a service for the religious community in that, by exposing a given concept of God as an idol, they indirectly clear the way for a new self-manifestation of the divine in still another form.[36] Quoting Heidegger, Marion notes that "god-less thinking" is in this sense more open

34. Marion, *God Without Being,* 30.
35. Marion, *God Without Being,* 31.
36. Marion, *God Without Being,* 32.

to the full reality of God than so-called "ontotheologic" or classical metaphysics is prepared to admit.[37]

G[⊠]D, on the other hand, represents God beyond the reference to any objective predicate or determination, even the most fundamental predicate of all, the predicate of Being. For, as Marion comments, "[t]he thought that thinks Being as such cannot and must not apprehend anything but beings, which offer the path, or rather the field of a meditation, of Being. Any access to something like 'God,' precisely because of the aim of Being as such, will have to determine him in advance as a being."[38] For one thinking in the context of Being, God inevitably is conceived as a being among other beings and thus as something less than the full reality of God. But how is one to understand the reality of God vis-à-vis creatures except as a being, albeit a transcendent being? Marion's answer is to refer to the pages of the Christian Bible and to describe God as Love: "God can give himself to be thought without idolatry only starting from himself alone: to give himself to be thought as love, hence, as gift; to give himself to be thought as a thought of the gift."[39]

Much as I agree with Marion that God is most aptly described as self-giving love in line with the Gospel of John, I suggest that there is a fundamental ambiguity here which dulls the sharpness of his insight. For love is, after all, an activity. But an activity does not exist on its own; it is always the activity of a subject of experience. Hence, as I see it, behind the affirmation of God as transcendent Love and Gift is the reality of God as the ontological source of that love and gift, namely, God as the transcendent Subject of experience who manifests Godself in and through the gift of perfect love to creatures. But, be it noted, this is not to ascribe to God still another objective perfection like that of Being. Subjectivity by definition is not an objective perfection but the ontological source of objective perfections like Being or Goodness or Love. In itself, it is more a potentiality than an actuality. And yet it is not a pure potentiality, the logical equivalent of nothingness. Rather it is a dispositional potentiality, one which is antecedently structured by its own past free decisions to

37. Marion, *God Without Being*, 35.
38. Marion, *God Without Being*, 43.
39. Marion, *God Without Being*, 49.

manifest itself in this way rather than that way. Thus God as Love can be trusted to behave consistently toward human beings in a loving way because this is the way that God has revealed Godself over the centuries, as becomes evident through the prayerful reading of the Bible.

Does this demand of the believer an act of faith, a trust in the enduring goodness of God? To be sure, so it does. But so also does our confidence in the goodness of another human being demand an implicit act of faith, a trust in the other's fidelity. No more than with the subjectivity of God, can we read the subjectivity of another human being and be absolutely certain that the other will continue to act toward us as he or she has acted in the past. This is the nature of intersubjective relationships which removes them from the certitudes of the logical order and gives them an existential quality which can be at times unnerving but which in the end is the source of their deep attraction for us. As Marion notes in his chapter on the reversal of vanity, for one locked within the scheme of his own logical abstractions, life is secure but ultimately very boring.[40]

Finally, at the end of the chapter on "The Crossing of Being," Marion distinguishes between two types of giving in the context of Being. There is, on the one hand, the giving implicit in the German *es gibt* and, on the other, the French *il y a* in which there is no implicit reference to the giver of the gift. Attention is focused simply on the constancy of the giving of being or existence as pure fact.[41] On the other hand, there is a giving within the context of Being which "must be understood by reference to the giver. . . . The gift gives the giver to be seen, in repeating the giving backward."[42] Here a distance opens up between the gift of being and the giver of the gift. God is seen as the author of the gift of being. But, for that same reason, God "does not have to be, nor therefore to receive the name of a being, whatever

40. Marion, *God Without Being*, 115-19. Marion, to be sure, sees boredom arising from the neglect of the ontological difference between Being and beings. But I would see this as akin to a basic disinterest in intersubjective exchange. One no longer sees the Other, whether divine or human, as a challenge to one's own self-appointed goals and values. Hence, one remains locked within one's own narrow world without the urge to transcend it.

41. Marion, *God Without Being*, 103.

42. Marion, *God Without Being*, 104.

it may be."[43] What is important is that one acknowledge the divine Giver in the gift of being and return the love implicit therein. "To return the gift, to play redundantly the unthinkable donation, this is not said, but done. Love is not spoken, in the end, it is made."[44] Yet, as I see it, such a proposed exchange of love between God and the human being implicitly sets up an ontological context of intersubjectivity where both God and the human being are understood as dynamically interrelated subjects of experience rather than as logically related objects of thought within an abstract causal scheme (as in classical metaphysics).

C. The Symbolic Order in the Theology of Louis-Marie Chauvet

Much like Marion in the preface to *God Without Being,* Chauvet makes clear in the introduction to *Symbol and Sacrament* that he takes quite seriously the critique of classical metaphysics by Heidegger, Derrida, and others and will attempt accordingly to sketch a non-metaphysical approach to Christian sacraments. That is, instead of analyzing Christian sacraments as instrumental causes of grace in line with the causal scheme of Aristotelian-Thomistic metaphysics, he will attempt a new foundational understanding of sacraments in terms of symbol and ritual.[45] The first four chapters of his book, accordingly, are focused on a critique of the classical metaphysics un-

43. Marion, *God Without Being,* 105. Cf. also David N. Power, *Sacrament: The Language of God's Giving* (New York: Crossroad, 1999), 276-81. Commenting on Marion's understanding of gift as something purely gratuitous and therefore unexpected, Power adds: "Another feature of gift that is brought to the fore is that there is no fusion between giver and gifted, that the giving gives rise to participation and mutuality, but never means total identification with one another and does not require a representation of the giver to the given which obscures the distance between them, or their otherness." In my judgment, the giving that "gives rise to participation and mutuality" is best explained in terms of a conscious metaphysics of intersubjectivity, such as I have in mind with this book.

44. Marion, *God Without Being,* 107.

45. Louis-Marie Chauvet, *Symbol and Sacrament: A Sacramental Reinterpretation of Christian Existence,* trans. Patrick Madigan, S.J. and Madeleine Beaumont (Collegeville, Minn.: Liturgical Press, 1995), 1-4.

dergirding the treatise on sacraments in the *Summa Theologiae* of Thomas Aquinas, and it is to this part of the book that we will primarily devote our attention here.

He begins by asking a question. Why did Aquinas and others in the classical tradition deal with sacraments in causal terms, namely, as instrumental causes of divine grace? He answers: "The Scholastics were *unable to think otherwise;* they were prevented from doing so by the ontotheological presuppositions which structured their entire culture."[46] That is, the classical metaphysical tradition beginning with Plato consistently gave priority to Being over Becoming. As a result, processes were understood teleologically, in terms of a limit in which the process would end and a state of being would ensue. Even relationships between persons, as Plato makes clear in the *Philebus* (according to Chauvet),[47] should not be treated as ongoing processes which by definition are never fully complete. Rather they should be analyzed teleologically as finished products or achievements of the causal activities of the persons vis-à-vis one another.

In classical terms, for example, through loving another human being I cause that person to become my beloved. But this effectively ignores the possibility that the beloved may refuse my advances and thus terminate the relationship. Thus I cannot directly cause the other to be truly my beloved, that is, to love me even as I love him or her. It was presumably this awareness of the tentative and necessarily unfinished character of human interpersonal relationships which prevented Aquinas and other scholastics from employing this analogy for the relationship of God to the human being in terms of grace and sacraments. An omnipotent God should not be dependent upon the response of a human being to achieve what God wants with respect to that person. Likewise, the presupposition of divine immutability would argue against a scheme for the understanding of grace and sacraments in terms of an ongoing exchange between God and the individual human being.

Thus, even though Aquinas altered his understanding of the sacraments from causal remedies for sin in the *Commentary on the Sentences* to sacred signs which sanctify human beings in the *Summa*

46. Chauvet, *Symbol and Sacrament,* 8.
47. Chauvet, *Symbol and Sacrament,* 22-26.

Theologiae,[48] in the end he still had to say that sacraments effect what they signify, that is, that they are instrumental causes of grace. He could not, in other words, make use of the notion of sacraments as symbols which mediate or facilitate an exchange between persons, and which in effect create a common world in which God and human beings can relate to one another on an interpersonal basis. Part of his difficulty, as Chauvet likewise points out,[49] was the strictly instrumentalist approach to language which Aquinas inherited from Aristotle: words are signs of ideas, and ideas are likenesses of things.[50] Words, in effect, are the instruments of self-disclosure for intelligent beings as they share with one another objective knowledge of an already existing world. Lost, accordingly, is the appreciation of words or gestures as symbols of a world still in the making, an intersubjective world of shared meanings and values which is more hinted at than fully expressed in any given word or gesture.

To get a better sense of this implicit world of intersubjective meanings and values, Chauvet turns to a series of twentieth-century philosophers, beginning with Martin Heidegger. " 'A word is not simply a handle, a tool for giving a name to something that is already there and represented; it is not merely a means for showing what presents itself by itself. On the contrary, *it is the word which bestows the coming-into-presence,* that is, being — that in which something can make its appearance as an entity.' "[51] Chauvet comments: "It is only in language — itself the voice of Being — that humans come into being. It is only within this matrix, that of a universe always-already spoken into a 'world' before they arrive, that each subject comes to be."[52] Elsewhere he refers to this reality constituted by language as a

---

48. Chauvet, *Symbol and Sacrament,* 11-21.

49. Chauvet, *Symbol and Sacrament,* 29-36.

50. Thomas Aquinas *Summa Theologiae* I, Q. 13, art. 1 resp.

51. Chauvet, *Symbol and Sacrament,* 56; the citation is from the French translation of *Unterwegs zur Sprache: Acheminement vers la parole* (Paris: Gallimard, 1976), 212: "Le mot n'est pas seulement une simple prise, un simple instrument pour donner un nom à quelque chose qui est là, déjà représenté: il n'est pas seulement un moyen pour exhiber ce qui se presente tout seul. Tout au contraire, *c'est le mot qui accorde la venue-en-présence,* c'est-à-dire l'être — en quoi quelque chose peut faire son apparition comme étant."

52. Chauvet, *Symbol and Sacrament,* 57.

"symbolic order": "It is in the symbolic order that subjects 'build' themselves; but they do this only by building the world, something that is possible for them insofar as they have inherited from birth a world already culturally inhabited and socially arranged — in short, a world already spoken."[53] He then concludes: "Humans do not preexist language; they are formed in its womb. They do not possess it like an 'attribute,' even if of the utmost importance; they are possessed by it. Thus, language does not arise to translate after the fact a human experience that preceded it; it is *constitutive* of any truly *human* experience, that is to say, significant experience."[54]

As I will indicate in chapter two, there are limits to the validity of Heidegger's and Chauvet's thesis that language is constitutive of human experience; otherwise, a type of linguistic determinism results. For the moment, however, let us continue to document Chauvet's movement away from the thought-patterns of classical metaphysics toward a new understanding of the validity of intersubjective linguistic experience as the basis of philosophical analysis. Turning, for example, to Jacques Derrida's celebrated maxim, "There has never been anything but writing," Chauvet comments: "Obviously, this proposition escapes absurdity only if the concept of 'writing' designates not just the convenient tool that humans invented at a certain point in their history, but a component of all language."[55] Thus language for Chauvet "is a radical given that *precedes* each person and is *law* for each person, as it is for the group as a whole. This law is an institution, a convention so profoundly cultural that the marking off of sounds into phonemes is as diversified as the different linguistic groups. However, it has this unusual characteristic, that no one person ever sat down one day and decided to be its creator."[56] Hence, the "writing" to which Derrida makes reference is not writing in the popular sense but an "arch-writing" present in the structure of language itself to which human beings both in speaking and in writing have to conform if they are to make sense to their fellow human be-

---

53. Chauvet, *Symbol and Sacrament*, 86.
54. Chauvet, *Symbol and Sacrament*, 87. Cf. also below, chapter two, pp. 49-50, where I cite Hans-Georg Gadamer, writing in *Truth and Method*, to much the same effect.
55. Chauvet, *Symbol and Sacrament*, 142.
56. Chauvet, *Symbol and Sacrament*, 141.

ings. It is the "trace" of the law invisibly at work in the cultural world of a given set of human beings to give them their identity as a group and to distinguish them from other groups operating under a different cultural and linguistic law.

If the materiality of language, its rootedness in a given culture with preset institutions and laws, offers a clue to the "symbolic order" spoken of above, even more so does the human body. Like language, it is not simply an instrument for the person to express himself or herself. Rather, the body is *the primordial place of every symbolic joining of the 'inside' and the 'outside.' "*[57] What transpires inside, namely, thought, cannot be divorced from what happens outside in and through the body. As Chauvet citing Merleau-Ponty comments, thought is " 'in no way interior' because 'it does not exist outside of the world and outside of words,' because, like the painting of an artist, 'language is not the illustration of a thought already formed, but the taking possession of this thought itself.' "[58] Chauvet concludes: "in short, it is the body which speaks, this body — my body — that is 'made of the same flesh as the world.' "[59]

What Chauvet is trying to address here is the corporeality of "being-in-the-world" (Heidegger's *in-der-Welt-sein*). Each individual human being is simultaneously a "triple body" of culture, tradition, and nature. As he notes, "each person's own body is structured by the system of values or symbolic network of the group to which each person belongs and which makes up his or her *social and cultural body.*"[60] At the same time, each person's body is a "living memory" of the historic tradition in which the individual and the group stand and to which they contribute here and now. Finally, each human body "is in permanent dialogue with the *universe*" in that it participates "in the alternations of day and night, the cycle of the seasons, and in the fundamental oppositions of earth-sky, water-fire, mountains-abysses, light-shadow, and so forth."[61] Thus the living body is " 'the arch-symbol of the whole

57. Chauvet, *Symbol and Sacrament*, 147.
58. Chauvet, *Symbol and Sacrament*, 146. Reference is to M. Merleau-Ponty, *Phénoménologie de la perception* (Paris: Gallimard, 1945), 213, 446.
59. Chauvet, *Symbol and Sacrament*, 146. Reference is to M. Merleau-Ponty, *Le Visible et l'invisible: Notes de travail* (Paris: Gallimard, 1964), 302.
60. Chauvet, *Symbol and Sacrament*, 150.
61. Chauvet, *Symbol and Sacrament*, 150.

symbolic order.' For it is in it that the within and the without, myself and others, nature and culture, need and request, desire and word are joined together."[62]

If we now reflect upon these passages out of Chauvet's *Symbol and Sacrament* and ask what their underlying thrust and direction seem to be, what emerges is in my judgment an incipient philosophy of intersubjectivity. Admittedly, Chauvet shares with Marion the same deeply rooted suspicion that metaphysics in any guise is necessarily ontotheological, a form of "totalizing" thinking which substitutes a set of logical abstractions for the richness and diversity of the empirically real. Hence, he prefers to talk about the realm of the symbolic or, as noted above, the "symbolic order" as the proper starting-point for a foundational theology of sacramentality. Yet, as I see it, the "symbolic order" as described above by Chauvet needs to be incorporated into a broader scheme of universal intersubjectivity in which objectivity in terms of the symbolic order comes into being in and through the dynamic interrelation of subjects of experience. The symbolic order, in other words, is the product of innumerable subjects of experience, past and present, responding to one another in such a way as to create relatively fixed patterns or structures of existence and activity through space and over time. This, moreover, is what I will describe as the "horizontal dimension" of a philosophy/theology of intersubjectivity in a subsequent chapter.

It is curious that Chauvet who, in my judgment, so accurately points out the "foundational way of thinking" characteristic of classical metaphysics, namely, thinking in terms of hierarchically-ordered schemes of causes and effects, does not recognize that his own symbolic approach to sacraments and by implication to the whole of Christian theology, is likewise characterized by a "foundational way of thinking."[63] As I see it, his own foundational way of thinking pre-

---

62. Chauvet, *Symbol and Sacrament,* 151. Reference is to D. Dubarle, "Pratique du symbole et connaissance de Dieu," *Le mythe et le symbole* (Paris: Beauchesne, 1977), 243.

63. According to Chauvet, classical metaphysics "allows itself to be ruled by a logic of 'foundations,' which requires a 'foundational being' " (*Symbol and Sacrament,* 27). Hence, a "foundational way of thinking" is for him invariably a form of ontotheology, namely, the belief that God is the necessary Ground or First Cause of finite beings. But a much simpler explanation of the term "foundational way

supposes subjects of experience, both human and divine, in dynamic interrelation in and through the medium of the body and of language. God, for example, in Chauvet's scheme "embodies" God's self in the person of the disfigured Man on the Cross and thus disabuses human beings of their preconceived ideas of God according to human standards of perfection.[64] He refers to this new approach to the reality of God in and through reflection on the symbol of the crucified Jesus as a "metontology" which stands in opposition to ontotheology or classical metaphysics.[65] But what is the theoretical basis for that distinction? Chauvet comments: metontology "springs from another epistemology: the symbolic epistemology of the *Other,* and not the metaphysical one of the most real *Being.*"[66] Then two pages later he notes: "Otherness is the symbolic place where all communi-

---

of thinking" is to assert that one is consciously working with a paradigm or model for the interpretation of a range of phenomena so as to render one's statements about the reality in question more consistent. Moreover, the model or paradigm does not have to be seen as a "foundation-being" or metaphysical *Grund,* if one respects Ian Barbour's *caveat* regarding the use of models in both religion and science: Models "are to be taken seriously but not literally; they are neither literal pictures nor useful fictions but limited and inadequate ways of imagining what is not observable. They make tentative ontological claims that there are entities in the world somewhat like those postulated in the models" (Ian Barbour, *Religion and Science: Historical and Contemporary Issues* [San Francisco: Harper, 1997], 117).

64. Chauvet, *Symbol and Sacrament,* 492-99.

65. Chauvet, *Symbol and Sacrament,* 499-502; cf. also pp. 70-76 where Chauvet discusses the thought of Stanislas Breton, *Le Verbe et la croix* (Paris: Desclée, 1981). For valuable commentary and further explanation of Breton's philosophy, cf. Power, *Sacrament,* 287-90. Power points out the Neoplatonic orientation of Breton's thought, namely, the way in which he conceives God as the transcendent One who can only be discovered indirectly in various "traces" to be found in "human memory, action, and story" rather than directly in different conceptual representations. While I am sympathetic to the idea that subjectivity, whether divine or human, can never be fully objectified in anything concrete and particular, I am at the same time wary of a Neoplatonic approach to reality with its focus on the One as utterly transcendent of the Many. Instead, with Colin Gunton, I favor a more dynamic understanding of the One as emergent out of the interplay of the Many with one another, beginning with the notion of the Trinity as one God in virtue of the perichoretic relation of the three divine persons with one another (cf. above, Introduction, pp. 5-6; also below, Appendix, pp. 180-85).

66. Chauvet, *Symbol and Sacrament,* 500.

cation can take place, because the other is a subject, and not an object."[67] As I see it, all this would be greatly simplified if he made clear from the start that his "symbolic epistemology of the Other" was grounded in a corresponding metaphysics of intersubjectivity in which subjects of experience in dynamic interrelation via word and gesture or some other sensible medium co-create a common world.

D. Catherine LaCugna and Elizabeth Johnson on Intersubjectivity

Among Catholic theologians writing on the doctrine of the Trinity and the God-world relationship in the last twenty years, unquestionably two of the most prominent have been Catherine LaCugna and Elizabeth Johnson. LaCugna's book *God for Us* with its strong emphasis on a strictly pastoral approach to the doctrine of the Trinity provoked even more discussion than Karl Rahner's *The Trinity* if only because it advanced the logic of Rahner's own position even further than he himself was ready to carry it.[68] Likewise, Johnson's book, *She Who Is,* by reason of its judicious selection of arguments for female images of God, quickly became a standard reference work for all those interested in promoting the cause of feminism within the framework of orthodox Christian doctrine.[69] For Johnson's strategy was to claim that female images and female names should not displace male images and male names for God but rather complement them so that Christians both in private prayer and in public worship would feel comfortable with both sets of images and names.[70]

Moreover, both LaCugna and Johnson exhibit in their work this shift to an intersubjective model for the understanding of the God-world relationship within contemporary Roman Catholic systematic theology. While, on the one hand, I find this very encouraging for the pursuit of my own project in this book, I still have reservations

67. Chauvet, *Symbol and Sacrament,* 503.
68. Cf. Catherine Mowry LaCugna, *God for Us.*
69. Cf. Elizabeth A. Johnson, *She Who Is: The Mystery of God in Feminist Theological Discourse* (New York: Crossroad, 1992).
70. Johnson, *She Who Is,* 42-57, esp. 56-57.

about the extent to which they use a strictly intersubjective model for the understanding of the God-world relationship. Like Rahner, they seem, in my judgment, to occupy a middle-ground position between classical Thomistic metaphysics and a thoroughgoing intersubjective approach to reality. In the following paragraphs, accordingly, I will make clear where my own position on the God-world relationship would differ from that of LaCugna and Johnson.

After setting forth her hypothesis about the emergence and eventual "defeat" of the doctrine of the Trinity in both the Western and Eastern church traditions, LaCugna at the beginning of the second part of her book sets forth her own understanding of a trinitarian God-world relationship. Distinguishing between *theologia,* our human understanding of the internal life of the three divine persons apart from creation, and *oikonomia,* our human understanding of the economy of salvation as proceeding from the Father, in Christ and through the Spirit, she concludes:

> *Oikonomia* is not the Trinity *ad extra* but the comprehensive plan of God reaching from creation to consummation, in which God and all creatures are destined to exist together in the mystery of love and communion. Similarly, *theologia* is not the Trinity *in se,* but, much more modestly and simply, the mystery of God. . . . An immanent theology of the Trinity is thus ineluctably a theology of the 'internal' structure of the economy of redemption.[71]

Elsewhere I have argued that LaCugna, in thus focusing so strongly on the *oikonomia* or economic Trinity to the virtual exclusion of *theologia* or the classical doctrine of the immanent Trinity, is in danger of losing an objective referent for the reality of God apart from the process of creation.[72] More important for our purposes in this chap-

---

71. LaCugna, *God for Us,* 223-24.

72. Cf. "Trinity: Economic and Immanent," *Horizons* 25 (1998): 7-22, esp. 19-21. N.B.: One may also legitimately question, it seems to me, the objective referent for the word "Us" in the title *(God for Us).* If God's self-revelation is so closely linked with salvation history in the biblical sense, do any individuals besides Christians ultimately put their trust in the one true God and thus qualify for salvation? The issues involved in interreligious dialogue, in other words, do not seem to be part of the context for LaCugna's reinterpretation of the doctrine of the Trinity.

ter, however, she sets forth in the following chapter an "ontology of relation" as the theoretical basis for her new understanding of the God-world relationship. It is the metaphysical presuppositions in this chapter that I wish to review here.

Relying heavily upon the Greek Orthodox theologian John Zizioulas, she notes that the Cappadocian Fathers (Basil, Gregory of Nyssa, and Gregory of Nazianzus) "predicated *relation* or *person (hypostasis)* as the mode of God's *ousia* [being]."[73] But this means that God " 'exists' on account of a person, the Father, and not on account of a substance."[74] Or, put in more general terms, "being is traced back not to substance but to person."[75] As I see it, this is where LaCugna stands midway between the classical Thomistic metaphysics of being and a new metaphysics of intersubjectivity. A person is, after all, an individual entity even when it is conceived as relational by nature, always in dynamic interrelation with other persons. But, as noted above, a *bona fide* social ontology should begin not with an individual entity, however conceived, but with a group of entities that are dynamically one even before they are regarded as distinct from one another. The totality or group rather than the individual entity should be the necessary starting-point for a genuine social ontology.

This is not to deny, of course, that *person* is a more dynamic term than *substance*. *Person* refers to a living subject of experience rather than to an inert object of thought as with *substance*. But, even so, it is in my judgment a mistake to identify *person* with *being* or *ousia*, as do LaCugna and Zizioulas, for *being* is the term used to describe all of reality, everything that exists, not just the reality of a person. Being within the context of a social ontology may well be described as intersubjective; within Whitehead's metaphysical scheme, for example, being is intersubjective in that every actual occasion or momentary subject of experience is internally related to every other subject of experience. But there seems to be no way logically to affirm that being is intrinsically personal or even interpersonal. There are many

73. LaCugna, *God for Us*, 243.
74. LaCugna, *God for Us*, 245; cf. also John Zizioulas, *Being as Communion* (Crestwood, N.Y.: St. Vladimir's Seminary Press, 1985), 41-42.
75. LaCugna, *God for Us*, 245; Zizioulas, *Being as Communion*, 41n. 37.

other entities that exist which are not persons or necessarily ordered to persons as the *raison d'être* of their existence.[76] The term *being* must describe the reality of their existence as well as the reality of persons.

To sum up, then, while I applaud the efforts of Catherine La-Cugna to set forth an "ontology of relation" as the theoretical basis for her own understanding of the God-world relationship, I do not think that she thought out carefully enough the logical implications of such a metaphysical scheme. If she had done so, perhaps her revised trinitarian approach to the God-world relationship would have been more acceptable to critics like myself who believe that she overstated the logic of Karl Rahner's position on the Trinity.

I turn now to a consideration of the way in which Elizabeth Johnson uses intersubjectivity as a model for the God-world relationship both in *She Who Is* and in her latest book, *Friends of God and Prophets*.[77] It is clear, to be sure, that the hermeneutical principle for Johnson in writing both of these books is not fidelity to a model of intersubjectivity but rather fidelity to women's experience. Quoting Rosemary Radford Ruether, she notes: "The critical principle of feminist theology is the promotion of the full humanity of women. Whatever denies, diminishes, or distorts the full humanity of women is, therefore, appraised as not redemptive."[78] Yet, given the difficulty of properly naming what is meant by the term "women's experience," something which Johnson herself concedes,[79] it is at least arguable whether or not a consistently worked out metaphysics of intersubjectivity might in the end better serve the ideal of achieving "the full humanity" both of women and of men than a criterion, however well-intentioned, which will inevitably be one-sided in its application.[80] At least, this will be the presupposition of my argument in the next few paragraphs.

76. Cf. on this point my article "Trinity: Economic and Immanent," 16-19.

77. Elizabeth A. Johnson, *Friends of God and Prophets: A Feminist Theological Reading of the Communion of Saints* (New York: Continuum, 1998).

78. Johnson, *She Who Is,* 30; cf. also Rosemary Radford Ruether, *Sexism and God-Talk: Toward a Feminist Theology* (Boston: Beacon, 1983), 18.

79. Johnson, *She Who Is,* 29.

80. Cf., however, Elizabeth A. Johnson, "Forging Theology: A Conversation with Colleagues," in *Things New and Old: Essays on the Theology of Elizabeth A.*

With reference to the doctrine of God in *She Who Is*, for example, Johnson employs the classical Thomistic doctrine of analogy to make clear that God as the "Pure Act of Being" is infinitely removed from anything that we human beings could say about Godself: "Human words, images, and concepts with their inevitable relationship to the finite are not capable of comprehending God, who by very nature is illimitable and unobjectifiable." She then quite properly concludes: "God can be pointed to in symbols shaped by women's reality as well as in imagery taken from the world of nature and of men."[81] While fully agreeing with her on this point, I would still question whether or not in the light of my own projected philosophy/theology of universal intersubjectivity it might be possible to revise the classical understanding of divine infinity with its exclusive emphasis on God's transcendence of creation so as to achieve a new understanding of di-

---

Johnson (New York: Crossroad, 1999), 98-104, where she argues strongly against my attempt to impose a uniform metaphysical system on systematic theology and, above all, on her own feminist project: "I also make ontological claims and draw inferences about the way things truly are, but these are not beholden to any complete metaphysical system. They may in truth be compatible with many systems. With regard to the Trinity, I play with multiple models, convinced that pushing only one alone inevitably leads to a regrettable univocity in speech about the divine" (100-101). While I would certainly agree with Johnson "on the legitimacy of pluralism at every level of thinking" (99), I am not convinced that "playing with multiple models" of the Trinity or of the God-world relationship on the part of the individual theologian is especially productive. Instead, I follow the counsel of Alfred North Whitehead that God should not be seen as an exception to a set of metaphysical categories but, as far as possible, as "their chief exemplification" (Whitehead, *Process and Reality*, 343). There is, accordingly, a major difference between Johnson and me on the function of analogy in constructing philosophical and theological models of the God-world relationship. As I see it, analogy should be operative between rival systematic conceptions of the God-world relationship since each of them is no more than a model or symbolic representation of a reality beyond human comprehension. Johnson, on the other hand, employs the classical notion of analogy to justify multiple models for the God-world relationship within one and the same system (Johnson, *She Who Is*, 113-20). While this certainly is in accord with her basic project in *She Who Is*, namely, to liberate language about God from exclusive male imagery, in my judgment it weakens the systematic character of her argument and perhaps, as I shall indicate below, does an unconscious disservice to the long-range goals of Christian feminism.

81. Johnson, *She Who Is*, 112.

vine infinity which would allow for the affinity of God to creatures in the exercise of subjectivity and yet preserve the divine transcendence in terms of the depth of that subjectivity.

As I indicated earlier in this chapter with reference to the philosophy of Jean-Luc Marion, every subjectivity, whether divine, human, or other than human, is "infinite" or indeterminate in the sense that it cannot fully objectify itself at any given moment. Otherwise, it would cease to be a subjectivity and become a fully determinate actuality with no possibility of further self-expression or communication with other subjects of experience. At the same time, there are different kinds of subjectivity, each with a greater or lesser range and depth of experience. Hence, the doctrine of analogy can be applied anew but this time with respect to levels of subjectivity rather than levels of objective perfection. Every human being and, at least in Whitehead's scheme, every created (actual) entity thus participates in the divine subjectivity in some limited way.

The advantage of this new approach to the notion of infinity, of course, is that it opens up the possibility of a metaphysics based on the principle of universal intersubjectivity which in turn could integrate and render more coherent Johnson's vision of a "liberating community of all women and men characterized by mutuality with each other and harmony with the earth."[82] Furthermore, as I have argued elsewhere,[83] the same metaphysics of intersubjectivity would enable Johnson to solidify her understanding of the Christian doctrine of the Trinity in terms of a communion of life and love among the three divine persons which is then shared with their creatures as the gift of eternal life. Johnson herself, to be sure, employs the communion model for her understanding of the doctrine of the Trinity and finds much in it which resonates deeply with her feminist sensibilities.[84] But in line with her classical understanding of divine infinity, she prefers to use a number of other models as well.[85] Likewise, she is apparently apprehensive about the tritheistic overtones implicit in an exclusive use of the communion model for the doc-

82. Johnson, *She Who Is,* 31.
83. Cf. Joseph A. Bracken, S.J., "The Theology of God of Elizabeth Johnson," in *Things New and Old,* 21-38.
84. Johnson, *She Who Is,* 219.
85. Johnson, *She Who Is,* 197-205.

trine.[86] But, as I have also argued, given the persuasive power of the controlling image of God in human life, something which Johnson readily concedes in terms of her feminist project,[87] a communitarian understanding of the doctrine of the Trinity set within a metaphysics of universal intersubjectivity would present a compelling vision of the ethical goals and values which Johnson herself so deeply espouses.

Furthermore, I would suggest that characterizing the God of Christian belief as "Three Who Are One" rather than "She Who Is" might likewise be to the long-range benefit of Christian feminists like Johnson who do not wish to reject the biblical understanding of God but only to revise it in accord with women's experience. For, as I see it, "She Who Is" curiously perpetuates the problem which it seeks to solve, namely, the attribution of sexual images to God as a transcendent tripersonal reality. That is, substituting "She Who Is" for "He Who Is" only confirms the tendency to think of God as an individual entity in strictly anthropomorphic terms. If, on the other hand, one conceives personhood as strictly correlative with the notion of community so that one becomes genuinely a person (as opposed to simply an individual) only to the extent that one is able to enter into community with other persons, then personhood is freed from its individualistic sexual overtones and connotes rather spiritual agency, the capacity for growth in knowledge and love together with other persons, quite irrespective of one's sexual orientation. The focus, in other words, is then on the community and the contribution which each member can and should make to the common good with no prejudgments as to what roles this or that person should play simply by

---

86. Johnson, *She Who Is*, 209. In the final analysis, of course, the issue is whether one sees the world as primordially constituted by individual entities who then enter into various forms of social organization with one another or whether one, on the contrary, sees the world as archetypally constituted by specifically social realities (e.g., communities, environments, even individual organisms when understood as complexes of interrelated parts or members). In line with the first worldview, describing the Trinity as a community of divine persons inevitably raises the suspicion of tritheism; whereas in line with the second worldview the corporate unity of the Trinity as a divine community is simply taken for granted as the model for the way finite reality is organized and structured.

87. Johnson, *She Who Is*, 222-23.

reason of gender. As I have indicated elsewhere,[88] I think that there is a "sexual revolution" already taking place in the United States somewhat along these lines. Such a basic equalization of roles within the community on the part of both men and women would in my judgment be significantly enhanced, at least for Christians, by a communitarian image of the Trinity, especially if it were conceived in terms of a metaphysics of universal intersubjectivity such as I will set forth later in this book.

Here Johnson and other feminists may object that I as a male am once again consciously or unconsciously discounting the value of women's experience as a resource for doing theology.[89] That is certainly not my intention. As I have indicated elsewhere,[90] I completely endorse Johnson's project of liberating language about God from exclusively male connotations. My point, however, is that feminist theology along with other theologies originating within hitherto marginalized groups within contemporary society (e.g., black theology, Hispanic-American theology) must in the end impact and help to reshape theology as a broadly conceived academic discipline for both men and women, blacks and whites, Hispanic-Americans and Anglo-Americans, etc. The insights of all the subgroups within the theological community must be widely shared if they are to have their proper effect: that is, if they are not simply to justify the existence of a given subgroup but to enrich the discipline as a whole.

Yet, if this "cross-cultural" enterprise is to succeed, then one needs a more broadly-based criterion for validity than simply women's experience, the experience of blacks, the experience of Hispanic-Americans, etc. In the final analysis one needs a commonly accepted philosophical conceptuality which all parties to the discussion agree is suitable for incorporating their own perspectives and interests without evident bias or discrimination. In my judgment, a metaphysics of universal intersubjectivity such as I will propose in Part Two of this book could provide such an objective format for free and open discussion among those who inevitably represent different per-

---

88. Bracken, "The Theology of God of Elizabeth Johnson," 34-37.
89. Cf., e.g., Johnson, "Forging Theology: A Conversation with Colleagues," 103-4.
90. Bracken, "The Theology of God of Elizabeth Johnson," 21-22.

spectives on the contemporary tasks of theology. As we will see later, Jürgen Habermas seems to have come to much the same conclusion in setting forth his own theory of communicative praxis for making necessary policy-decisions within democratically-organized Western societies.[91]

To sum up, then, in this chapter I have tried to document a shift to intersubjective modes of thought as the preferred way to conceive the God-world relationship within contemporary Roman Catholic theology. Obviously, many other authors could have been cited.[92] Furthermore, I believe that much the same shift in perspective is also taking place among Protestant systematic theologians working on the God-world relationship. I have already mentioned a few of them in my introductory chapter and will analyze their work in more detail in the final chapter of this book. All that I tried to make clear in this chapter is that this shift in perspective is already significantly present among representative thinkers in the Catholic tradition and, even more importantly, that it has not yet come to completion. My assumption in this chapter has been that Roman Catholic theologians are for the most part midway between the classical Thomistic understanding of the God-world relationship and an explicit social ontology. That is, whereas in my view an explicit social ontology has its starting-point in the group or community rather than in an individual entity, contemporary Roman Catholic systematic theology is for the most part neo-Thomistic in its orientation. Its starting-point is the human being with an inbuilt capacity for self-transcendence in the direction of the Other, both divine and human. While, as noted

91. Cf. below, chapters two and five.
92. Bernard Lonergan, for example, seems to exemplify this shift to inter-subjective modes of thought in *Method in Theology* (New York: Herder & Herder, 1972), especially when it is compared with his approach to the notion of transcendental method in *Insight: A Study of Human Understanding* (London: Long-mans, Green & Co., 1957). That is, where *Insight* evidently focuses on the individual human being moving by degrees toward full rational self-consciousness, *Method in Theology* lays emphasis on method as a "framework for collaborative creativity" (*Method in Theology*, xi) and envisions the work of theology in terms of "functional specialties" carried out by a team of theologians working in concert on a given issue. Cf. below, chapter two, where I cite Lonergan's collaborative approach to theology in *Method in Theology* as an instance of achieving truth and objectivity through intersubjectivity.

above, this certainly represents a significant advance beyond the limits of the epistemology adopted by Immanuel Kant and various contemporary neo-Kantians, it still does not measure up in my judgment to the requirements of a *bona fide* social ontology. My efforts in the second part of this book will be directed, accordingly, to sketching the main lines of such a social ontology.

Beforehand, however, in the remaining two chapters of this first part of the book, I will try to respond to two interrelated objections coming from those in the academy who are profoundly suspicious of any form of metaphysics, whether classical or neo-classical. The first objection is that language not only conditions thought but in effect predetermines it. Thus there is no way for a given conceptual scheme to set forth structures of intelligibility with even a provisional claim to truth and objectivity beyond the boundaries of its cultural-linguistic context. In response to this objection, I will offer arguments primarily from Whitehead's theory of symbolism but also from the metaphysical schemes of Jürgen Habermas and Bernard Lonergan to the effect that language, properly used, liberates human beings from sociocultural constraints so as to enable them to imagine and conceive the new and unexpected. Then in the following chapter I will address some of the objections of deconstructionists to the "logocentrism" implicit in classical metaphysics. My strategy will be twofold. First of all, I will point out the remarkable affinity between Jacques Derrida's notion of *différance* and the function of creativity within Whitehead's metaphysical scheme. In this way, I will be equivalently saying that there might be a "logos" in Derrida's philosophy, but, if so, that (as in Whitehead's scheme) it is based on a principle of becoming rather than a principle of being. Then in the second half of the chapter I will examine what might be identified as residual elements of classical logocentrism in Whitehead's philosophy, especially as it was subsequently developed by Charles Hartshorne and his followers. Yet, as I see it, a better understanding of the Whiteheadian category of "society," especially as it will function within my own metaphysics of universal intersubjectivity, will free Whitehead's thought from the charge of logocentrism. Thus the way will finally be cleared for an initial presentation of my own projected metaphysics of intersubjectivity in Part Two.

2 Language and Objectivity in an Intersubjective Context

Language is not just one of man's possessions in the world; rather, on it depends the fact that man has a *world* at all. The world as world exists for man as for no other creature that is in the world. But this world is verbal in nature. . . . Not only is the world world only insofar as it comes to language within it, but language, too, has its real being only in the fact that the world is presented in it. Thus, that language is originarily human means at the same time that man's being-in-the-world is primordially linguistic.[1]

1. Hans-Georg Gadamer, *Truth and Method,* trans. Joel Weinsheimer and Donald G. Marshall, 2nd revised edition (New York: Crossroad, 1992), 443. N.B.: Gadamer, to be sure, is not a linguistic determinist, as an initial reading of this citation might imply. For, as he also makes clear in *Truth and Method,* "world" in this context is not the same as "physical environment" but closer in meaning to "worldview," an implicit orientation to life which can only be expressed in language and through which language itself achieves its highest meaning and value: "The truth is that because man can always rise above the particular environment in which he happens to find himself, and because his speech brings the world into language, he is, from the beginning, free for variety in exercising his capacity for language" (444). Yet there are times when worldviews clash as people of different cultural-linguistic backgrounds try in vain to understand one another. Gadamer's solution is to appeal to a "fusion of horizons" (306-7) whereby one's antecedent worldview is subject to expansion and revision through ongoing contact with the worldview of others. Gadamer thus lays out the problematic for which the authors discussed in this chapter (Whitehead, Habermas, and Lonergan) seek more specific solutions.

Hans-Georg Gadamer thus sums up in his celebrated book *Truth and Method* what has been described as "the linguistic turn" in contemporary philosophy whereby human access to reality is seen as heavily preconditioned by language. Human beings, in other words, have no choice but to express their understanding of the world around them in whatever language is at hand for their self-expression and communication with their peers. Even more, as we have already seen in chapter one, the way in which reality or "Being" becomes present to us humans seems to be in and through language. We do not first have an insight into the nature of reality and then find words to express it. Rather, we gain the insight into reality only insofar as we think of the right word to give it determinate form and meaning. As Chauvet, referring to Heidegger, claims, "it is only in language — itself the voice of Being — that humans come into being."[2]

How is one to interpret such an approach to reality?[3] On the one hand, language seems to provide a form of objectivity for human beings in their efforts at communication with one another. As Jürgen Habermas has made clear with his theory of "communicative rationality," human beings enter into a dialogue-situation with the ideal of achieving consensus or at least mutual understanding of their differing positions on some issue.[4] Thus, in using the same language, human beings gain an understanding of one another's deepest con-

2. Cf. above, chapter one, p. 33. Likewise, Louis-Marie Chauvet, *Symbol and Sacrament: A Sacramental Reinterpretation of Christian Existence*, trans. Patrick Madigan, S.J., and Madeleine Beaumont (Collegeville, Minn.: Liturgical Press, 1995), 57.

3. Admittedly, there are many different language-oriented philosophies at the present time with quite different methodologies and presuppositions. Language analysis as practiced in England and North America, for example, has traditionally been non-metaphysical, focusing on the ordinary usage of words in strictly empirical contexts. Gadamer and Heidegger, on the other hand, are clearly more metaphysical in their analysis of the way that language molds human experience. My focus in this chapter will be on the more metaphysical approach to language, above all, in Paul Ricoeur's and Alfred North Whitehead's analysis of the meaning and function of symbols in human life.

4. Jürgen Habermas, *The Theory of Communicative Action*, trans. Thomas McCarthy, 2 vols. (Boston: Beacon Press, 1984 & 1987); cf. also Jane Braaten, *Habermas's Critical Theory of Society* (Albany, N.Y.: State University of New York Press, 1991), 9-18.

victions and values and can come to share a more or less common worldview. Hence, objectivity about the nature of reality between different human subjects of experience is achieved through the proper use of language. Yet the appeal to language as the basis for objectivity in human relations may be too simple: for if different languages embody a wisdom or worldview to be found only in different language-groups, then the problem of objectivity has only been transferred from the level of the individual to the level of the group. Objectivity, in other words, is only possible within a language-group, not between language-groups. Between language-groups, subjectivity reigns once again since each language represents a different worldview, appropriate to one group but not to all the others.

Certain anthropologists and sociologists might at this juncture simply comment that this is the way things are, given the fact of different languages and different cultures or worldviews implicitly expressed in those languages.[5] But for a realist philosopher like Alfred North Whitehead, this is an impossible situation. As he notes in the introduction to *Process and Reality,* "Speculative Philosophy is the endeavor to frame a coherent, logical, necessary system of general ideas in terms of which every element of our experience can be interpreted."[6] By "our experience" he evidently did not mean only the experience of those who are familiar with the English language and the worldview it may or may not imply. Rather, in Whitehead's mind "our experience" refers in principle to the experience of any human being who is sufficiently self-reflective on the recurrent data of consciousness. Admittedly, the terms used in his philosophy are derived from the English language and would have to be carefully translated into other languages in order for those familiar with only those other

5. Cf., e.g., Richard Bernstein, *Beyond Objectivism and Relativism: Science, Hermeneutics, and Praxis* (Philadelphia: University of Pennsylvania Press, 1983), 25-30, 93-108. Bernstein himself, of course, believes that it is possible to move beyond classical objectivism and relativism through the right kind of intersubjective communication, that is, "dialogical communities in which *phronesis* [ethical reflection mediating between the universal and the particular], judgment, and practical discourse become concretely embodied in our everyday practices" (223). Thus understood, Bernstein's project is very much akin to my own in this book.

6. Whitehead, *Process and Reality: An Essay in Cosmology,* corrected edition, ed. David Ray Griffin and Donald W. Sherburne (New York: The Free Press, 1978), 3.

languages to grasp his basic meaning and intent. But the very idea of a Speculative Philosophy such as Whitehead sets forth in *Process and Reality* is that through concepts originating in one language-system he is attempting to describe reality as it exists independently of the language-systems of human beings. He is, in other words, writing a cosmology, that is, a treatise on the reality of the natural world, which includes human beings, but which existed in its basic features long before human beings with their different languages appeared on the scene.

The big question, of course, is whether Whitehead is correct in this assumption or whether he is to be dismissed as a naive realist insufficiently aware of the inevitable limitations on human understanding which arise out of different historical-cultural contexts. Here the reflections of Professor Isamu Nagami of Rikkyo University in Tokyo may be helpful. Presenting a paper at a conference on the philosophy of Alfred North Whitehead in Claremont, California, Nagami first takes note of Whitehead's own skepticism about the capabilities of ordinary language to express fundamental philosophical insights, and quotes him: "It is true that the general agreement of mankind as to experienced facts is best expressed in language. But the language of literature breaks down precisely at the task of expressing in explicit form the larger generalities, the very generalities which metaphysics seeks to express."[7] Whitehead, therefore, says Nagami, has recourse to metaphoric language in *Process and Reality,* language which deliberately sets aside the conventional meaning of words and phrases so as to point to dimensions of reality that cannot otherwise be readily described in human language, even the most scientific.

Whitehead's image of the flight of an airplane is pertinent here: "The true method of discovery is like the flight of an aeroplane. It starts from the ground of particular observation; it makes a flight in the thin area of imaginative generalization; and again it lands for renewed observation rendered acute by rational interpretation."[8] As Nagami notes, " 'The ground of particular observation' symbolizes a socio-cultural condition based on a specific linguistic culture. No phi-

---

7. Whitehead, *Process and Reality,* 14. Quoted in Isamu Nagami, "Whitehead's Thought and Metaphoric Language," unpublished paper, p. 3.

8. Whitehead, *Process and Reality,* 5.

losopher can escape from this situation."[9] But the flight in the thin air of imaginative generalization liberates one, at least for the moment, from the customary thought-patterns of one's "earth-bound" socio-cultural condition and allows one to construct a model of the reality in question, so to speak, from a higher viewpoint. One inevitably loses thereby certain details, since every model represents a necessary simplification of a very complex situation. What is gained as a result, however, is a new insight into the way things work along with powerful new motivation to reorder one's life accordingly.

Yet, even if one has thereby personally gained a "higher viewpoint," a new feeling of objectivity, with respect to the world in which one lives, is the problem of objectivity thereby solved? Is objectivity ever achieved apart from an intersubjective context in which new theories have to be first shared with others and then broadly accepted by the group before they are recognized as more or less objective, that is, corresponding to the way things are? Josiah Royce's triadic community of interpreters comes to mind here: the interpreter of a sign, the one referred to by the sign, and the one to whom the interpretation of the sign is offered.[10] Furthermore, as Royce makes clear in *The Problem of Christianity,* these mini-communities of interpretation should by degrees expand into a Universal Community of Interpretation corresponding to the human race as a whole.[11] For only when a virtually universal consensus on a given point obtains can one be assured of genuine objectivity.[12] As we shall see below, Jürgen Habermas espouses much the same approach to truth and objectivity in his theory of "formal pragmatics." For the moment, however, let us return to Whitehead's notion of metaphor or symbolic language and, above all, explore the metaphysics which he proposes by way of validation for his theory of symbolic reference.

9. Nagami, "Whitehead's Thought," 7.
10. Cf. Josiah Royce, *The Problem of Christianity* (Chicago: University of Chicago Press, 1968), 312-17.
11. Royce, *The Problem of Christianity,* 340-41.
12. Royce himself seems to have had misgivings about his own consensus-oriented approach to truth and objectivity in hat he likewise postulated that the ultimate reality and objectivity of this process of communal interpretation must be guaranteed by an omniscient spirit who grasps it in its totality within the unity of a single comprehensive insight. Cf. on this point *The Problem of Christianity,* 340.

A. Whitehead's Hermeneutical Metaphysics[13]

As Nagami also made clear in his talk, Whitehead stands closer to Paul Ricoeur than to Aristotle in his understanding of metaphor. Aristotle, after all, thought of metaphor as a figure of speech, the substitution of a more colorful expression for the literal meaning of the word.[14] Ricoeur, on the other hand, thought of metaphor primarily as a semantic innovation, a conscious stretching of the meaning of a word to convey a hitherto unsuspected dimension of the reality in question. A deliberate tension is thus set up in the mind of the reader or hearer between the literal meaning and the new metaphorical meaning of the term.[15] One has to struggle to understand what the speaker or writer is trying to communicate. As Nagami comments, "[i]n so doing metaphors tell us something new about reality."[16] Moreover, it is clear that this is also Whitehead's understanding of the function of metaphor. As he comments in the opening chapter of *Process and Reality*, when one seeks to set forth metaphysical first principles, "[w]ords and phrases must be stretched toward a generality foreign to their ordinary usage; and however such elements of language be stabilized as technicalities, they remain metaphors mutely appealing for an imaginative leap."[17] For Whitehead, accordingly, metaphor refers to an imaginative new understanding of this world

13. I owe this expression to Stephen Franklin, who, in his book *Speaking from the Depths* (Grand Rapids: Eerdmans, 1990), refers to Whitehead's philosophy as a "Hermeneutical Metaphysics of Propositions, Experience, Symbolism, Language, and Religion." Franklin explores in much greater detail what I merely sketch in this section of the chapter. I have also greatly profited from careful reading of Ronald L. Farmer's book, *Beyond the Impasse: The Promise of a Process Hermeneutic* (Macon, Ga.: Mercer University Press, 1997).

14. Aristotle *Poetics* 1457b: "Metaphor consists in giving the thing a name that belongs to something else."

15. Cf., e.g., Paul Ricoeur, *Interpretation Theory: Discourse and the Surplus of Meaning* (Fort Worth: Texas Christian University Press, 1976), 51: The functioning of a metaphor "is, in effect, a calculated error, which brings together things that do not go together and by means of this apparent misunderstanding it causes a new, hitherto unnoticed, relation of meaning to spring up between the terms that previous systems of classification had ignored or not allowed."

16. Nagami, "Whitehead's Thought," 8.

17. Whitehead, *Process and Reality*, 4.

which in its own way transcends the limitations of language, at least insofar as it has been used up to that point by the language-users.

There is a difference, however, between the approaches of Ricoeur and Whitehead on the subject of metaphor. That is, even though they both differ from Aristotle in thinking of metaphor as a semantic innovation rather than simply as a figure of speech, they differ from one another in the way that they employ metaphor within their respective philosophical schemes. Ricoeur distinguishes between symbol and metaphor: "The latter [metaphor] is a free invention of discourse; the former [symbol] is bound to the cosmos," that is, the structure of the sacred universe, in which correspondences exist "between creation *in illo tempore* and the present order of natural appearances and human activities."[18] Metaphors, accordingly, spell out in different ways the deeper meaning of primordial symbols already present within human experience. As such, metaphors are operative in literature, above all in poetry, but likewise in the sciences. In both cases, an extended metaphor or model "creates its own world"[19] in trying to describe a symbolic reality more real than appearances.

Whitehead's treatment of metaphor has much in common with Ricoeur's analysis of the connection between symbol and metaphor. But it is also clear that his emphasis is primarily on the conscious use of metaphor in creating a philosophical system. He sees metaphor, for example, as the only way consciously to direct attention to those features of human experience which are universally present but seldom attended to, features which, if properly reflected upon, could unexpectedly link together otherwise disparate spheres of human existence and activity.[20] The original insight in many cases may very well have been spontaneous, what the Japanese philosopher Kitaro Nishida calls an "action-intuition" emergent out of one's unconscious mind.[21] But, once in possession of such an insight, says Whitehead, one must think it through in all its logical consequences.

18. Ricoeur, *Interpretation Theory*, 61-62.

19. Ricoeur, *Interpretation Theory*, 67.

20. Whitehead, *Process and Reality*, 5.

21. Cf. Robert E. Carter, *The Nothingness Beyond God: An Introduction to the Philosophy of Kitaro Nishida*, 2nd ed. (St. Paul, Minn.: Paragon House, 1997), 105-10. Cf. also below, chapter four, for further discussion of Nishida's philosophy.

One thus begins with a relatively simple concept or idea drawn from some already familiar area of human experience and ends with a full-scale model or conceptual scheme with an applicability well beyond its original parameters.

One way to make this last point clear is to set forth Whitehead's theory of symbolic language as articulated in his lectures at the University of Virginia in 1927, published under the title *Symbolism: Its Meaning and Effect*. For, beginning with an empirical overview of the different kinds of symbols in human experience, Whitehead expands his original insight into the workings of symbols in human life so as to ground a conceptual scheme for the self-constitution of all subjects of experience (actual occasions), even the most primitive, such as the ultimate components of inanimate objects. His initial definition of symbolism in human consciousness, for example, runs as follows: "The human mind is functioning symbolically when some components of its experience elicit consciousness, beliefs, emotions, and usages, respecting other components of its experience. The former set of components are the 'symbols,' and the latter set constitute the 'meaning' of the symbols."[22] But he then adds: "There are no components of experience which are only symbols or only meanings. The more usual symbolic reference is from the less primitive component as symbol to the more primitive as meaning."[23] Accordingly, both "symbol" and "meaning" within human experience are real rather than contrived, since they both make reference beyond themselves to something extra-mental.

Whitehead gives the example of the word "tree" and asks why we regard the word "tree" as a symbol for the physical reality of an actual tree when, in point of fact, the physical tree could likewise be a symbol for the word "tree."[24] A poet, for example, takes a walk in the forest to enkindle his imagination for the composition of a poem on the beauties of nature. In this case, "the trees are the symbols and the words are the meaning. He [the poet] concentrates on the trees in order to get at the meaning."[25] But, once the poem is

22. Whitehead, *Symbolism: Its Meaning and Effect* (New York: G. P. Putnam's Sons, 1959), 8.
23. Whitehead, *Symbolism*, 10.
24. Whitehead, *Symbolism*, 11-12.
25. Whitehead, *Symbolism*, 12.

published, the poet's readers "are people for whom his words refer symbolically to the visual sights and sounds and emotions he wants to evoke."[26] Thus in the use of language there is a double symbolic reference: "from things to words on the part of the speaker, and from words back to things on the part of the listener."[27] What Whitehead is proposing, therefore, is that both words and things "enter into our experience on more or less equal terms."[28] As such, they both have a physical component and a conceptual component. The spoken word, for example, is a physical sound with a definite meaning attached for potential hearers; in like manner, a written word is a set of physical marks on a page with significance for the reader. Finally, the extra-mental reality to which the spoken or written word has reference likewise comes into human experience with both physical and conceptual dimensions, quite apart from its explicit designation here and now in terms of a spoken or written word.

To make this last point clear, Whitehead introduces two technical terms for the analysis of human perception of extra-mental reality: namely, "causal efficacy" and "presentational immediacy" (cf. Glossary). Through causal efficacy an extra-mental reality conveys both information and a feeling-tone about itself and the outside world to the individual perceiving it; through presentational immediacy, the individual assimilates that same information and feeling-tone so as imaginatively to represent that extra-mental reality within his or her mind in the same way that it exists outside the mind.[29] Only when these two autonomous modes of perception operate in combination does a human being or other higher-level animal organism properly see, hear, and feel reality all around it. Shortly I will indicate how, in Whitehead's view, causal efficacy is likewise at work in the self-

26. Whitehead, *Symbolism,* 12
27. Whitehead, *Symbolism,* 12.
28. Whitehead, *Symbolism,* 11. One could quibble here with Whitehead on the strict equivalence of words and things. Words are a special kind of "thing" in that their whole function is to refer beyond themselves in a way that is not peculiar to extra-mental things as subsistent realities. What Whitehead seems to have in mind is that both words and things are dual-dimensional. That is, both possess a physical and mental component.
29. Cf. here Farmer, *Beyond the Impasse,* 84-88, 101 (Fig. 4-3).

constitution of all actual occasions, even those which are constitutive of inanimate things. For the moment, however, it is enough to note that in Whitehead's mind there is a necessary prelinguistic component to human awareness of the outside world. That is, in terms of causal efficacy, an individual *feels* the impact of the outside world even before he or she is prepared to name or otherwise describe that experience through language.

The value of this approach to language and symbolism by Whitehead, as I see it, is that it meets the challenge posed by Wilfrid Sellars and other language analysts in their opposition to the so-called "myth of the given," that is, the belief that our sensations are accurate representations of the external world.[30] Sellars and others assert on the contrary that no such experiences are simply given to human consciousness but that one and all are antecedently determined with respect to their meaning and value for the percipient by the intersubjective language conventionally used to describe the experience.[31] Whitehead, to be sure, in no way denies that language heavily conditions the way in which we experience reality. As Stephen Franklin points out, for Whitehead language elicits "propositional prehensions" (cf. Glossary), that is, different ways in which to interpret and shape our human experience.[32] Thus, depending upon the vocabulary at our disposal at any given moment, we will tend to notice some things and overlook other things; likewise we will attend only to certain features even of the things that we notice and unconsciously ignore still other features because once again we have the vocabulary at hand to name some differences but not others.[33] The key point, however, as Franklin likewise points out, is that prior to the naming of things in terms of propositional prehensions human beings are at first simply receptive to data from the outside world in

---

30. Cf., e.g., Wilfrid Sellars, *Science, Perception and Reality* (London: Routledge & Kegan Paul, 1963), 127-34, 164-70.

31. Sellars, *Science, Perception and Reality*, 190-96. Cf. also Willard Van Orman Quine, *From a Logical Point of View: Nine Logico-Philosophical Esssays*, 2nd ed. (New York: Harper Torchbook, 1963), 20-46; also Richard Rorty, *Philosophy and the Mirror of Nature* (Princeton, N.J.: Princeton University Press, 1979), 165-212.

32. Franklin, *Speaking from the Depths*, 295. Cf. also Farmer, *Beyond the Impasse*, 91-93.

33. Franklin, *Speaking from the Depths*, 295-96.

terms of "physical prehensions" or feeling-level experiences of the outside world.[34]

Whitehead's model for his analysis of the way in which presentational immediacy and causal efficacy work is, of course, his key concept of an actual occasion; in Whitehead's view, for example, a human being at a preconscious level is actively integrating from moment to moment sense data from the external world into his or her self-awareness. Keeping this in mind, we note what he says about presentational immediacy:

> Presentational immediacy is our immediate perception of the contemporary external world, appearing as an element constitutive of our own experience. . . . This appearance is effected by the mediation of qualities, such as colours, sounds, tastes, etc., which can with equal truth be described as our sensations or as the qualities of the actual things which we perceive. These qualities are thus relational between the perceiving subject and the perceived things.[35]

Once again, we note the insistent realism of Whitehead's metaphysical scheme. Sense data are neither purely mental nor simply physical in character, but pertain with equal force to the reality of the perceiver and the thing perceived.

Furthermore, they are presented to us in terms of a spatial scheme within our imagination which more or less accurately corresponds to the way in which they are to be found outside the mind in the spatio-temporal world. "Thus the disclosure of a contemporary world by presentational immediacy is bound up with the disclosure of the solidarity of actual things by reason of their participation in an impartial system

---

34. Franklin, *Speaking from the Depths,* 127: "The primary instance of a perception in the mode of causal efficacy is an actual entity's simple physical prehension of a past actual entity, such a simple physical prehension occurring in the first, conformal stage of the concrescing entity's development." Cf. also Farmer, *Beyond the Impasse,* 223-24; likewise, Christine Hardy, *Networks of Meaning: A Bridge between Mind and Matter* (Westport, Conn.: Praeger, 1998), 17: "Sensorimotor processes are loaded with meaning, far beyond their connection with language; in the same way, affects and feelings — some of the most meaningful individual experiences — are largely beyond language. For most of us, love and passion are a depth of experience and meaning that words cannot adequately describe."

35. Whitehead, *Symbolism,* 21-22.

of spatial extension."[36] Unlike Immanuel Kant, therefore, in his *Critique of Pure Reason,* space and time for Whitehead are not the mind's pure forms of sensibility which are imposed upon sense data in order to organize the latter into a coherent whole.[37] Rather, space and time for Whitehead are, in the first place, part of the makeup of the real world out of which an actual occasion in human experience is here and now emerging. Furthermore, those same spatial and temporal relations are necessarily part of that actual occasion's self-constitution so that it can afterwards as a "superject" or completed actual occasion take its place within that same world out of which it came. As Whitehead comments, "the world discloses itself to be a community of actual things, which are actual in the same sense as we are."[38]

Yet, granted the indispensable role of presentational immediacy in human sense perception, Whitehead nevertheless reminds his audience that presentational immediacy is a very limited representation of external reality. In his own words, presentational immediacy is "vivid, precise, and barren."[39] It is barren because it presents to us nothing more than the geometrical relations of things to one another within the world of our imagination. The full richness and texture of the extra-mental world are presented to us by the other mode of perception, causal efficacy. Furthermore, while presentational immediacy is an important factor in the experience of human beings and other animals with a power of imagination, causal efficacy is at work in the self-constitution of all actual occasions, even those which are constitutive of inanimate things like tables and chairs. Here Whitehead differs dramatically from David Hume on the notion of causal efficacy in human experience. Whereas Hume regards causal efficacy as "the importation, into the data, of a way of thinking or judging about those data,"[40]

---

36. Whitehead, *Symbolism,* 23.

37. Immanuel Kant, *Critique of Pure Reason,* trans. Norman Kemp Smith (New York: St. Martin's Press, 1965), 67-78.

38. Whitehead, *Symbolism,* 21.

39. Whitehead, *Symbolism,* 23.

40. Whitehead, *Symbolism,* 39. Whitehead also makes reference here to Immanuel Kant as one for whom notions of causality arise only with reflective experience. This at least appears to be a misreading of Kant by Whitehead. For Kant in *The Critique of Pure Reason* is quite clear that causality is constitutive of human experience, not merely an inference from experience.

thus as characteristic of human beings in their more reflective moments, Whitehead urges that causal efficacy, understood as the conformation of present fact to immediate past in the self-constitution of actual occasions, "is more prominent both in apparent behavior and in consciousness, when the organism is low grade. A flower turns to the light with much greater certainty than does a human being, and a stone conforms to the conditions set by its external environment with much greater certainty than does a flower."[41]

Causal efficacy, accordingly, is the mode of perception at work in the self-constitution of all actual occasions, even in those without the power of imagination. Paradoxically, it works more effectively the less it is constrained in its operation by the alternate mode of perception, namely, presentational immediacy. Presentational immediacy, in other words, by reason of its precision and vividness distracts human beings and other higher-level organisms from attention to the massive deliverances of causal efficacy, the information and feeling-tones streaming in from the outside world through the sense-organs at every moment. Thus human beings and other higher-level organisms may ignore, sometimes at their own peril, what simpler organisms and even the actual occasions constitutive of inanimate things (like stones) are on a feeling-level immediately aware of and responsive to.

In the concluding pages of *Symbolism: Its Meaning and Effect,* Whitehead focuses on the way in which symbolism works, not simply in the consciousness of individuals, but in the functioning of communities and other human social institutions. He notes initially, however, that the longest-lasting "societies" have been those of inanimate things vis-à-vis their constituent actual occasions; a rock, for example, might keep its basic shape and texture for millions of years.[42] Physical organisms of various kinds, on the other hand, have a much shorter time-span, paradoxically because they sustain life which in Whitehead's view is a bid for freedom, "a bid for a certain independence of individuality with self-interests and activities not to be construed purely in terms of environmental obligations."[43] The price to be paid for this freedom, however, is a much shorter life-history. Hu-

41. Whitehead, *Symbolism,* 42.
42. Whitehead, *Symbolism,* 64-65.
43. Whitehead, *Symbolism,* 65.

man beings, moreover, have normally a much shorter life span than the communities or other social groupings to which they belong, for they are born into a given community and usually die as a member of that same community. In the meantime, the community survives because of commonly-held symbols which shape the lives of its members. Symbols, in other words, channel the energies of community members for the achievement of common purposes even as the members remain basically free to interpret, critique, and in some measure modify those same symbols. "In the place of the force of instinct which suppresses individuality, [human] society has gained the efficacy of symbols, at once preservative of the commonweal and of the individual standpoint."[44]

Chief among these symbols operative within human communities is, of course, language, especially when language is understood to be not simply a medium for the transmission of information about the external world but as a vehicle for the expression of feeling and desire in an intersubjective context. "[L]anguage," says Whitehead, "binds a nation together by the common emotions that it elicits, and is yet the instrument whereby freedom of thought and of individual criticism finds its expression."[45] By way of explanation, he notes, first of all, that "a social system is kept together by the blind force of instinctive actions, and of instinctive emotions clustered around habits and prejudices."[46] Hence, innovations to the social order, if not carefully introduced, often provoke a violent reaction among members of the society who feel that their customary way of life is thereby threatened. Reason must be brought to bear upon the turbulent emotions aroused by unexpected and (at least initially) unwanted changes in the traditional way of life. Here conscious attention to the basic linguistic symbols governing the thinking and the behavior of the group is all-important since a careful reordering of these operative symbols can do much to restore peace and tranquility to the group. Individual community members, to be sure, may not pay much attention to the theoretical meaning of a given symbol, but its power to guide the practical behavior of those same individuals can be enormous. As

44. Whitehead, *Symbolism*, 66.
45. Whitehead, *Symbolism*, 68.
46. Whitehead, *Symbolism*, 68.

Whitehead comments, "the symbol evokes loyalties to vaguely conceived notions, fundamental for our spiritual natures. The result is that our natures are stirred to suspend all antagonistic impulses, so that the symbol procures its required response in action."[47]

One of the basic differences between the American and French revolutions in terms of their social consequences, for example, was that the American Revolution involved only a modest reordering of the prevailing symbols operative in the lives of the former English colonists: "When George Washington had replaced George III, and Congress had replaced the English Parliament, Americans were still carrying on a well-understood system so far as the general structure of their social life was concerned. . . . The ordinary signs still beckoned people to their ordinary actions, and suggested the ordinary common-sense justification."[48] By contrast, the symbols characteristic of ordinary civil life for French citizens were so completely uprooted by the French revolution that total anarchy was prevented only by the institution of a reign of terror which was itself terribly unsettling and unpredictable.

Likewise in this context, Whitehead returns to his basic metaphor, namely, the actual occasion as a fleeting moment in the consciousness of a human being. Noting that the unity of an actual occasion is a dynamic process wherein many disparate components (not only sense data but feeling-level responses toward those same sense data) have to be adjusted to one another,[49] he nevertheless insists that none of these components in their dynamic interrelation are "necessarily determined by the primitive phases of experience" from which they emerged.[50] Hence, the actual occasion enjoys a certain freedom to order its private world of symbols derived from the past and to fashion itself into a new objective reality full of meaning and significance for the future, namely, for its successor actual occasions in their own processes of self-constitution. This relative freedom of self-constitution for the actual occasion, of course, does not guarantee ultimate success for the society (societies) to which the individual

47. Whitehead, *Symbolism*, 74.
48. Whitehead, *Symbolism*, 76-77.
49. Whitehead, *Symbolism*, 86.
50. Whitehead, *Symbolism*, 87.

occasion belongs and to which it contributes its momentary "satisfaction." As Whitehead comments, it is not true that "the mere workings of nature in any particular organism are in all respects favorable either to the existence of that organism, or its happiness, or to the progress of the society in which the organism finds itself."[51] But this is the price to be paid for the emergence of novelty.

In similar fashion, a community will survive only if its language and other symbol systems function successfully to adjust the aims and purposes of individuals to the goals and values of the community and vice versa. Yet with the passage of time, changes in the prevailing symbol systems will inevitably become desirable, if not indeed necessary. Here the risk of freedom of expression in the realm of symbols is just as dangerous for communities as it is for individuals. But it is a task which must be undertaken. "The art of free society consists first in the maintenance of the symbolic code; and secondly in fearlessness of revision, to secure that the code serves those purposes which satisfy an enlightened reason. Those societies which cannot combine reverence to their symbols with freedom of revision, must ultimately decay either from anarchy, or from the slow atrophy of a life stifled by useless shadows."[52] Whitehead, then, is evidently committed to the belief that language liberates as well as constrains human beings in their dealings with one another.

B. Habermas's Theory of Communicative Rationality

At this point, we may profitably turn to Jürgen Habermas's extended reflections on the role of language in the formation and maintenance of human communities. These reflections, to be sure, are embedded within a much larger project for his two-volume work, *The Theory of Communicative Action*. As Thomas McCarthy notes in his translator's introduction, Habermas has three interrelated goals which he wishes to achieve in this work: "(1) to develop a concept of rationality that is no longer tied to, and limited by, the subjectivistic and individualistic premises of modern philosophy and social theory; (2) to construct a two-

---

51. Whitehead, *Symbolism*, 87.
52. Whitehead, *Symbolism*, 88.

level concept of society that integrates the lifeworld and system paradigms; and, finally, (3) to sketch out against this background a critical
theory of modernity which analyzes and accounts for its pathologies in
a way that suggests a redirection rather than an abandonment of the
project of enlightenment."[53] Our interest in this chapter will be mostly
limited to an analysis of his first goal, namely, a theory of communicative rationality which puts emphasis on the critical use of language to
establish a sense of objectivity among human beings who are participants in an ongoing dialogical or communitarian way of life.

Habermas's basic contention is that in speaking to one another
"we are constantly making claims, even if usually only implicitly,
concerning the validity of what we are saying, implying, or presup-
posing."[54] These claims have to do in some measure with the truth of
what we say about the objective world around us here and now; in
some measure with the rightness or legitimacy of the values which we
thereby express in terms of our membership in the intersubjective
world to which we belong together with our contemporaries; finally,
in some measure with the truthfulness and sincerity in the way we
present to our contemporaries these other two claims to what is true
and right here and now.[55] Other individuals, in turn, can challenge
these claims, ideally not by a show of force, but by reasoned argument to the contrary. Our counter-response, accordingly, must likewise be in terms of reasoned argument in defense of our validity
claims to be speaking the truth about the objective world, or to be
expressing values consonant with the accepted mores of the community, and to be truthful rather than devious in thus giving expression
to our innermost feelings and desires.

The projected result of this idealized speech-situation, of course,
will be that the participants will achieve a sense of objectivity about
what is in fact the case here and now and/or what ought to be striven
for in terms of common values and norms of behavior. In effect, they
will have given new meaning and value to a common "lifeworld"
which, even without their explicitly reflecting upon it, gives consistency and purpose to their lives both as individuals and as members

53. Habermas, *Theory of Communicative Action*, translator's introduction, I:vi.
54. Habermas, *Theory of Communicative Action*, I:x.
55. Habermas, *Theory of Communicative Action*, I:10-22.

of a given community.[56] The lifeworld, in other words, is the implicit store of shared meanings and values upon which individual members unconsciously draw in their ongoing communication with one another and to which, as noted above, they contribute here and now by their efforts at mutual understanding and cooperative activity. As such, the notion of the lifeworld bears a strong resemblance to what Whitehead had in mind with the abiding power of various cultural symbols to elicit deep feeling and spontaneous desire among the members of a community.

At the same time, likewise in line with Whitehead's remarks on the role of symbols in community life, a lifeworld is not rigidly fixed in its basic structure and design. Since by definition it came into being and took shape only through sustained efforts at mutual understanding and communication among its members, it can over time be suitably revised as those members grow in knowledge both of one another and of the external world in which they live. Yet all of this is made possible for human beings only because of language. Provided that it is used in the right way, namely, in the interests of "communicative rationality" with its implicit claims to validity in the matter of truth, moral values, and personal authenticity, as Habermas proposes, language is both the "glue" that binds human beings to one another so as to sustain a common lifeworld and the indispensable instrument for their ongoing critique of at least some of the traditional meanings and values embedded in that same lifeworld.

Habermas, of course, is no naive idealist in this matter. He fully recognizes that individuals, more often than not, act out of self-interest in their dealings with one another. They employ what Habermas calls "cognitive-instrumental" rationality as opposed to communicative rationality.[57] That is, the rationality of their behavior is primarily exhibited in the skill with which they adjust means to ends so as to achieve the goals which they set for themselves as individuals. In Habermas's view, however, this more individualistic approach to rationality can and should be incorporated into the broader context of communicative rationality whereby individuals consciously work together to achieve common goals.

56. Habermas, *Theory of Communicative Action,* II:119-35.
57. Habermas, *Theory of Communicative Action,* I:10.

Only responsible persons can behave rationally. If their rationality is measured by the success of goal-directed interventions, it suffices to require that they be able to choose among alternatives and to control (some) conditions in their environment. But if their rationality is measured by whether processes of reaching understanding are successful, recourse to such capacities does not suffice. In the context of communicative action, only those persons count as responsible who, as members of a communication-community, can orient their actions to intersubjectively recognized validity claims.[58]

Habermas is distinguishing his own position here from that of his distinguished predecessor in social theory, Max Weber, who concluded somewhat pessimistically that human beings are only capable of cognitive-instrumental rationality in dealing with one another and that this ultimately leads to a "disenchantment of the world" wherein religious/metaphysical worldviews have been thoroughly "rationalized" and wherein as a result there is no commonly acknowledged higher meaning and value to human life beyond the self-centered pursuit of particular goals and values by individuals.[59] As Habermas sees it, Weber was led in this direction because of his starting-point for the analysis of human sociality in the philosophy of consciousness with its traditional focus on the individual as opposed to the group. If one instead begins with the primacy of the group or individuals in dynamic interaction, then it is possible to maintain that communication with others for the sake of achieving common goals is a more comprehensive form of rationality than the simple means-end orientation involved in the satisfaction of personal interests and, furthermore, that the underlying meaning and value of language is precisely to achieve this deeper level of communication and cooperation among individuals within the group.[60]

At the same time Habermas does not question Weber's other ba-

---

58. Habermas, *Theory of Communicative Action*, I:14.

59. Habermas, *Theory of Communicative Action*, I:243-54; see also McCarthy's introductory remarks: I, xvii-xviii.

60. Cf. here Braaten, *Habermas's Critical Theory of Society*, 64: "The theory of communicative competence holds that there is at least one end (mutuality) to which we are committed in virtue of being capable of communication and that this end is prior to personal ends."

sic contention that the modern tendency to "rationalization" of life in society demands that the varied activities of individuals vis-à-vis one another be subjected to analysis in terms of "systems" theory rather than simply through the paradigm of the common "life-world." As we shall see more in detail in chapter five, systems theory allows for the analysis and interpretation of the interaction of subgroups within society, quite apart from the specific interactions of individuals on one another. The lifeworld, to be sure, is both logically and temporally prior to the organization of society in terms of interacting systems (economic, political, etc.). But, given the gradual erosion of traditional structures of authority and of longstanding patterns of behavior within contemporary society, the practical reorganization of community life in terms of relatively impersonal "systems" seems inevitable.

Yet Habermas is wary of the tendency within systems analysis to explain the interaction of groups with one another simply in terms of impersonal "steering mechanisms" far removed from the discourse-situation characteristic of communicative rationality. In a sense, language as the privileged medium of interpersonal communication is thus being set aside in favor of a conceptual scheme in which impersonal factors like money and its various uses in the economic order or power and its various manifestations in the political order are the focus of attention for those seeking an explanation of current conditions in the social order. Hence, says Habermas, while systems analysis is very useful for explaining the broader configurations of life in contemporary society, ways must be worked out for human beings to reassert control over their lives through language, that is, through discourse-situations in which the merits and demerits of various public policies are argued out and a consensus achieved with respect to a common course of action.

C. Lonergan's Notion of a World Mediated by Meaning

Another twentieth-century philosopher who has reflected deeply on the issues of truth and objectivity within an interpersonal context is Bernard Lonergan, S.J. As he sees it, truth and objectivity can be virtually guaranteed if only one is faithful to what he calls "transcendental method," that is, "a basic pattern of [mental] operations employed in every cognitional enterprise,"[61] whether in the day-to-day activities of ordinary life or in more specialized academic disciplines such as the humanities and the various natural and social sciences. These mental operations, says Lonergan, are organized in terms of four different levels of conscious experience:

> There is the *empirical* level on which we sense, perceive, imagine, feel, speak, move. There is an *intellectual* level on which we inquire, come to understand, express what we have understood, work out the presuppositions and implications of our expression. There is the *rational* level on which we reflect, marshal the evidence, pass judgment on the truth or falsity, certainty or probability, of a statement. There is the *responsible* level on which we are concerned with ourselves, our own operations, our goals, and so deliberate about possible courses of action, evaluate them, decide, and carry out our decisions.[62]

Transcendental method, then, consists in recognizing the inherent dynamism of human conscious activity in progressively moving through these four levels of experience in the course of whatever we think, say, and do. Thus, in becoming self-aware of one's implicit mental operations, one can gradually become aware of different realms of meaning in which these collective operations of experiencing, understanding, judging, and deciding are exercised analogously but at the same time differently. What counts as a valid procedure in the realm of common sense, for example, will be defective in the realm of scientific theory where more specialized rules for data-gathering, forming hypotheses on the basis of the data, making judgments about the validity of the hypothesis, and finally deciding how to test or otherwise implement the hypothesis come into play. The goal, of course, is a differentiated self-consciousness in which one is fully aware of what one is doing in each of these distinct realms of meaning.[63]

---

61. Bernard J. F. Lonergan, S.J., *Method in Theology* (New York: Herder & Herder, 1972), 4.
62. Lonergan, *Method in Theology*, 9.
63. Lonergan, *Method in Theology*, 81-85.

In his first major work, *Insight*,[64] Lonergan's attention was primarily directed to an analysis of transcendental method as operative within the consciousness of the individual human being. But in a sequel to that work, namely, *Method in Theology*, Lonergan applied transcendental method, in the first place, to theology as a collective academic enterprise, but likewise by implication to other projects in which human beings find themselves working as a team or community. As a result, he was able to show how transcendental method functions within these groups or communities of human beings as well as within individuals. Not only individuals, therefore, can achieve differentiated self-awareness; likewise, specialized groups of individuals or even entire communities of human beings can, at least in principle, achieve a form of self-transcendence in adhering to what Lonergan calls the "transcendental precepts": namely, be attentive, be intelligent, be reasonable, be responsible.[65]

For our purposes in this chapter, it is sufficient to note that Lonergan, along with Whitehead and Habermas, thus affirms the capacity of human beings to use language so as to achieve truth and objectivity in their dealings with one another. As he notes in *Method in Theology*, "[b]y its embodiment in language, in a set of conventional signs, meaning finds its greatest liberation. For conventional signs can be multiplied almost indefinitely. They can be differentiated and specialized to the utmost refinement. They can be used reflexively in the analysis and control of linguistic meaning itself."[66] Accordingly, if a group through collective attention to the transcendental precepts noted above is sufficiently self-aware of how it is using language and in which realms of meaning it is operating, then that group in Lonergan's view runs only a modest risk of being overly conditioned or even fully determined by the language which it employs. The transcendental precepts, in other words, keep both the individual and the group mindful of the need to be self-critical in the use of language. Naturally, if an entire community has gone awry in interpreting its basic traditions and commonly held values,

---

64. Bernard J. F. Lonergan, S.J., *Insight: A Study of Human Understanding* (London: Longmans, Green & Co., 1957).
65. Lonergan, *Method in Theology*, 20.
66. Lonergan, *Method in Theology*, 70.

then, "in the measure a subject takes the tradition, as it exists, for his standard, in that measure he can do no more than authentically realize unauthenticity."[67] But, even if the bulk of individuals within the group thus find themselves inadvertently living inauthentically, Lonergan's conviction is that others in the same pursuit of genuine authenticity will find a way to hold the group accountable for its inauthentic behavior. Sustained reliance on the transcendental method, in other words, will sooner or later work those changes both in the individual and in the group which are needed for authentic existence.

D. Concluding Remarks

Thus far in this chapter, I have summarized the views of three prominent twentieth-century thinkers on the way in which language can be used to liberate as well as to constrain human beings in their efforts to communicate with one another and understand the world in which they live. Hence, the question naturally arises whether both in the content of their thought and in the methodology which they each use in arriving at their conclusions, these philosophers are saying the same things, that is, making the same claims about truth and objectivity within human experience. The answer to that question, in my judgment, is yes, albeit with certain modest reservations about the methodologies of Habermas and Lonergan vis-à-vis that of Whitehead. For, as I see it, with his stipulation that human beings have a prelinguistic feeling-level experience of the external world through the operation of causal efficacy upon their consciousness at every moment, Whitehead more successfully than either Habermas or Lonergan meets the challenge posed by Sellars and other contemporary philosophers to the effect that language effectively controls our human experience. That is, if there is a necessary prelinguistic component to human experience as Whitehead contends, then human beings, quite irrespective of their language-context and cultural history, have common access to an external reality which somehow serves as a check on their subjective efforts at interpretation and con-

67. Lonergan, *Method in Theology,* 80.

trol.[68] The category of causal efficacy within Whitehead's philosophy, therefore, with its assumption of an immediate contact of human beings with the world around them, gives a realistic orientation to Whitehead's thought which, as I see it, is not so readily available in the schemes of either Habermas or Lonergan. This is not to say, of course, that Habermas and Lonergan are naive idealists, but only that their schemes seem to presume a direct feeling-level access to external reality on the part of human beings for which Whitehead quite explicitly accounts with his detailed exposition of the self-constitution of actual occasions in terms of causal efficacy and presentational immediacy.

In addition, both Habermas and Lonergan impress me as dealing with the key postmodern issue of "otherness" less effectively than Whitehead. I will have much more to say on this point in the next chapter, which deals with the philosophy of Jacques Derrida. But for now I will bring this chapter to a close with my estimate of the way that Whitehead better deals with the fact of "otherness" than does either Habermas or Lonergan. First of all, with respect to Habermas's project, I have some reservations with his emphasis on rational consensus as the goal of a theory of "communicative rationality." Naturally, consensus should be aimed at as far as possible in communication between human beings on matters of import. But there are frequently times when such consensus is not available even after considerable deliberation and even soul-searching on the part of the participants to the discussion. People simply have to agree to disagree at a certain point.[69] As I see it,

68. Cf., however, Farmer, *Beyond the Impasse*, 89-90: "Because one perceives data only in relation to the significance the data have for oneself *perception is always perspectival.*" Hence, even though human beings are in touch with the real world through causal efficacy, as Whitehead prescribes, they have to share perceptions of that external world with one another in order to get a more objective understanding of the world around them. This is, of course, still another argument for the notion of truth and objectivity as a consequence of intersubjectivity, communication between distinct subjects of experience, rather than simply human subjectivity as such.

69. Cf. here Bernstein, *Beyond Objectivism and Relativism*, 197-223, where he notes the difference in approach to dialogue between Gadamer and Habermas, on the one hand, and Richard Rorty and Hannah Arendt, on the other. Where Gadamer and Habermas focus on consensus as the projected goal of dialogue, Rorty and Arendt are more content to think of dialogue as the best way to make clear necessary differences of viewpoint.

within Habermas's scheme this would have to be seen as a failure in rational communication, something which would have to be remedied by further discussion and argument at a later date.

Within Whitehead's account of the self-constitution of an actual occasion, on the other hand, "contrast" plays a key role. As he notes in *Process and Reality,* "the many components of a complex datum [for the self-constitution of an actual occasion] have a unity; this unity is a 'contrast' of entities."[70] These "entities" are both past actual occasions or physical facts and "eternal objects" or potential structures of intelligibility. In both cases, the concrescing actual occasion is obliged either to harmonize these latent contrasts between facts and possibilities or to dismiss them as irrelevant to its self-constitution here and now through what Whitehead calls "negative prehensions."[71] Hence, within Whitehead's scheme in my judgment, there is, at least in principle, a greater tolerance for otherness or difference as a *normal* feature of reality. Whitehead, in other words, better than Habermas, anticipates the regular occurrence of otherness and finds a way to incorporate it positively into his metaphysical scheme, that is, as a way to enhance the intensity of experience through a delicate harmony of contrasting features.[72] In the practical order, of course, there are limits to what a human being or a group can tolerate by way of differences with other individuals and other groups, and this is why Whitehead allows for the dismissal of irrelevant differences through negative prehensions. But Whitehead in any case does not have to regard it as a temporary breakdown in human communication when human beings have to agree to disagree on a given point. All the participants to the discussion can benefit from having somehow to assimilate the viewpoints of their logical opponents into their own assessment of the issue at hand even if it does not immediately result in some form of rational consensus.[73]

70. Whitehead, *Process and Reality,* 24.
71. Whitehead, *Process and Reality,* 83.
72. Whitehead, *Process and Reality,* 83.
73. Naturally, one could counterargue here that Habermas with his emphasis on consensus is more practical than Whitehead with his focus on tolerance of differences. For only with consensus can cooperative action be effectively taken for the good of the group. Even while conceding this point, however, one could still maintain with Whitehead that a respect for differences which is not simply based

Similarly, with respect to Lonergan's metaphysical scheme, I suspect that he would be in principle less tolerant of otherness in the way that human beings think and behave than Whitehead. His key notion of transcendental method, for example, with its four-step procedure in the movement toward the goal of full rational self-consciousness would necessarily seem to exclude any other epistemology, that is, any other way for human beings to think and behave rationally. As he notes in *Method in Theology*, "[w]here other methods aim at meeting the exigences and exploiting the opportunities proper to particular fields, transcendental method is concerned with meeting the exigences and exploiting the opportunities presented by the human mind itself. It is a concern that is both foundational and universally significant and relevant."[74] But there are language-situations and even entire cultures in which full rational self-consciousness is not highly prized; it is, in fact, seen as a liability to "enlightenment" or salvation. The goal of human life within such a context, therefore, is through an extended process of meditation to lose a distinct sense of self-awareness and to become totally absorbed in an object of contemplation, ultimately in the world as an all-enveloping totality.[75]

Here, too, I believe that Whitehead, with his metaphysical scheme based on momentary subjects of experience which, in principle at least, can assimilate otherwise conflicting dimensions of reality into the subjective harmony of their own self-constitution, is better prepared to accept the fact of radical otherness in today's highly pluralistic world than is Lonergan with his notion of transcendental method. This is not to deny, of course, the obvious advantages of transcendental method for the purposes of clear and effective thinking and behavior among those individuals who are antecedently trained for this purpose by their previous education and who accordingly place a very high value on rational self-consciousness. But, given the generic character of Whitehead's notion of an actual occa-

---

on expediency but grounded in the very nature of reality (i.e., the self-constitution of actual occasions) is indispensable for the peaceful coexistence of human beings in today's pluralistic society. Cf. on this point, chapter three.

74. Lonergan, *Method in Theology*, 14.

75. What I have in mind here, of course, are the various East Asian religions: classical Hinduism, Buddhism, and Taoism, in which totally "selfless" behavior is extolled as the highest human virtue and accomplishment.

sion as a momentary subject of experience which constitutes itself largely out of the data presented to it by its own past world (for human beings, its own past cultural world), his scheme allows for a variety of epistemologies or ideals of rationality, depending upon the particular cultural context in which they are operative.[76]

In the next chapter I will return to this elusive notion of otherness within the philosophy of the French deconstructionist, Jacques Derrida. My aim will be, first of all, to explore the possibility that even with his strong emphasis on otherness and nonidentity, Derrida's own thought seems to imply some kind of process-relational understanding of reality, above all if the latter be articulated in terms of a logic of intersubjectivity as argued for in this book. In line with this latter theme, I will investigate the parallels between Derrida's key notion of *différance* and the function of "creativity" within Whitehead's metaphysical scheme. Secondly, I will assess whether Whitehead's philosophy itself escapes the objections which Derrida lodges against classical metaphysical schemes in terms of their implicit passion for achieving unity or sameness at the price of genuine plurality. My contention will be that a reinterpretation of Whitehead's category of society as a structured field of activity for its constituent actual occasions seems to liberate his metaphysical scheme from the charge of "logocentrism" which Derrida customarily levels at metaphysical schemes. Then, with potential objections from radical deconstructionists thus cleared away, I will be in a position in the second part of this book to set forth an outline of my proposed metaphysics of intersubjectivity.

---

76. Cf. here Joseph A. Komonchak, *Foundations in Ecclesiology*, Supplementary Issue of the *Lonergan Workshop Journal*, vol. 11, ed. Fred Lawrence (Chestnut Hill, Mass.: Boston College, 1995), 100. Referring to Lonergan's transcendental method, he comments: "There has always been a danger, however, that this turn to the concrete subject will itself suffer from a certain abstractness, conceiving of the individual, if not as a Leibnizian monad, then as a lonely existential hero. But incarnate subjectivity is not envisaged in its full concreteness if it is referred only to the embodied character of the human spirit. The analysis must include as well the fact that this embodied spirit is also always concretely located communally and socially, economically, politically, and culturally."

3 The One and the Many Revisited

As mentioned at the end of the preceding chapter, the theme of "otherness" is prominent in academic circles within the United States and Western Europe at present. Here the influence of Emmanuel Levinas, with his ground-breaking work *Totality and Infinity*, is clearly evident.[1] That is, the drive within classical Western philosophy toward "totalizing" schemes in which genuine individuality is sacrificed to the logical exigencies of a set of universal concepts, in Levinas's view, must be countered by a heightened awareness of the "infinity" present in the "face" of the other.[2] While granting the legitimacy of Levinas's insight here, one may still object that an overly strong emphasis on otherness creates its own conceptual dilemma. For how is one to understand the notion of otherness except in terms of its conceptual counterpart, namely, sameness? That is, to be genuinely other than something else, one must somehow be the same as the other, in effect, be in some way comparable or in relation to the other.[3] Men and women, for example, are sexually other only because

---

1. Cf. Emmanuel Levinas, *Totality and Infinity: An Essay on Exteriority*, trans. Alphonso Lingis (Pittsburgh: Duquesne University Press, 1969); cf. also by the same author, *Otherwise than Being, or Beyond Essence*, trans. Alphonso Lingis (The Hague: Martinus Nijhoff, 1981). Likewise, cf. *Eglise et Theologie* 30:1 (1999), in which the entire issue is dedicated to a critical appreciation of Levinas's thought.

2. Levinas, *Totality and Infinity*, 33-52.

3. Cf., e.g., Jacques Derrida, "A Conversation with Jacques Derrida," in *Deconstruction in a Nutshell*, ed. John D. Caputo (New York: Fordham University

they share in different ways human nature and thus are comparable with one another in the matter of sexuality. Human beings are other than apes because they both are different types of primates (in distinction from non-primates). Total otherness, accordingly, seems to be unthinkable since it cannot be defined or otherwise known in terms of its relation to anything else. Even if one claims, for example, that God is totally other than anything finite, the resulting notion of God is distinguishable from pure nothingness only because God is then likewise conceived as Creator with reference to a world of creatures or, within a trinitarian understanding of God, because God in Godself is internally differentiated as three persons in dynamic interrelation even apart from creation.[4]

Keeping these reflections in mind, I turn now to what I regard as an unfortunate lacuna in the reflections of many postmodern thinkers on the subject of otherness. My thesis is that their efforts to conceive the other as genuinely other tend to be inconclusive since they do not give a *principled* reason why the other must remain other and thus may not be reduced to sameness in the interests of some overriding theoretical or practical concern. As Colin Gunton remarks in *The One, the Three and the Many,*[5] there is a tendency in contemporary thought theoretically to acknowledge the primacy of the other and yet in practice to reduce the other to the

---

Press, 1997), 13: "Singularity is not simply unity or multiplicity. . . . You see, pure unity or pure multiplicity — when there is only totality or unity and when there is only multiplicity or disassocation — is a symbol of death. What interests me is the limit of every attempt to totalize, to gather, *versammeln* . . . the limit of this unifying, uniting movement, the limit that it had to encounter, because the relationship of the unity to itself implies some difference." Hence, every true identity is internally self-differentiated, and every real difference only makes a difference if it can be compared with something else and thus share some measure of identity with the other thing.

4. Cf. Roland Faber, "Trinity, Analogy, and Coherence," in *Trinity in Process: A Relational Theology of God,* ed. Joseph A. Bracken, S.J., and Marjorie Hewitt Suchocki (New York: Continuum, 1997), 147-71, esp. 150-52. Faber points out that the Fourth Lateran Council in 1215 decreed that any analogy between God and creatures must be grounded in an even greater dissimilarity. But, by the same token, some analogous understanding of the reality of God on the basis of human experience is both possible and necessary for Christian life and worship.

5. Cf. below, Appendix, pp. 180-81.

hegemony of the same under a new guise, if only to bring order out of chaos in dealing with masses of individuals. Hence, only if one has thought through the necessary dialectical relationship between otherness and sameness and realized that neither is basically intelligible without the other,[6] can one offer a *principled* reason to maintain the genuine otherness of the other, quite apart from the pressure to reduce the other to the same all over again in the name of some alleged value or goal.

Here one might object that this was in fact the ideal of G. W. F. Hegel in working out his philosophy of Absolute Spirit as the dynamic identity of unity and difference. But as Mark C. Taylor points out, Hegel remained true to the Western philosophical tradition in that he privileged unity over plurality: "His overriding concern [was] to establish the *union* of union and nonunion and the *identity* of identity and difference."[7] Hence, any metaphysical scheme which will legitimately uphold the otherness of the other will, in conscious opposition to Hegel, have to privilege otherness over sameness even while maintaining their dialectical interdependence. Yet, as I see it, this is precisely the presupposition of the metaphysics of intersubjectivity which I hope to develop in the course of this book. That is, within the context of intersubjectivity, (human) subjects of experience are, in Levinas's words, "infinitely" different from one another. Yet paradoxically, from moment to moment, they are in vital contact with one another; in effect, they bridge that infinite difference, through various forms of communication. The objectivity or sameness thus established is, to be sure, strictly dependent upon the continued interplay of those same or still other subjects of experience with one another through language or some other medium of communica-

6. Cf. here Mark C. Taylor, *Deconstructing Theology* (New York: Crossroad, 1982), 56: "Determinate identity is born of ontological intercourse with otherness. . . . Identity and difference, unity and plurality, oneness and manyness are thoroughly co-relative — joined in a dialectical relation of reciprocal implication." Taylor's guide for the analysis of the dialectical relationship between identity and difference is primarily Hegel, as Taylor makes clear again and again in this book, even though he readily acknowledges that Hegel erred in giving so much weight to identity over difference.

7. Mark C. Taylor, ed., *Deconstruction in Context: Literature and Philosophy* (Chicago: University of Chicago Press, 1986), Introduction, 8-9.

tion.[8] Hence, within a metaphysics based on intersubjectivity, the focus has to be more on otherness than on sameness, even though, as noted above, sameness in the form of shared patterns of thought and behavior must likewise be present as a check against a Leibnizian atomism in which each monad or self-enclosed subject of experience would be in effect a world unto itself.

To provide theoretical justification for my proposal here, I will in the first part of this chapter carefully analyze some of Jacques Derrida's key terms so as to indicate how they actually seem to make better sense in the context of a metaphysics of intersubjectivity than in the context of the classical metaphysics of being which he evidently had in mind in mounting his critique of the Western philosophical tradition. In particular, I will focus on his key notion of *"différance"* as the systematic play of differences and indicate its affinity with Whitehead's notion of creativity (cf. Glossary) as that principle whereby "[t]he many become one and are increased by one."[9] In both cases, as I see it, Whitehead and Derrida were trying to capture in words the dynamism of becoming, the moment of creative advance.[10] Then in the second part of the chapter, I will make clear

8. Taylor, *Deconstructing Theology,* 76. Noting that human work or self-objectification calls forth a response from other human beings so as to invest themselves in the same work, Taylor comments: "The object produced by the subject's labor harbors potentiality that *necessarily* remains unrealized by the acting subject. The work is finished through the activity of responsive agents."

9. Whitehead, *Process and Reality: An Essay in Cosmology,* corrected edition, ed. David Ray Griffin and Donald W. Sherburne (New York: The Free Press, 1978), 21. Cf. also Luis G. Pedraja, "Whitehead, Deconstruction and Postmodernism," *Process Studies* 28 (1999): 68-84, esp. 75, 82-83. Pedraja's reflections on the relation between Whitehead and Derrida in the matter of postmodernism are remarkably similar to my own even though neither of us was antecedently aware of the other's work on the same theme.

10. More than Whitehead, Derrida focuses on the future as the unexpected, that which would seem to be impossible from the vantage point of the past (cf. John Caputo's commentary on "A Conversation with Jacques Derrida," *Deconstruction in a Nutshell,* 117-18: "History, thus, is not a course set in advance headed toward its *telos* as toward a future-present, a foreseeable, plannable, programmable, anticipatable, masterable future. History means, rather, to set sail without a course, on the prowl for something 'new.' Such an open-ended, non-teleological history is just what Derrida means by 'history,' which means for him that something — an 'event' — is really happening, e-venting *(é-venir)."* At the

how process-relational metaphysics still runs the risk of what Derrida calls the "logocentrism" (cf. Glossary) implicit in the entire Western philosophical tradition. But I will at the same time indicate how this charge of logocentrism can be deftly avoided if one gives closer attention to the logical consequences of the notion of society within Whitehead's conceptual scheme. That is, I will set forth below my own understanding of how a democratically-organized society of actual occasions can be understood as a network of interrelated differences which exist in virtue of creativity but for the same reason operate without a logical centerpoint or *Logos* in the sense critiqued by Derrida.

A. *Différance* and Creativity Compared

In his book *Margins of Philosophy,* Derrida has an essay simply titled *"Différance"* in which he lays forth at some length his understanding of this key term in his philosophy. He begins with reference to the fact that *différance,* when spoken aloud, is indistinguishable from another more common French word, namely, *différence.*[11] He then adds: *"Différance is not,* does not exist, is not a present-being *(on)* in any form."[12] Thus "it has neither essence nor existence. It derives from no category of being, whether present or absent."[13] This is remarkably similar to Whitehead's description of creativity as that which is actual in terms of its accidents or instantiations: "It is only then capable of characterization through its accidental embodiments, and apart from these accidents is devoid of actuality."[14] In both cases, we are dealing with something that may be seen as a principle of activity

---

same time, Whitehead's notion of the self-constitution of an actual occasion is that, while clearly dependent upon its past, it is, at least in principle, a new and original moment in an ongoing process. Hence, Whitehead is like Derrida on principle opposed to the teleological mind-set of classical metaphysics which subtly undercuts any real possibility of evolution in the sense of unplanned change.

11. Jacques Derrida, *"Différance,"* in *Margins of Philosophy,* trans. Alan Bass (Chicago: University of Chicago Press, 1982), 3-5.

12. Derrida, *"Différance,"* 6.

13. Derrida, *"Différance,"* 6.

14. Whitehead, *Process and Reality,* 7.

rather than as an entity.[15] Both *différance* and creativity, therefore, empower entities to be themselves, in effect, to make a difference in a world of individual entities.

This is not to ignore, of course, that the overall thrust of the philosophy of Derrida is quite different from that of Whitehead. Derrida's focus is on detecting subtle differences of perspective within established identities so as to set free a creative rethinking of those same identities. Deconstruction, he says, insists "not on multiplicity for itself but on the heterogeneity, the difference, the disassociation, which is absolutely necessary for the relation to the other. What disrupts the totality is the condition for the relation to the other."[16] Whitehead, on the other hand, as a metaphysician is focused on principles of order and continuity within the creative process. Yet both thinkers, as noted above, have tried to capture the creative moment when something new emerges from the old without cutting off all sense of continuity with the old. As I will indicate below, the notion of "trace" and the dialectic of presence and absence which are so prominent in Derrida's philosophy likewise have their counterpart in the philosophy of Whitehead.

In the meantime, however, note should be taken of still another feature of *différance* in Derrida's philosophy which can be matched with Whitehead's understanding of creativity. Derrida points out that the notion of *khora* (receptacle) in Plato's *Timaeus* is basically incompatible with the so-called "philosophy of Plato" with its emphasis on a graded hierarchy of forms up to and including the Idea of the Good as the Form of Forms.[17] But Plato, after all, must have had

---

15. Taylor, *Deconstructing Theology*, 100-101: "Saussurean *difference* and Derridean *différance* are variations of Hegel's notion of negativity. . . . When negativity is adequately grasped in its infinity and absoluteness, it reveals itself to be the essence, the *Wesen* or *Inbegriff* of everything. Essence is pure negative activity that relates itself to itself in otherness. . . . Essence realizes itself through active self-negation in which it posits itself as other, that is, as determinate being, and returns to itself from this otherness by negating its own negation." Common to Saussure, Derrida, Hegel, and Whitehead, therefore, is the insight that an infinite activity underlies all the finite determinations to be found in this world. It is this necessarily indeterminate activity which establishes the dynamic identity-indifference of all determinate individual entities with one another.

16. Derrida, "A Conversation with Jacques Derrida," 13.

17. Derrida, "A Conversation with Jacques Derrida," 9. Cf. also "Khora," in

some reason for discussion of this term in the *Timaeus*. Since *khora* represents for Plato a receptacle devoid of any determinations apart from the entities to be found within it, it seems to be his expression for the principle of pure potentiality which stands in necessary opposition to the Idea of the Good as the principle of pure actuality in his philosophy. Yet, like Aristotle with his term *hyle*, Plato conceived *khora* or the receptacle as a purely passive reality, namely, that which receives forms (as opposed to that which produces forms). Derrida, on the other hand, thinks of *khora* in active terms as linked to *différance*, the systematic "play" of differences.[18] In the same way, Whitehead notes that creativity "is another rendering of the Aristotelian 'matter,' and of the modern 'neutral stuff.' But it is divested of the notion of passive reception, either of 'form,' or of external relations; it is the pure notion of the activity conditioned by the objective immortality of the actual world."[19]

Thus what both Derrida and Whitehead seem to be getting at here is the way in which the relation between the principles of potentiality and actuality is curiously reversed when one switches from a metaphysics of Being to a metaphysics of Becoming. Within a metaphysics of Being the principle of actuality is active, so to speak, "from the top down," with the principle of potentiality as the necessary receptacle for the play of forms within it. Within a metaphysics of Becoming, on the other hand, the principle of potentiality is active "from the bottom up" to produce as products or effects of its activity the various actualities encountered in the world. For the same reason, neither Derrida nor Whitehead wants to associate *différance* or creativity with the actuality of God understood as the Supreme Being.

Derrida, for example, is emphatic that *différance* is not to be identified with God, even the God of negative theology, since negative theologies "are always concerned with disengaging a super-

---

On the Name, trans. Ian McLeod, ed. Thomas Dutoit (Stanford, Calif.: Stanford University Press, 1995), 87-127.

18. Derrida, "Khora," 126. Derrida does not explicitly use the term *différance* here, but I rely upon the judgment of John Caputo that *différance* is what is intended with Derrida's reference at this point to "a necessity which is neither generative nor engendered" (cf. Caputo, *Deconstruction in a Nutshell*, 96-105).

19. Whitehead, *Process and Reality*, 31.

essentiality beyond the finite categories of essence and existence, that is, of presence, and always hastening to recall that God is refused the predicate of existence, only in order to acknowledge his superior, inconceivable, and ineffable mode of being."[20] In similar fashion, Whitehead declares that "God is its [creativity's] primordial, non-temporal accident."[21] God is an instance of the operation of creativity, not the transcendent source of creativity. Within my own conceptual reworking of Whitehead's metaphysical scheme, to be sure, I modify Whitehead's understanding of creativity so as to avoid the otherwise inevitable consequence of two Ultimates, God and creativity.[22] That is, I propose that creativity is the nature or principle of activity first for God and then by a free decision on God's part likewise for all creatures.[23] But even within my scheme creativity is not operative from above, but, properly understood, from below. That is, within God creativity is the *underlying* principle for the existence and interrelated activity of the three divine persons. Likewise, within creation, creativity is the *underlying* principle for the existence and interrelated activity of all creatures. Hence, even though coeternal with God as the Supreme Being, creativity is immanent within creatures rather than transcendent to them. It may be aptly described as the "divine matrix" within which the three divine persons and all their creatures exist in dynamic interrelation.[24]

Somewhat later in his essay, Derrida notes that *différance*, like the Latin *differre*, has two meanings. The first, less common, meaning is to put off until later or to "temporize": "to take recourse, consciously or unconsciously, in the temporal and temporizing mediation of a de-

20. Derrida, *"Différance,"* 6; cf. also John D. Caputo, *The Prayers and Tears of Jacques Derrida: Religion without Religion* (Bloomington, Ind.: Indiana University Press, 1997), 1-19. Caputo is emphatic that deconstructionism and negative theology of God are not to be conflated: *"Différance* does not settle the God question one way or the other; in fact, the point is to unsettle it, to make it more difficult, by showing that, even as we love the name of God, we must still ask what it is we love."

21. Whitehead, *Process and Reality,* 7.

22. Cf., e.g., Whitehead, *Science and the Modern World* (New York: The Free Press, 1967), 173-79.

23. Cf. below, chapter four, pp. 126-27.

24. Cf. my recent book *The Divine Matrix: Creativity as Link between East and West* (Maryknoll, N.Y.: Orbis Books, 1995), esp. ch. 4.

tour that suspends the accomplishment or fulfilment of 'desire' or 'will,' and equally effects this suspension in a mode that annuls or tempers its own effect."[25] The second, more common, meaning of *différance* or *differre* is "to be not identical, to be other, discernible, etc."[26] Here I would argue that the same two meanings are to be found in Whiteheadian creativity as the metaphysical principle whereby "[t]he many become one, and are increased by one."[27] That is, in virtue of creativity a new actual occasion is created which is different from its predecessors but whose ultimate identity lies not in itself but in the nexus or social configuration of actual occasions out of which it arose and to which it contributes its own momentary pattern of intelligibility even as it passes out of existence. No single actual occasion has, therefore, any enduring significance; its significance lies in its being the latest member of a temporally ordered nexus or "society" of actual occasions. In Derrida's terms, its ultimate meaning is "deferred" to the ongoing context of the society to which it belongs. As Whitehead notes in *Adventures of Ideas:* a society "enjoys a history expressing its changing reactions to changing circumstances. But an actual occasion has no such history. It never changes. It only becomes and perishes."[28]

Derrida also notes that *différance* designates "a constitutive, productive, and originary causality, the process of scission and division which would produce or constitute different things or differences."[29] But is not Whiteheadian creativity also a "constitutive, productive, and originary causality" whereby "the many become one, and are increased by one"? Furthermore, perhaps even better than with Derrida's notion of *différance,* Whitehead's category of creativity makes clear that, even though each actual occasion is different from its predecessors and successors, an unmistakable affinity or sameness between these separate actual occasions is likewise present in that they are all instantiations of one and the same originary causality. As noted above, differences only make a difference when there is a dialectical

25. Derrida, *"Différance,"* 8.
26. Derrida, *"Différance,"* 8.
27. Whitehead, *Process and Reality,* 21.
28. Alfred North Whitehead, *Adventures of Ideas* (New York: The Free Press, 1967), 204.
29. Derrida, *"Différance,"* 9.

connection between the individuals thus distinguished from one another. At the same time, postulating this underlying unity does not in and of itself imply a covert return to "logocentrism" (cf. Glossary) where all differences are ultimately dissolved into a unitary sameness. For everything depends upon how one conceives this sameness: namely, as the sameness of an immanent activity or the sameness of a transcendent entity. Only in the latter case, as I see it, can one raise the question of logocentrism. For an activity which is immanent in various entities so as to enable them to exist must by definition operate somewhat differently in each entity. Hence, it is the principle of radical otherness within these entities even as it simultaneously functions as the underlying principle of unity between them.

Derrida also proposes that *différance* as "temporizing" involves temporalization and spacing, "the becoming-time of space and the becoming-space of time."[30] His argument here is somewhat convoluted since he begins with an analysis of language rather than an analysis of extra-mental reality in which space and time are key coordinates. His initial reference, therefore, is to Ferdinand de Saussure's celebrated hypothesis that language is an arbitrary system of signs whose significance is determined by their relation to one another rather than by their common relation to an external reality.[31] Derrida then continues: "The first consequence to be drawn from this is that the signified concept is never present in and of itself, in a sufficient presence that would refer only to itself. Essentially and lawfully, every concept is inscribed in a chain or in a system within which it refers to the other, to other concepts, by means of the systematic play of differences."[32] Basically, the same statement can be made about an

30. Derrida, *"Différance,"* 8.

31. Derrida, *"Différance,"* 11: " 'Whether we take the signified or the signifier, language has neither ideas nor sounds that existed before the linguistic system, but only conceptual and phonic differences that have issued from the system.' " As I indicated already in chapter two, I follow Whitehead in arguing that language does have an extra-mental reference but on the level of feeling in terms of causal efficacy rather than on the level of presentational immediacy in terms of perceptions or concepts. Hence, within the limits of what is immediately present to consciousness by way of perceptions or concepts, Saussure is correct in proposing that language is a self-enclosed system of signs without reference to extramental reality.

32. Derrida, *"Différance,"* 11.

actual occasion as a member of an ongoing social nexus or "society." Its coming-to-be has meaning and value only in terms of the society to which it belongs. The key difference, of course, is that, while Derrida refers to *différance* as the "systematic play of differences" within language, Whitehead's notion of creativity is operative within extramental reality to insure the *ordered* sequence of actual occasions according to a "common element of form" or shared pattern of intelligibility (cf. Glossary). Yet Derrida is not thereby insensitive to the possibility that there is more at work in language than language itself. For he immediately adds that as the systematic play of differences, "*différance* is thus no longer simply a concept, but rather the possibility of conceptuality, of a conceptual process and system in general."[33] This reference to the possibility of conceptuality and of "system in general," as we shall see below, will eventually lead Derrida into more overtly metaphysical reflection by way of explanation for the reality of *différance*. Here it is sufficient to note that creativity for Whitehead, like *différance* for Derrida, is not in itself the actuality of conceptual process, system, or any other determinate reality, but rather the ontological possibility for the latter.

Derrida's second conclusion from Saussure's hypothesis runs as follows:

> It is because of *différance* that the movement of signification is possible only if each so-called 'present' element, each element appearing on the scene of presence, is related to something other than itself, thereby keeping within itself the mark of the past element, and already letting itself be vitiated by the mark of its relation to the future element, this trace being related no less to what is called the future than to what is called the past, and constituting what is called the present by means of this very relation to what it is not: what it absolutely is not, not even a past or a future as a modified present.[34]

Once again, the parallel with Whitehead's notion of an actual occasion is remarkable. An actual occasion always bears the mark of its past in

33. Derrida, *"Différance,"* 11.
34. Derrida, *"Différance,"* 13. Cf. also on this point Pedraja, "Whitehead, Deconstructionism and Postmodernism," 82.

that it is largely constituted out of "prehensions" (cf. Glossary), both physical and conceptual, of its predecessor actual occasions. Likewise, it anticipates the impact which it as a "superject" or completed actual occasion will have on its successors, above all, within the same society of actual occasions. Hence, it is in a very real sense constituted here and now by its (anticipated) future. Thus an actual occasion like an "element" in the quotation from Derrida is never really present to itself but always in transition from past to future.

Finally, Derrida arrives at an explanation of what he referred to above as "the becoming-space of time" and "the becoming-time of space":

> An interval must separate the present from what it is not in order for the present to be itself, but this interval that constitutes it as present must, by the same token, divide the present in and of itself. . . . In constituting itself, in dividing itself dynamically, this interval is what might be called *spacing*, the becoming-space of time or the becoming-time of space *(temporization)*. And it is this constitution of the present, as an 'originary' and irreducibly nonsimple (and therefore, *stricto sensu* nonoriginary) synthesis of marks, or traces of retentions and protentions . . . that I propose to call archi-writing, archi-trace, or *différance*. Which (is) (simultaneously) spacing (and) temporization.[35]

Here, too, there seems to be a significant parallel with Whitehead's account of the self-constitution of an actual occasion. It must separate itself from its predecessors on which it heavily depends for its self-constitution in order to be itself. Likewise, it must somehow distinguish itself from its successors in order to assess its anticipated impact upon those same successor actual occasions. In the process, the actual occasion together with its predecessors and successors sets up a space-time system governing the society as a whole. That is, the Whiteheadian society does not exist in space and time but creates its own space-time parameters in virtue of the ordered succession of its member actual occasions.[36]

35. Derrida, *"Différance,"* 13.
36. Cf. Whitehead, *Process and Reality*, 92: "Thus the physical relations, the geometrical relations of measurement, the dimensional relations, and the various grades

The point of this extended comparison of Whitehead's concept of creativity and Derrida's notion of *différance,* of course, is not to suggest that Derrida was somehow dependent upon Whitehead's philosophy for his own understanding of the nature of language, but rather to insinuate that Derrida is perhaps more of a metaphysician than he himself is prepared to admit. That is, even though he sees himself as working within the tradition of classical metaphysics in order to deconstruct it, that is, to set it free from its own rigidified presuppositions,[37] his own more positive efforts to understand the nature of language, when systematically organized, themselves seem to presuppose an inchoative metaphysics, a new way of understanding not only human language but reality as a whole. In this respect, the sage remark of Etienne Gilson to the effect that philosophy buries its undertakers,[38] may be vindicated once again. That is, one cannot think systematically without explicitly or implicitly making certain claims not only about one's specific subject matter but also about how one's subject matter fits into the broader scheme of things, in the end, the nature of reality.

Derrida seems indirectly to confirm this observation with his remarks about language and self-consciousness in the second half of the article on *différance.* He begins by citing Saussure once more to the effect that language is not an effect of the speaking subject but rather that the speaking subject is a function of language: "The subject (in its identity with itself, its self-consciousness) is inscribed in language, is a 'function' of language, becomes a *speaking* subject only by making its speech conform . . . to the system of the rules of language as a system of differences, or at the very least by conforming to the general law of *différance.*"[39] He then cites Nietzsche, Freud, and Heidegger in

---

of extensive relations involved in the physical and geometrical theory of nature, are derivative from a series of societies [of actual occasions] of increasing width of prevalence, the more special societies being included in the wider societies."

37. Cf., e.g., Derrida, "A Conversation with Jacques Derrida," in *Deconstruction in a Nutshell,* 6: "That is what deconstruction is made of: not the mixture but the tension between memory, fidelity, the preservation of something that has been given to us, and, at the same time, heterogeneity, something absolutely new, and a break."

38. Etienne Gilson, *The Unity of Philosophical Experience* (Westminster, Md.: Four Courts Press, 1982), 306.

39. Derrida, *"Différance,"* 15.

support of his basically metaphysical claim that consciousness is a function of language rather than an entitative reality in its own right, that is, the self-presence of the subject to itself "before distributing its signs in space and in the world."[40] Nietzsche, for example, argued that consciousness is the effect of unconscious forces within the psyche. Derrida comments: "Force itself is never present; it is only a play of differences and quantities. There would be no force in general without the difference between forces."[41] For that matter, as Derrida sees it, Nietzsche's entire philosophical project is an implicit affirmation of *différance* when the latter is understood as "the displaced and equivocal passage of one different thing to another, from one term of an opposition to another" (e.g., for Nietzsche, from the sensible to the intelligible, from nature to culture, etc.).[42]

Likewise, within Freudian psychological theory the two notions of differing and deferring are inextricably tied together:

> A certain alterity — to which Freud gives the metaphysical name of the unconscious — is definitively exempt from every process of presentation by means of which we would call upon it to show itself in person. In this context, and beneath this guise, the unconscious is not, as we know, a hidden, virtual, or potential self-presence. It differs from, and defers, itself; which doubtless means that it is woven of differences, and also that it sends out delegates, representatives, proxies; but without any chance that the giver of proxies might "exist," might be present, be "itself" somewhere, and with even less chance that it might become conscious.[43]

The parallel with Whitehead's notion of consciousness is once again quite striking. For Whitehead, too, consciousness is not the permanent presence of the human subject to itself, but a varying function of mental processes, most of which are not conscious. That is, for Whitehead consciousness arises only at an advanced stage in the concrescence (cf. Glossary) of some (but by no means all) actual occasions when "intellectual feelings" provide a contrast between ac-

40. Derrida, *"Différance,"* 16.
41. Derrida, *"Différance,"* 17.
42. Derrida, *"Différance,"* 17.
43. Derrida, *"Différance,"* 20-21.

tuality and potentiality, that is, a contrast between a de facto set of actual occasions and some imaginative possibility that could be accepted or rejected by the current actual occasion in its process of self-constitution: "Consciousness is the way of feeling that particular real nexus, as in contrast with imaginative freedom about it."[44] As a result, Whitehead concludes, "[c]onsciousness flickers; and even at its brightest, there is a small focal region of clear illumination, and a large penumbral region of experience which tells of intense experience in dim apprehension."[45] Finally, for Whitehead as well as for Derrida, language plays a key role in the emergence of consciousness. For, while non-human animal species exercise consciousness to some degree, their inability to communicate with one another by means of language severely restricts the range of possibilities available to them in consciousness. Language, in other words, elicits in human beings the above-named "intellectual feelings" which even prior to conscious awareness set forth a variety of new possibilities for what is perceived to exist and thus add notably to the intensity of consciousness here and now.[46]

My purpose, once again, in this extended comparison between Whitehead and Derrida on various topics is simply to suggest that Derrida is indirectly constructing a new metaphysics even as he seeks systematically to deconstruct the implicit presuppositions of classical Western metaphysics. Yet, insofar as the informal metaphysics of Derrida appears to have a natural affinity with the metaphysical system of Whitehead, one is further led to surmise that, if Derrida himself or one of his disciples were more thoroughly to systematize his reflections on the nature of language, this resemblance might well be even more striking.[47] Derrida, in other words, however tentatively,

---

44. Whitehead, *Process and Reality*, 261. Cf. also Stephen Franklin, *Speaking from the Depths: A Hermeneutical Metaphysics of Propositions, Experience, Symbolism, Language and Religion* (Grand Rapids: Eerdmans, 1990), 27-29.

45. Whitehead, *Process and Reality*, 267.

46. Cf. Franklin, *Speaking from the Depths*, 245-46.

47. Cf. on this point Caputo's commentary on Derrida's style of writing: "So, if Derrida has a style, a signature, a dominant tone, a unity of purpose, if his works weave a certain fabric, it is up to someone else to trace that signature out later on, to countersign it for him. It is not his business and it would be stultifying for him to have to obey any such internal imperative, to censor himself, to

seems to be at work on a metaphysics of becoming which is governed by a logic of intersubjectivity much akin to what I have proposed in these pages in reliance on the philosophy of Whitehead. My surmise here is, I believe, unexpectedly confirmed when one reviews in the final pages of *"Différance"* Derrida's comments on the philosophy of Heidegger and the latter's key insight into the ontological difference between Being and beings.

Derrida begins by noting the alterity of past and future to the present. That is, there is a "past" which is necessarily other than the present and a "future" which never will be present.[48] Time, in other words, is not a succession of "nows" which move uniformly out of the future into the present and thence into the past. Rather, much akin to what Whitehead says about the self-constitution of an actual occasion, Derrida says that the present moment always contains the "trace" of the past and the "trace" of the future. The specific content of what is meant by past and future may vary from moment to moment, but the relation of past and future to the present moment never varies. In similar fashion, the meaning of Being is not exhausted by the beings, particular entities, which it empowers to exist here and now in the present. Thus, while in one sense *différance* can be understood as "the historical and epochal *unfolding* of Being or of the ontological difference," from another angle *différance* is " 'older' than the ontological difference or than the truth of Being."[49] For the latter terms are simply historical manifestations of the deeper reality of *différance* or "the trace": "Always differing and deferring, the trace is never as it is in the presentation of itself."[50]

Derrida illustrates this point by reference to a text of Heidegger, *Der Spruch des Anaximander* (1946), in which Heidegger first distinguishes between what is present and the act of presencing and then indicates that the nature or essence of this act of presencing and the relation of the act of presencing to what is present still remains hid-

---

pursue such an image, to abide by a contract that has been signed for him without his consent" (*Deconstruction in a Nutshell,* 46). By the same token, of course, a systematization of Derrida's thought along the lines that I have suggested in this chapter is not out of place.

48. Derrida, *"Différance,"* 21.
49. Derrida, *"Différance,"* 22.
50. Derrida, *"Différance,"* 23.

den.[51] As Derrida comments, the difference between Being and beings has disappeared without leaving a trace. For, when the activity of presencing appears as something present, indeed, as the highest being present (" 'in einem höchsten Anwesenden' "),[52] then "erasure" belongs to the reality of the "trace." That is, not only can the "trace" be regularly erased, but in fact it is constantly being erased.[53] Only thus can one explain the historical oblivion of the distinction between Being and beings from the beginning of Western philosophy. At the same time, as Heidegger also notes, the trace curiously remains in the very language that is used to talk about Being.[54]

Pursuing this last point further, Derrida calls attention to Heidegger's translation of Anaximander's word *(to khreon)* as *Brauch* (usage), that which primordially discloses and conceals the reality of Being.[55] As Derrida sees it, Heidegger's *Brauch* is equivalent to his own term *différance;* but for that same reason he questions whether Heidegger or anyone else can through reflection on *Brauch* (or *différance)* arrive at a knowledge of the essence of Being *(Wesen des Seins).* "There is no essence of *différance;* it (is) that which not only could never be appropriated in the *as such* of its name or its appearing, but also that which threatens the authority of the *as such* in general, of the presence of the thing itself in its essence."[56] Grammatically speaking, *différance* is a noun, a name for a thing; but it is not a thing but rather an activity "which unceasingly dislocates itself in a chain of differing and deferring substitutions."[57] Heidegger's search for a unique word to describe the reality of Being is, in Derrida's view, a remnant of metaphysical thinking in Heidegger's reflections. Yet Derrida shares with Heidegger the nostalgic desire or perhaps

51. Derrida, *"Différance,"* 23.

52. Derrida, *"Différance,"* 24; compare also M. Heidegger, *Holzwege,* sixth ed. (Frankfurt: V. Klosterman, 1980), 360.

53. Derrida, *"Différance,"* 24.

54. Derrida, *"Différance,"* 25: " 'However, the distinction between Being and beings, as something forgotten, can invade our experience only if it has already unveiled itself with the presencing of what is present *(mit dem Anwesen des Anwesenden);* only if it has left a trace *(eine Spur geprägt hat)* which remains preserved *(gewährt bleibt)* in the language to which Being comes.' " See Heidegger, *Holzwege,* 360.

55. Derrida, *"Différance,"* 25.

56. Derrida, *"Différance,"* 25-26.

57. Derrida, *"Différance,"* 26.

even hope that in language Being or *différance* will "always and every-where" somehow make itself felt.[58]

Derrida's focus, accordingly, here at the end of his essay on *différance* is still on the deconstruction of the classical metaphysics of Being in which Being is given a name and thus assigned a place within a hierarchically-ordered metaphysical scheme. But inadvertently he is setting forth in my judgment a new metaphysics of becoming with *différance* as its archetypal principle. That is, while his preferred subject matter is the elusive character of language as an ongoing play of differences, he affirms with Heidegger that something more is at stake in language than language itself. *Différance* is somehow descriptive of Being (in the sense of universal Becoming) as well as of language. In that respect, there is a deep, even if somewhat oblique, affinity of Derrida's philosophy with that of Whitehead. That is, the basic metaphysical instincts of both men flow in the same direction: namely, an affirmation, on the one hand, of the universal fluidity of reality and, on the other hand, of the interconnectedness of everything with everything else as a result. Whitehead is clearly the more systematic thinker; but Derrida may be more insightful with respect to the issue of "logocentrism." As I shall indicate below, Whitehead's notion of the God-world relationship is somewhat ambiguous and the efforts of his disciples, notably Charles Hartshorne, to clear up these ambiguities have resulted in what appears to be a subtle form of logocentrism. But, as I will explain below, there should be a way for disciples of Whitehead to remedy that oversight in conventional process-relational metaphysics and at the same time to remain faithful to Whitehead's own deeper instincts in terms of the God-world relationship.

B. Overcoming the Residual Logocentrism in Process-Relational Metaphysics

In the final chapter of *Process and Reality*, Whitehead discusses what he means by the "consequent nature" of God as opposed to the "primordial nature" of God (cf. Glossary). By virtue of the divine primor-

---

58. Derrida, *"Différance,"* 27; Heidegger, *Holzwege*, 362.

dial nature, God "is the unlimited conceptual realization of the absolute wealth of potentiality."[59] That is, in one comprehensive valuation God brings order and coherence out of the vast plurality of eternal objects (cf. Glossary) or patterns of intelligibility pertinent to the world of creation. But this nontemporal conceptual prehension of possibilities on God's part must then be linked with God's physical prehension of the actual course of events within creation (cf. Glossary). This is accomplished in Whitehead's view through the divine consequent nature, which is as a result the objectification of the world in God. God thus "shares with every new creation its actual world; and the concrescent creature is objectified in God as a novel element in God's objectification of that actual world. This prehension into God of each creature is directed with the subjective aim, and clothed with the subjective form, wholly derivative from his all-inclusive conceptual valuation."[60] Like all other actual entities, therefore, God is dipolar in nature. But whereas a finite actual entity begins its concrescence with the physical prehension of past actual occasions and then adds from a variety of sources conceptual prehensions pertinent to its own self-constitution, God begins with an unlimited conceptual prehension of possibilities and then adds physical prehensions or physical feelings to that all-embracing conceptual vision in line with actual events taking place in the world.

Thus far Whitehead's concept of the God-world relationship is consistent with his overall theory for the self-constitution of actual entities. What is not clear, however, is whether or not God as a result equivalently constitutes the transcendent ground or objective principle of unity for the cosmic process from moment to moment.[61] For,

59. Whitehead, *Process and Reality*, 343.

60. Whitehead, *Process and Reality*, 345.

61. This, of course, presumes that the cosmic process has an objective unity, i.e., that it constitutes a universe rather than a number of loosely related "pockets of order" (cf. below, Appendix, p. 206). In line with my field-oriented approach to Whiteheadian societies, I assume here that the physical universe even with its myriad subdivisions is a single all-comprehensive structured field of activity for the events taking place within it. Likewise, I presume that changes take place in the field as a result of these events instantaneously rather than simply at the speed of light as prescribed by Einstein's theories of special and general relativity. Hence, from moment to moment there is an objective state of affairs in the universe which has been effected by the subjective agencies of all actual occasions in existence up

even though each actual entity unifies the physical and conceptual data proper to its world, and even though subsequent actual entities can prehend the actual world(s) proper to their predecessors,[62] the actual worlds of all these finite actual entities are strictly perspectival. They are limited, in other words, by what Whitehead calls their "subjective aim" (cf. Glossary) at internal self-constitution in one way rather than another.[63] Only God has a non-perspectival vision of the wealth of conceptual possibilities in virtue of the divine primordial nature; and only God has a non-perspectival physical prehension of the events taking place in the world of creation. Thus it would appear that if the world has an objective unity, if it in effect constitutes a single, all-comprehensive process, then only God in virtue of the divine consequent nature is able to give it that all-embracing unity and order. As Whitehead comments with respect to the completeness of the divine consequent nature, "[i]n it there is no loss, no obstruction. The world is felt in a unison of immediacy."[64]

But is there not a perspectival character even to God's unification of the world process within the divine subjectivity? For, as Whitehead notes further, "[t]he revolts of destructive evil, purely self-regarding, are dismissed into their triviality of merely individual facts; and yet the good they did achieve in individual joy, in individual sorrow, in the introduction of needed contrast, is yet saved by its relation to the completed whole."[65] Thus, to achieve the harmony proper to the divine being, God must downplay the immediate significance of certain events taking place in creation and give consider-

---

to that point. I recognize the controversial character of this presupposition. But, as far as I know, it has not been refuted by discoveries in the natural sciences; in fact, within the thought-world of quantum mechanics as a result of the empirical refutation of the Einstein-Podalsky-Rosen *Gedankenexperiment,* there have been cautious proposals along these same lines about the "non-locality" of interrelated quantum-events separated from one another by a distance greater than the speed of light (cf. here Ian Barbour, *Religion and Science: Historical and Contemporary Issues* [San Francisco: HarperCollins, 1997], 175-77).

62. Whitehead, *Process and Reality,* 230.

63. Whitehead, *Process and Reality,* 25: "The 'subjective aim,' which controls the becoming of a subject, is that subject feeling a proposition with the subjective form of purpose to realize it in that process of self-creation."

64. Whitehead, *Process and Reality,* 345-46.

65. Whitehead, *Process and Reality,* 346.

ably more significance to those same events from a long-range perspective. As a result, there is an inevitable selectivity present even in God's prehension of the unity of the world process. God's consequent nature is equivalently God's judgment on the world, losing nothing that can be saved.[66] But presumably there are events or in any case dimensions of events which cannot be saved.

Furthermore, as Whitehead also makes clear in the final paragraphs of *Process and Reality*, "God and the world are the contrasted opposites in terms of which Creativity achieves its supreme task of transforming disjointed multiplicity, with its diversities in opposition, into concrescent unity, with its diversities in contrast."[67] From this perspective, there would seem to be no possibility of residual logocentrism in Whitehead's notion of the God-world relationship since God and the world are actually opposed to one another within the cosmic process with no hint of the world being thereby subordinated to God. But in that case the earlier question returns with even greater urgency. Does the world as the dialectical counterpart to God possess an objective unity and cohesiveness in itself over and above God's subjective prehension of it from moment to moment? Here the ambiguity in Whitehead's conception of the God-world relationship becomes apparent, for the consequent nature of God does indeed appear to be the unifying principle for the events taking place in the world within the following key passage out of *Process and Reality*.

Whitehead begins with the comment that there are "four creative phases in which the universe accomplishes its actuality."[68] The first phase is that of "conceptual origination, deficient in actuality, but infinite in its adjustment of valuation."[69] Presumably this phase has reference to the primordial nature of God which is, as noted above, God's initial valuation of all the eternal objects pertinent to the world process. The second phase is that of "physical origination, with its multiplicity of actualities."[70] This phase evidently has to do with the sheer multiplicity of finite actual entities concrescing within the

66. Whitehead, *Process and Reality*, 346.
67. Whitehead, *Process and Reality*, 348.
68. Whitehead, *Process and Reality*, 350.
69. Whitehead, *Process and Reality*, 350.
70. Whitehead, *Process and Reality*, 350.

world process at any given moment. As Whitehead notes, "[i]n this phase full actuality is attained; but there is deficiency in the solidarity of individuals with one another."[71] As a result, a third phase is needed "in which the many are one everlastingly, without the qualification of any loss either of individual identity or of completeness of unity."[72] The reference to "everlastingness" implies that the multiple finite actual entities find their unity with one another within the divine consequent nature; hence, the objective unity of the world process would seem to be from moment to moment contained within the divine consequent nature. This impression is confirmed by the fourth and last phase of the world process in which "the perfected actuality [of the world process and/or the divine consequent nature at any given moment] passes back into the temporal world, and qualifies this world so that each temporal actuality includes it as an immediate fact of relevant experience."[73] The unity of the world process thus achieved from moment to moment within God serves as the basis for the divine initial aims to initiate the process of self-constitution for the next set of creaturely actual entities.

From the perspective of Jacques Derrida and other deconstructionists, accordingly, this might well be interpreted as a blatant instance of logocentrism whereby the One as a transcendent reality serves as the principle of unity for the empirical Many. There is, however, as I see it, a relatively easy way in which to deflect possible criticism of Whitehead's thought on this point by contemporary deconstructionists. Furthermore, this new line of thought should unequivocally clear up the residual ambiguity in Whitehead's thought, noted above, whereby the *objective* unity of the world process appears to be confused with the strictly *subjective* unity of the divine consequent nature.

As I have indicated throughout this book, Whitehead seems to have not specified carefully enough the need for some kind of objective unity for societies as ontological totalities which are more than the sum of their constituent parts or members. He distinguishes, for example, between social and non-social nexuses of actual entities.

71. Whitehead, *Process and Reality*, 350.
72. Whitehead, *Process and Reality*, 350-51.
73. Whitehead, *Process and Reality*, 351.

Societies are social nexuses in that they perpetuate a "common element of form" (cf. Glossary) among their constituent actual entities from one moment to the next.[74] Likewise, he distinguishes between personally-ordered societies of actual entities (cf. Glossary), which like the soul within a human being have no spatial thickness but simply transmit a "common element of form" from one moment of experience to the next, and corpuscular societies (cf. Glossary), which are made up of spatially-interconnected "strands" of such personally-ordered societies of actual entities.[75] But what remains unclear therewith is the extent to which personally-ordered societies and, even more so, corpuscular societies are ontological totalities greater than the sum of their parts, that is, their constituent actual occasions. Especially since Whitehead likewise claims in the same chapter of *Process and Reality* that "the ultimate metaphysical truth is atomism,"[76] the exact ontological status of such societies in Whitehead's philosophy is ambiguous. Societies as "Public Matters of Fact" evidently exist.[77] But are they ultimately reducible to the interplay of individual actual occasions or do they in some sense constitute an objective reality over and above those same occasions?

As I will explain more in detail in chapter five, Charles Hartshorne provided for most Whiteheadians the standard resolution for this philosophical issue many years ago with his proposal that a distinction should be made between compound and composite individuals in common sense experience.[78] Compound individuals are those complex or "structured" societies of actual occasions (cf. Glossary) which are governed by a regnant subsociety of actual occasions (equivalently a soul or animating principle). Through its latest actual occasion at any given moment, this regnant subsociety gives an objective unity and coherence to all the other subsocieties of actual occasions within the overall structured society which is the compound individual entity at the level of common sense experience (e.g., a hu-

74. Whitehead, *Process and Reality,* 34.
75. Whitehead, *Process and Reality,* 34-35.
76. Whitehead, *Process and Reality,* 35.
77. Whitehead, *Process and Reality,* 22.
78. Charles Hartshorne, "The Compound Individual," in *Philosophical Essays for Alfred North Whitehead,* ed. F. S. C. Northrup (New York: Russell & Russell, 1936), 193-210.

man being or any other higher-order animal organism). All other more democratically-organized "structured" societies in which there is no such "soul" or regnant subsociety of actual occasions are to be regarded in Hartshorne's view as composite individuals or "virtual aggregates" of actual occasions (e.g., the societies of actual occasions making up rocks and other strictly inanimate objects in the macroscopic world).

My counterargument for some years now has been that most Whiteheadian societies are not governed by a regnant subsociety or "soul." Both in the suborganic world of atoms and molecules and in the supraorganic world of communities and environments, Whiteheadian societies are best understood as democratically organized and thus as without a regnant subsociety to give them some kind of objective unity. Accordingly, I propose that all Whiteheadian societies without exception are the product of the coordinated activity of their various subsocieties and constituent actual occasions. Where a regnant subsociety is present, naturally it exercises a predominant influence on the functioning of the structured society as a whole (as the mind or soul exercises a predominant influence on the functioning of a human being); but all the other subsocieties (the heart, the liver, the lungs, etc.) likewise play a role in the overall functioning of the structured society (the human being as a whole). Hence, even though a Whiteheadian structured society does not exercise agency except in and through its subsocieties and their constituent actual occasions, it is nevertheless an objective ontological unity in its own right through the dynamic interplay of those same subsocieties and constituent actual occasions. The human being, in effect, is a whole greater than the sum of its functioning parts or members.

Most important for our discussion in this chapter, however, is that this understanding of Whiteheadian structured societies is quite consciously non-logocentric. Within a Whiteheadian structured society, whether it be monarchically organized in terms of a regnant subsociety (e.g., a human being or some other animal organism with a "soul") or democratically organized as the byproduct of subsocieties in strictly coordinate interaction (e.g., a community or environment), there is no single unifying center of activity but instead an ongoing interplay of multiple centers of activity which together constitute the ontological unity of some macroscopic reality. Furthermore, if one grants the legitimacy of this extension of Whitehead's thought on the nature of societies, one can clear up the ambiguity surrounding his presentation of the God-world relationship in *Process and Reality.* That is, one can say that the world as an all-embracing structured society with a myriad number of subsocieties and constituent actual occasions possesses its own ontological unity even prior to its prehension by God into the divine consequent nature. God's prehension of the world from moment to moment is needed, to be sure, in order to provide an objective basis for the divine initial aims initiating the process of self-constitution for the next set of actual occasions. But God's prehension of the predecessor actual occasions is not needed to give the world an objective unity which it otherwise would not have. Thus there is no question of logocentrism either within the world as a complex social reality in its own right or between God and the world in terms of God's unification of the multiple actualities of the world at any given moment through incorporation into the divine consequent nature.

The importance of this modest further specification of Whitehead's categorical scheme is even more apparent when one compares it with Charles Hartshorne's attempt to clarify Whitehead's understanding of the God-world relationship. In line with his understanding of a Whiteheadian structured society as a "compound individual," sketched above, Hartshorne suggests that the God-world relationship is best presented in "soul-body" terms.[79] That is, the world is the "body" of God, the physical component of the divine being; and God is the soul of the world, its inner animating principle. Yet this analogy, as I see it, is implicitly logocentric; for God, as a transcendent individual entity, is evidently the unifying principle for the world as an aggregate of societies and their constituent actual occasions. On the other hand, as I will elaborate in Part Two of this book, if God be understood in trinitarian terms as a community of three interrelated divine subjects of experience, then the prevailing image of the God-world relationship is not that of an organism with God as its unifying principle. It is rather the image of an all-comprehensive society in which the

---

79. Cf., e.g., Charles Hartshorne, "The Compound Individual," 218-20; likewise by the same author, *Man's Vision of God and the Logic of Theism* (Hamden, Conn.: Archon Books, 1964), 174-211.

three divine persons of the Christian doctrine of the Trinity are indeed the primordial members, but in which all creatures are likewise members adding their specific pattern of intelligibility to the overall shape or structure of the cosmic society as an objective ontological reality.[80]

Thus there is no single focal point for the understanding of the operation of this cosmic society. The three divine persons by their dynamic interrelation give a necessary order and structure to the cosmic community, but the *Logos* or ontological principle of unity is distributed among all its members, both divine and creaturely, in terms of their dynamic interrelation to one another and their collective contribution to the order and well-being of the whole. Logocentrism is thereby avoided in that the unity of the God-world relationship is not found in a transcendent entity (namely, God as an individual being) but in a transcendent activity, namely, Whiteheadian creativity insofar as it first constitutes the tripersonal reality of God as a divine community and then the ongoing reality of creation as a sub-community within the divine communitarian life, that is, as a comprehensive "structured society" of subsocieties and their constituent actual occasions in dynamic interrelation.[81]

80. Cf. here Ian Barbour, *Religion and Science*, 322. Like me, Barbour is unhappy with the standard soul-body analogy for the God-world relationship among process-oriented thinkers and prefers instead the notion of God as "the leader of a cosmic community." Such a cosmic community "is neither a monarchy nor a democracy, since one member is preeminent but not all powerful." If, however, instead of thinking of God as an individual entity within this cosmic community, Barbour would imagine God as a primordial divine community within which the community of finite beings would take its origin and be sustained, then his emphasis on a "social" approach to the God-world relationship, i.e., on a plurality of interacting centers of activity, would be much stronger.

81. Cf. here Robert Magliola, *Derrida on the Mend* (West Lafayette, Ind.: Purdue University Press, 1984), 144-45. Magliola likewise argues that the unity of the three divine persons of the Christian doctrine of the Trinity is to be found in their dynamic relations of opposition to one another and not in some common ontological substrate. Hence, the Trinity thus understood is a non-logocentric reality in that each divine person is *a* center of unity but none is *the* center of unity for their conjoint existence as one God. Cf. also on this point Anselm Kyonsuk Min, "Solidarity of Others in the Body of Christ: A New Theological Paradigm," *Toronto Journal of Theology* 14 (1998): 239-54. Min interprets the solidarity of Christians with one another as members of the Mystical Body of Christ within an explicitly trinitarian

This is not to deny, of course, that God is necessary to the world in a way that the world is not necessary to God. For, even within a radically communitarian understanding of the God-world relationship, the world shares in the divine communitarian life only through the gracious free decision of the divine persons. The divine persons, in other words, freely choose to extend their own divine principle of communal existence and activity to creatures, thereby empowering those same creatures to exist in relation to one another as well as to the divine persons. But, as I see it, the key point in the charge of logocentrism, namely, that the One effectively controls the relations of the empirical Many to one another through their conjoint relation to itself as a transcendent individual entity, is thereby countermanded. For reality is then no longer understood in terms of a graded hierarchy of individual entities up to and including God as a transcendent individual entity who is their Creator. Rather, reality is set forth as a hierarchically-ordered network of social totalities or interrelated "systems" with individual entities or subjects of experience as their constituent parts or members (beginning with the community of the divine persons but extending into the vast network of interrelated systems or communities within creation). The *Logos,* as noted above, is as a result never concentrated in an individual entity since even God is a community of divine persons who share equally a common principle of existence and activity. Furthermore, within creation the *Logos* is always distributed among the members of a given social totality or system so that the members by their dynamic interrelation constitute the unity of that totality. The net result, accordingly, is a specifically social understanding of reality in which individual entities are, on the one hand, ontologically subordinate to the social totalities of which they are members but yet, on the other hand, are naturally equipped by their dynamic interrelation to modify the ongoing character or structure of those same social totalities.[82]

context: "The Holy Spirit creates, redeems and re-creates all things by bringing them together in Christ as the primordial model of the creature created in the image of God. If Christ is the model of solidarity, the Holy Spirit is the agent of solidarity, and God the source of solidarity" (250). In this way, Min moves away from the inevitable limitations of an organismic model for the understanding of the God-world relationship toward the societal model advocated in this chapter.

82. Cf. below, chapter five, pp. 138-39.

C. Concluding Remarks

To sum up, then, in this chapter I have attempted to show how Jacques Derrida in his efforts at a systematic deconstruction of classical metaphysics is consciously or unconsciously at work on a new metaphysics of becoming. Furthermore, if my extended analysis and comparison of Derrida's *différance* and Whitehead's notion of creativity has any logical plausibility, then it would appear that Derrida's implicit metaphysics of becoming bears a strong affinity with the basic insights of Whitehead's process-relational metaphysics: namely, the overall fluidity of reality and yet for the same reason the interrelation of everything with everything else in the forward movement of the cosmic process. As I indicated in the second half of the chapter, however, there seem to be residual elements of the classical metaphysics of being in contemporary process-relational metaphysics. Above all if one subscribes to Charles Hartshorne's distinction between compound and composite individuals for the unity of structured societies of actual occasions and to his rethinking of the God-world relationship within Whitehead's philosophy along the lines of a soul-body analogy, a subtle form of logocentrism seems to be present.

At the same time, as I indicated above, there is a relatively easy way in which to meet the potential objections of contemporary deconstructionists to this feature of process-relational metaphysics. That is, by allowing for the objective unity of Whiteheadian societies in virtue of the coordinated activity of their constituent actual occasions, one can convert process-relational metaphysics into a more thoroughgoing social ontology in which the necessary emphasis on the autonomy of individual actual occasions is balanced off against an equally important emphasis on the objective reality of the societies of which they are constituent members. Hence, as noted above, the *Logos* or ontological principle of unity for the cosmic process is not located in a transcendent entity but rather in a transcendent activity, namely, what Derrida calls *différance* and what Whitehead calls creativity. *Différance* and creativity thereby play a dual role in their respective philosophies. That is, each serves both as the principle of differentiation and as the principle of unity for all the particular entities of this world. Paradoxically, what makes entities different from one another simultaneously links them together in ongoing patterns of dynamic interrelation.

Likewise, with this chapter I bring to a close the first part of this book, which was intended to make clear the legitimacy and appropriateness of a new metaphysics based on the principle of universal intersubjectivity. As I indicated in chapter one, there seems to be a shift taking place in contemporary Roman Catholic systematic theology away from the classical hierarchical understanding of the God-world relationship toward a more overtly intersubjective model for the understanding of that same relationship. At the same time, in my judgment this shift in perspective remains incomplete because of its focus on the exclusive relationship of God to human beings and vice-versa rather than, as in the philosophy/theology of Thomas Aquinas, on God's relationship to all of creation and vice-versa. What was set forth originally, in other words, by Karl Rahner, Bernard Lonergan, and other Catholic systematic theologians as a new theological anthropology needs to be expanded into a fully developed cosmology based on the same principles of intersubjectivity. As I will further explain in Part Two of this book, Whitehead's philosophy, albeit with some modest modifications, would seem to be well-suited as the basic philosophical conceptuality for taking this next step.

PART TWO

4 *Intersubjectivity: The Vertical Dimension*

Ever since the publication of *Ich-Du (I and Thou)* by Martin Buber in 1923,[1] the notion of intersubjectivity has become a philosophical commonplace. But, like many terms which for one reason or another rapidly gain wide acceptance, intersubjectivity still lacks precise philosophical definition. How is it, for example, to be distinguished from subjectivity, whether the latter term be understood either as empirical subjectivity or as transcendental subjectivity (as in the philosophy of Immanuel Kant and the German Idealists)? Can the "otherness" of the Other truly be accounted for if one undertakes an analysis of intersubjectivity from the perspective of the self as an individual subject of experience? Emmanuel Levinas's masterwork *Totality and Infinity* is grounded on the premise that this is impossible since the "face" of the Other according to Levinas bespeaks an "Infinity" to me which I can never rationally comprehend.[2] But is intersubjectivity then fully accounted for in terms of the ontological priority of the Other to the Self (as Levinas would claim) or is this latter move simply the logical

1. Martin Buber, *I and Thou*, trans. Walter Kaufmann (New York: Scribner's, 1970).
2. Emmanuel Levinas, *Totality and Infinity: An Essay on Exteriority*, trans. Alphonso Lingis (Pittsburgh: Duquesne University Press, 1969), 51: "To approach the Other in conversation is to welcome his expression, in which at each instant he overflows the idea a thought would carry away from it. It is therefore to *receive* from the Other beyond the capacity of the I, which means exactly: to have the idea of infinity."

opposite of the priority of the Self to the Other in classical metaphysics?[3] Perhaps intersubjectivity is at least partially grounded in the reality of "the between" (Das Zwischen) in Buber's philosophy, that which is ontologically prior to the reality of both the I and the Thou. But in that case what do we mean by "the between"? Is it another name for God or whatever else is considered to be Ultimate Reality? Or is it somehow less than Ultimate Reality and yet transcendent to human subjects of experience in dynamic interrelation?

In the present chapter I will explore this notion of "the between" as a necessary context for the dynamic interplay of subjects of experience with one another. As I see it, it does not in itself offer a complete explanation of the reality of intersubjectivity; but it does present a necessary dimension of that reality, what I refer to in the title of this chapter as the "vertical" dimension of a metaphysics of intersubjectivity. For that purpose I will make extensive use of an essay by the Japanese philosopher Kitaro Nishida. In a work written shortly before his death and entitled "The Logic of the Place of Nothingness and a Religious WorldView," Nishida comments: "Religion, from the standpoint of philosophy at least, can be grasped only by means of the logic of place."[4] As Masao Abe notes in his explanation of this passage, Nishida was referring here not simply to Japanese "True Pure Land Buddhism," but to all forms of religion, including Christianity.[5] My intention in this chapter will be, with the help of Abe's commentary on this key notion in Nishida's philosophy, to set forth

---

3. Cf. here Andrew Tallon's Foreword to *Mystery and Method: The Other in Rahner and Levinas* by Michael Purcell (Milwaukee: Marquette University Press, 1998), vii: "Rahner and Levinas need each other. There's too much self and not enough other in Rahner, and there's too much other and not enough self in Levinas. They complement and correct each other, together achieving a balance that escapes both of them taken alone." Saying this is, of course, not to discount the enormous influence of Rahner and Levinas within their respective academic disciplines this past century, but simply to admit that the full complexity of the issue of intersubjectivity somehow escaped both of them.

4. Masao Abe, " 'Inverse Correspondence' in the Philosophy of Nishida: The Emergence of the Notion," trans. James L. Fredericks, *International Philosophical Quarterly* 32 (1992): 343; cf. also Kitaro Nishida, *Last Writings: Nothingness and the Religious World View*, trans. David A. Dilworth (Honolulu: University of Hawaii Press, 1987), 91.

5. Abe, " 'Inverse Correspondence,' " 343.

my own understanding of Nishida's "logic of place" and then to indicate how it approximates to what I am calling the vertical dimension of a logic of intersubjectivity. For I believe that Nishida, like Martin Buber, grasped the dynamic character of human and divine intersubjectivity. But, even better than Buber, he realized that this dynamic exchange between God and human beings, and among human beings even apart from God, must be grounded in a transcendent matrix or all-encompassing "place" which Nishida himself calls Absolute Nothingness, namely, that out of which all subjects of experience without exception emerge and then by their dynamic interrelation co-constitute a "world" or objective social order.[6]

A. The Logic of Place according to Nishida

Early in his philosophical career, above all, in *An Inquiry into the Good*,[7] Kitaro Nishida focused on the notion of "pure experience" as that which transcends the duality of subject and object within empirical consciousness. In some ways, he here recapitulated the efforts of Fichte and the other German Idealists to find a transcendental starting-point for systematic reflection on the nature of reality. That is, he tried to grasp the dynamic self-constituting activity of "pure experi-

6. The relationship between Nishida and Buber on the notion of intersubjectivity is, of course, not easy to evaluate. On the one hand, as James Heisig points out in "Non-I and Thou: Nishida, Buber, and the Moral Consequences of Self-Actualization," *Philosophy East and West* 50 (2000): 179-207, the primary relationship in Nishida's philosophy is not the I-Thou relationship between human beings as advanced by Buber, but the relationship between the finite self and Absolute Nothingness which then results in the religious conversion of the self-centered I into a non-I. For that same reason, Nishida's analysis of intersubjectivity is more mystical than properly social/historical; his analysis lacks the concreteness of actual human relationships in the historical order which is available to Buber through the category of *Beziehung* (connection). On the other hand, as I will indicate below, Nishida's notion of Absolute Nothingness quite possibly offers a better explanation of how God (or, in any case, the Transcendent) can be present to human beings in and through "pure" or "immediate" experience.

7. Kitaro Nishida, *An Inquiry into the Good*, trans. M. Abe and C. Ives (New Haven, Conn.: Yale University Press, 1990).

ence" before it solidified into the oppositional reality of subject and object in empirical consciousness:

> In pure experience, the intellect, emotions, and will are still undivided: they are a single activity, without any opposition between subject and object. Since that opposition arises from the demands of thinking, it is not a fact of immediate experience; in immediate experience, there is only a single, independent, self-sufficient event. There is neither a subject which sees nor an object which is seen.[8]

Later Nishida became uneasy about the "subjectivism" which was unavoidably associated with this approach to the nature of reality. As Abe comments, given this approach, "it is still unclear how the True Reality realized within Subjective Existence relates to the objective world."[9]

Accordingly, in subsequent years Nishida shifted his attention first to "self-awakening," understood as the transcendental unity of human consciousness, and from there to a careful analysis of Aristotle's notion of *hypokeimenon* or individual substance as the starting-point for an understanding of objective reality. In particular, he analyzed the relation between subjects and predicates within judgments about individual substances. In customary judgments, for example, the individual substance is subsumed within the class of things represented by the predicate. The judgment "I am a human being" subsumes me as a particular human being within the class of human beings in general. The distinguishing features which constitute me as an individual human being, however, are ignored in asserting the objective truth of the judgment that I am a human being. Thus what is represented by the predicate "human being" is an "abstract universal" since it only represents a partial truth about me as the subject of the sentence.

Nishida's aim, on the other hand, was to search for a "concrete universal," in which the individual entity which is represented by the subject of the judgment does not lose its particularity in being sub-

8. Masao Abe, "Nishida's Philosophy of 'Place,' " trans. Christopher Ives, *International Philosophical Quarterly* 28 (1988): 357. Reference is to *An Inquiry into the Good*, pp. 48-49.
9. Abe, "Nishida's Philosophy of 'Place,' " 358; cf. also *An Inquiry into the Good*, p. xxxi.

sumed under the predicate. But this would mean that the predicate is no longer a logical abstraction such as "human being" but refers to something which in its own way is even more "concrete" than the particular entity in question. The predicate, in other words, must represent a universal reality which assumes particularity or concreteness in becoming this individual entity. In such a truly subsumptive judgment, therefore, the particular entity which is represented by the subject of the sentence "does not lose its specific difference as it does when subsumed by an abstract universal — instead, a particular is grasped as the self-determination of a concrete universal (concrete in the sense that it concretizes rather than abstracts)."[10]

By way of interpretation of this paradoxical statement, I would say that Nishida is here implicitly returning to his earlier proposal that an all-embracing activity is the transcendental reality at the base of "pure experience." That is, Nishida's "concrete universal" in distinction from the abstract universals of Aristotelian formal logic would seem to be not a concept or logical abstraction but a transcendent activity which lies at the base of objective reality just as it lies at the base of empirical consciousness or subjective reality. It is then this universal activity which particularizes itself within individual entities as the potential subjects of truly subsumptive judgments. As such, it is both the individual entity and itself at the same time, for it is not limited to being just this one particular entity. Rather, it is simultaneously all particular entities at the same time that it is none of them exclusively. Furthermore, the individual entity is fully understood in its particularity only when it is subsumed under this "concrete universal." The "concrete universal," in other words, does not strip it of its distinguishing characteristics vis-à-vis other entities in the same class (as in the case of abstract universals), but rather invests the entity with those individuating differences in thus becoming identified with it here and now.

Nishida, to be sure, does not refer to this "concrete universal" as an activity, but rather as a "place." As Abe notes, "[h]e viewed a particular as 'that which lies within' a universal and a universal as the 'place' within which the particular lies."[11] On the other hand, it is also clear

10. Abe, "Nishida's Philosophy of 'Place,' " 360.
11. Abe, "Nishida's Philosophy of 'Place,' " 363.

that "place" for Nishida is not a static reality, simply the de facto context or environment within which a particular entity exists. Rather, it is evidently a dynamic reality which realizes or determines itself in giving shape or form to this particular entity. Abe in his commentary at this point makes a comparison with the notion of the "concrete universal" in the philosophy of Hegel: "According to Hegel, a concrete universal contains a principle of individualization, through which it develops distinctions within itself while maintaining self-identity. This self-differentiation is completely self-determined."[12] By comparison with Hegel's "concrete universal," Nishida's "concrete universal" is, therefore, likewise a dynamic, self-determining reality. Unlike Hegel's "concrete universal," however, Nishida's "concrete universal" does not in the end become a self-existing reality. For Hegel, the "concrete universal" is in the end Absolute Spirit. As such, it absorbs the reality of particular entities into its own all-encompassing subjective-objective reality. For Nishida, on the other hand, the "concrete universal" has no reality apart from the particular entities in which it manifests itself. In itself, it is Absolute Nothingness, a total lack of reality in and for itself; for, as we shall see below in connection with the notion of "inverse correspondence," it is simply the ontological ground or all-encompassing context for entities to arise and be related to one another in dynamic co-origination.

To sum up, then, "place" for Nishida would seem to imply both a transcendent activity and a transcendent context or space for its operation. Bringing the two ideas together, one might imagine Absolute Nothingness as an ontogenetic matrix (cf. Glossary) or all-encompassing energy-field for the various entities which take shape within it. As such, it would be both the collective field of consciousness at the base of the subject-object distinction within particular human consciousnesses and the transcendent source of all the particular energy-fields operative within the world of nature. The classical subject-object duality would thus be overcome in that the world of human consciousness and the world of nature would have a unitary origin in Absolute Nothingness understood as this all-embracing energy-field at the base of reality. In no sense is it a thing-like reality which would logically require still another "place"

12. Abe, "Nishida's Philosophy of 'Place,'" 364.

for its existence. Rather, as a strictly non-entitative reality or "field-being" it is simply the "place" within which everything else exists. Its only form of existence, paradoxically, is in terms of the entities which exist within it since it takes on determinate form in them as particular entities.[13]

Masao Abe illustrates this last point with reference to the celebrated *mu* koan in Zen Buddhism (When a monk asks Master Joshu, "Does a dog have Buddha nature?," Joshu replies, "Mu": literally, "Nothing" or "Nothingness"). Abe comments: "The true Buddha Nature is in no sense Being; it is the totally unobjectifiable *Absolute Nothingness* diverging from any 'Buddha Nature' about which one asks 'have . . . or have not.' A dog is truly a dog precisely because it is a self-determination of this true Buddha Nature."[14] Yet the monk will come to this realization only when it dawns on him that he too is a self-determination of Absolute Nothingness. Abe concludes: "*All individuals* are self-determinations of Absolute Nothingness and are at the same time self-determinations of themselves (this also involves a mutual determination between individuals) and that precisely in this way *the world* is a self-determination of Absolute Nothingness. . . . In short, the self-determination of Absolute Nothingness, the self-determination of individuals, the mutual determination between individuals, and the self-determination of the world are all the same thing."[15]

13. Cf. Robert E. Carter, *The Nothingness Beyond God: An Introduction to the Philosophy of Nishida Kitaro,* 2nd ed. (St. Paul, Minn.: Paragon House, 1997), 59-60: "Aristotle provided a logic which gave primacy to the grammatical subject, and thus to the unchanging substratum. Nishida wants to right this by placing full emphasis on the grammatical predicate, or to the underlying matrix of place out of which the subject arises, and which actually gives it its proper shape-as-contextualized. Still, it seems to this author that Nishida would have done better to have spoken not of his 'logic of place,' but to have stressed his logic of subject *and* predicate, or of object and place. It is not exactly a logic of place, but a logic of place as the matrix or context out of which all differentiations or determinations arise, and in which they and their mutual relationships are grounded."

14. Abe, "Nishida's Philosophy of 'Place,' " 369.

15. Abe, "Nishida's Philosophy of 'Place,' " 370. One possible way to understand better the philosophical issue at stake here is to reflect on the difficulty which first Thomas Aquinas and then Duns Scotus had with the principle of individuation within their respective metaphysical schemes. Aquinas appealed to

115

To understand this latter point more fully, however, we must have recourse to another key term in Nishida's philosophy, namely, "inverse correspondence." Inverse correspondence, says Abe, is a notion unique to Nishida's thought.[16] Although in itself a logical concept, it has mystical overtones; for it "precisely captures the essence of religion common to the various religious traditions."[17] In the above-cited article, Abe elaborates on how Nishida developed this concept through contact with a fellow Buddhist scholar, Risaku Mutai, who formulated a similar expression, namely, "correspondence in the place [of absolute nothingness]."[18] For our purposes, however, it will suffice simply to explain what is meant by the term "inverse correspondence" or, in terms of an earlier formulation by Nishida, "absolute contradictory self identity." In the process, it should become clear how this notion as part of the logic of place relates to my own project in this chapter of outlining the vertical dimension for a logic of intersubjectivity.

Abe begins by citing a text from Nishida: " 'The individual, by being opposed to another individual, is an individual.' "[19] Abe then elaborates:

In Nishida's case, to claim that 'the individual opposes the individual' never simply means that the individual and the other statically face each other in one and the same dimension. It means, instead, that they dynamically oppose each other and that this dynamic op-

---

"signate matter," that is, matter as somehow adding further specification to an essence or universal form; Duns Scotus invented a new universal form *haecceitas* which somehow became individuated through "informing" a particular entity (cf. here Frederick Copleston, S.J., *A History of Philosophy*, vol. 2, 2 [Garden City, N.Y.: Doubleday Image Book, 1962], 46, 235-36). But neither Aquinas nor Scotus simply appealed to Being itself as the necessary principle of individuation for all entities insofar as it causes them to be. If they had done so, they might have ended up with an understanding of Being very much akin to what Nishida and Abe describe as Absolute Nothingness, namely, a universal principle of activity which does not exist in itself but only in the entities which it empowers to be.

16. Masao Abe, " 'Inverse Correspondence,' " 329.
17. Masao Abe, " 'Inverse Correspondence,' " 329.
18. Masao Abe, " 'Inverse Correspondence,' " 331.
19. Masao Abe, " 'Inverse Correspondence,' " 334. Reference is to Nishida, *Last Writings*, 93.

position works mutually in the creation of something new. This mutual working of dynamic opposition means that the one tries to appropriate the other by means of a thorough negation of the other. It means that the other is negated and the self is affirmed and, at the same time, it means that the self negates itself and stands in the place of the universal beyond the self and the other. Finally, it means that the self is affirmed by means of an inverse determination arising out of this universal place.[20]

What Abe appears to be saying, at least in part, is that the self paradoxically affirms itself by admitting its essential dependence on its logical counterpart for its own self-identity. Its deeper self-identity, in other words, is to stand in dynamic relation to that which is opposed to it and thereby to create, in Abe's words, "something new." The greater the logical opposition between the self and the other, paradoxically the greater is their mutual identity as this new unitary reality. Hence, the self must radically negate itself as self-sufficient, that is, as independent of the other, in order to attain its own deeper identity.[21]

An obvious example of this notion of "inverse correspondence" is the way in which men and women are defined in terms of their identity-in-difference. To be a woman means not to be a man, and vice versa. Yet only together do men and women constitute "something new," namely, humanity as a bisexual reality. Likewise, the notion of inverse correspondence would seem roughly to correspond to Buber's logic of intersubjectivity in *I and Thou*. That is, I become truly myself only when I acknowledge you as Thou, someone both like me and yet different from me; otherwise, I tend to treat you as an It, an object of thought or desire for myself.[22] Yet what Nishida adds to this

20. Abe, " 'Inverse Correspondence,' " 334.
21. Cf. Carter, *The Nothingness Beyond God*, 58: "Two things cannot be self-contradictory unless they are related by an enveloping matrix which, at the same time, unites them. For things to be in opposition implies thereby a deeper, underlying and grounding unity/system/*basho* [place]." As we have seen already in chapter three, this dialectical understanding of self and other whereby they mutually presuppose "an enveloping matrix" or common ground might well resolve some of the hitherto insoluble problems associated with the notion of the Other and otherness to be found in contemporary postmodern philosophy.
22. Buber, *I and Thou*, 53-56.

117

explanation of intersubjectivity, which Buber only hints at with his reference to "the between," is an explicit reference to the ontological context for an I-Thou encounter, "the place of the universal beyond the self and the other." Only insofar as the self stands in the place of Absolute Nothingness, that is, sees its self-definition arising not only out of its relation to the other but even more fundamentally out of its relation to this ontological context of Absolute Nothingness, will it finally achieve its true self-identity as an "absolute contradictory self identity."[23]

Abe further explains this last point by borrowing an image from Nishida and then amplifying it to illustrate the difference between "religions of grace" such as Christianity and Pure Land Buddhism and "religions of awakening" such as Zen Buddhism in their respective understandings of God or Ultimate Reality.[24] In "The Logic of the Place of Nothingness and the Religious Worldview," Nishida makes reference to Nicholas of Cusa, who depicted the all-encompassing reality of God sometimes as an infinite circle, at other times as an infinite sphere. Nishida himself prefers the image of an infinite sphere to describe Absolute Nothingness: "Now because this infinite sphere has no circumference, every point, every act of consciousness, is a center radiating in infinity."[25] Abe's comment is that this image of an infinite sphere in which there is no absolute center but only mutually overlapping centers of activity radiating into infinity describes quite well Nishida's own understanding of Absolute Nothingness within Zen Buddhism as a "religion of awakening." Absolute Nothingness is everywhere within the sphere of the absolute present and yet nowhere since it only exists within the different centers of activity which it empowers to exist. In "religions of grace," however, says Abe, the relation between the self and God or the self and Amida Buddha is better represented by the image of an infinite circle (rather than an infinite sphere), since in an infinite circle there is nevertheless an absolute center-point which corresponds to God or Amida Buddha with the

---

23. Cf. Carter, *The Nothingness Beyond God*, 58-80.

24. Masao Abe, "The Problem of 'Inverse Correspondence' in the Philosophy of Nishida: Comparing Nishida with Tanabe," trans. James L. Fredericks, *The International Philosophical Quarterly* 39 (1999): 59-76.

25. Nishida, *Last Writings*, 53-54; cf. also 76, 89.

self existing "on the circumference" and thus in dependent relation on God or Amida Buddha for grace, the means of salvation.[26]

Abe's point is that Nishida was insufficiently aware of the difference between the image of the infinite circle and the image of the infinite sphere as representing two quite different ways for human beings to understand their relation to the Absolute. As a result, Nishida misunderstood the position of his junior colleague in the philosophy department at the University of Kyoto, Hajime Tanabe, who as a Pure Land Buddhist endorsed the notion of "other-power," reliance on Amida Buddha, for personal salvation. For the same reason, he misunderstood the reality of God for Christians. But, claims Abe, properly understood, the two approaches to God or the Absolute are complementary and should make room for one another through "self-negation."[27]

My own comment would be that Abe is exactly right on this point. That is, religions of awakening and religions of grace do address different understandings of the self's relation to God or the Absolute. Hence, individuals who ground their personal religious worldview in one or other of these understandings should upon reflection realize that they are in dynamic relation with only one dimension of the Absolute or Ultimate Reality. Hence, they should through a process of "self-negation" find a way to incorporate the basic stance of the rival worldview into their own understanding and

26. Abe, "The Problem of 'Inverse Correspondence' in the Philosophy of Nishida," 69-71. "Grace" is needed, of course, because within Pure Land Buddhism and Christianity human beings are unable to "save" themselves by their own "power," as in Zen Buddhism. Furthermore, at least within Christianity, the issue of salvation is further complicated by belief in the reality of "sin" as the principal obstacle to union with God. Detailed discussion of this matter lies outside the scope of the present work, but it should in any case be clear why within a Christian context a distinction must be made between the ontogenetic matrix or divine nature and God as a (tri-)personal being. For the ontogenetic matrix as an impersonal principle of existence and activity enables human beings to commit sin as well as to do good. Thereby the relation between the human being and a tri-personal God is put in jeopardy even as the ontogenetic matrix or divine nature paradoxically continues to support the human being in his or her self-centered sinful activity.

27. Abe, "The Problem of 'Inverse Correspondence' in the Philosophy of Nishida," 74-76.

appreciation of God or the Absolute.[28] As I will make clear below in my reinterpretation of Whitehead's philosophy, I believe that there is a way at least for Christians to incorporate both approaches to Ultimate Reality, that is, both the interpersonal and the transpersonal approach, into a full understanding of God. To this rethinking of Whitehead's understanding of the God-world relationship, therefore, we now turn.

B. A Whiteheadian Logic of Intersubjectivity

Certainly it is not common to think of the philosophy of Alfred North Whitehead in terms of a logic of intersubjectivity. Perhaps because Whitehead was initially a mathematician and natural scientist, one does not associate his philosophy with psychology and the realm of the intersubjective. But, in view of the fact that for Whitehead "the final real things that exist"[29] are actual entities or momentary subjects of experience, it makes sense to think of his philosophy as involving an implicit logic of intersubjectivity. Subjects of experience in dynamic interrelation make up the building-blocks of the universe in his philosophical scheme. Even inanimate things are ultimately composed of subjects of experience in dynamic interrelation (cf. Glossary). The conventional understanding of intersubjectivity, to be sure, focuses exclusively on human intersubjectivity, that is, on the relations of human persons to one another. But my contention is that Whitehead's broader understanding of intersubjectivity in terms of actual entities in dynamic interrelation is by no means a liability but rather an unexpected asset for a systematic understanding of the phenomenon of intersubjectivity. Provided that human intersubjec-

28. The implications of this insight for interreligious dialogue are obviously quite significant, even though they cannot be elaborated upon here. Briefly stated, what it seems to imply as a goal for interreligious dialogue is mutual enrichment for all the participants in an atmosphere of trusting acceptance of one another's cherished beliefs rather than seeking to establish a higher viewpoint from which to rank and order the various world religions.

29. Alfred North Whitehead, *Process and Reality: An Essay in Cosmology*, corrected edition, ed. David Ray Griffin and Donald W. Sherburne (New York: The Free Press, 1978), 18.

tivity in its mode of operation is basically akin to the operation of intersubjectivity among non-human subjects of experience (even among the submicroscopic components of inanimate things), one is in a position to think in terms of a metaphysics based on the principle of intersubjectivity rather than simply an anthropology derived from that same principle.

To illustrate this last point, I will now indicate how Whitehead's basic philosophical intuitions are more akin to those of Nishida as stated above than to the classical tradition of Western metaphysics represented by Aristotle and the medieval scholastics. As Masao Abe comments with respect to the notion of the individual in the philosophy of Nishida, "Aristotle's individual is a *seen* individual, not an acting one. If an individual is moved by an unmoved Prime Mover, it must be said not to change or act by itself. To Nishida, an individual is always the acting or actor that acts by itself."[30] The same, of course, may be said of Whiteheadian actual entities, at least in terms of their process of concrescence. They are not objects of thought like the grammatical subjects of sentences in Aristotle's formal logic. Rather, they are dynamic realities, subjects of experience which constitute themselves out of the data provided by their past world and which even as "superjects" for subsequent actual entities influence their successors in the latter's self-constitution.[31]

Still another way in which Whitehead and Nishida share the same intersubjective worldview is in their common refusal to think of individuals as in any sense isolated or self-sufficient. Abe comments with respect to Nishida's view: "Because an individual can be an individual only in opposition to other individuals, Nishida examines the *relationship* between one individual and another. (This is a natural result of his understanding of an individual as an actor). He thus understands this relationship as a dynamic inter-action between two or

30. Abe, "Nishida's Philosophy of 'Place,'" 363.

31. It is, of course, a matter of debate among Whiteheadian scholars how this influence of past actual occasions on their successors is de facto exercised and, even more, what Whitehead himself held on this subject. Cf. here Judith A. Jones, *Intensity: An Essay in Whiteheadian Ontology* (Nashville: Vanderbilt University Press, 1998) for a new and quite controversial reinterpretation of how actual occasions impact upon their successors; cf. also below, chapter five, concluding note.

myriad acting individuals."[32] Whitehead would heartily agree, given his own presupposition of "internal" as opposed to "external" relations between actual entities whereby actual entities enter into one another's self-constitution. Admittedly, actual occasions which are strict contemporaries do not directly influence one another's becoming. But, as Jorge Nobo has pointed out in recent publications, a proper understanding of Whitehead's notion of the extensive continuum allows one to say that strictly contemporary actual entities indirectly influence one another's becoming in that they anticipate one another's place within the extensive continuum and thereby one another's concrete actualization as this or that physical reality here and now.[33] For all practical purposes, therefore, contemporary actual entities mutually influence one another's self-constitution in the same way that individuals within Nishida's worldview are only defined in terms of their "inverse correspondence" with one another by way of self-negation and self-affirmation.

Finally, Abe notes that for Nishida the analysis of the individual "includes the factors of time and space, in that the spatial and temporal 'world' is inseparable from the individual."[34] In similar fashion for Whitehead, actual occasions are not to be found in space and time; rather, by their dynamic interrelation they generate specific spatial and temporal relations among themselves, thus creating a "world" in process of development. Whereas Aristotle, therefore, presupposed a "world" already fixed in its basic structure within which individual entities would take their place according to a hierarchically-ordered scheme of things, for both Nishida and Whitehead the "world" with its spatial and temporal dimensions is a historical reality, something which has gradually taken shape as a result of the dynamic interrelation of individuals/actual entities with one another

32. Abe, "Nishida's Philosophy of 'Place,'" 363.
33. Jorge Nobo, *Whitehead's Metaphysics of Extension and Solidarity* (Albany, N.Y.: State University of New York Press, 1986), 1-58; also "Experience, Eternity, and Primordiality," *Process Studies* 26 (1997): 171-204, esp. 176-80. Finally, cf. Stephen T. Franklin, *Speaking from the Depths* (Grand Rapids: Eerdmans, 1990), 187. A practical example of what is intended here is the way in which a batter in a baseball game swings the bat so as to make contact with a pitched ball elsewhere than where the ball is right now in his or her line of sight.
34. Abe, "Nishida's Philosophy of 'Place,'" 363.

both simultaneously and successively. As Nishida comments in "The Logic of the Place of Nothingness and the Religious WorldView," "I am an expressive monad of the world. I transform the world into my own subjectivity. . . . But this transactional logic of contradictory identity signifies as well that it is the world which is expressing itself in me. The world creates its own space-time character by taking each monadic act of consciousness as a unique position in the calculus of its own existential transformation."[35]

Perhaps the most striking similarity in Nishida's and Whitehead's respective worldviews, however, remains to be discussed. That is, both of them presuppose that subjects of experience in dynamic interrelation have a common relationship to a supraempirical reality which Whitehead calls creativity and Nishida terms Absolute Nothingness. Admittedly, I am here taking sides with a long-standing debate among Whiteheadian scholars about the status of creativity within Whitehead's metaphysical scheme.[36] But if, as Jorge Nobo maintains, the notion of creativity in Whitehead's metaphysical scheme should be linked with still another category in that scheme, namely, the notion of the "extensive continuum,"[37] so as to constitute what Nobo calls the "ontogenetic matrix" or ontological ground for the becoming and the being of actual entities, past, present, and future,[38] then the comparison with Absolute Nothingness as the "place" where individual subjects of experience are ultimately located, is quite striking. Neither the conjoint activity of creativity and the extensive continuum for Nobo nor Absolute Nothingness for Nishida are thing-like realities which need to be "placed" in some broader context in order to be understood properly. Both in that

35. Nishida, *Last Writings*, 52.

36. Cf. my earlier book *The Divine Matrix: Creativity as Link between East and West* (Maryknoll, N.Y.: Orbis Books, 1995), 52-56, for a brief summary of this discussion.

37. The extensive continuum is a metaphysical "given" for Whitehead in that it constitutes the necessary context or "place" for the interrelated existence of actual entities not only in our own "cosmic epoch" but also in any conceivable past or future cosmic epochs. Hence, the extensive continuum underlies the space-time continuum familiar to us from the natural sciences. Cf. on this point, Whitehead, *Process and Reality*, 61-82.

38. Nobo, "Experience, Eternity, and Primordiality, 190-94.

sense are the ultimate "place" where entities come into existence and are related to one another. Likewise, both Nobo's ontogenetic matrix and Nishida's Absolute Nothingness are dynamic realities which take on determinate existence in terms of the entities which they empower to exist. Every particular entity, therefore, is both itself and at the same time a self-determination of either the ontogenetic matrix or Absolute Nothingness.

Other philosophers of intersubjectivity like Martin Buber have suggested, to be sure, a transcendent source for the I-Thou relationship within human experience. In addressing another human being as Thou, one is intuitively aware of the co-presence of the divine Thou as an enabling transcendent reality.[39] But what is not so clear is how this co-presence of the divine Thou with the human Thou can be logically justified. One wonders how God or some other transcendent entity could thus identify with the being of a finite entity without undermining the latter's ontological status as an independent finite reality. Within the classical substance-oriented philosophy of Aristotle, for example, one substance cannot appropriate another substance without reducing the latter substance to an accidental modification of itself (as in the ingestion of food and drink).[40] Since Nobo's ontogenetic matrix and Nishida's Absolute Nothingness, however, as noted above, are to be conceived more as a dynamic context or place rather than as one of the entities thus in place, this problem seems to be obviated. Precisely as dynamic rather than fixed realities, Nobo's ontogenetic matrix and Nishida's Absolute Nothingness can "inform" a finite entity, that is, be co-present to it as the latter's enabling principle of existence and activity, without undermining the ontological status of the finite entity. In this way, a third party could legitimately feel or otherwise experience the presence and activity of a divine principle or transcendent context operative within the finite Thou.

The same philosophical issues, of course, are at stake in what Buddhists call "enlightenment" or "awakening." That is, for Buddhists enlightenment or awakening takes place when the human being somehow becomes aware of his or her identification with the transcendent

39. Buber, *I and Thou*, 123-24 and 180-82.
40. Aristotle *Metaphysics* 1040b10-17.

reality of Absolute Nothingness.[41] This would be logically impossible if Absolute Nothingness were itself a self-existing substantive reality. For, in that case, at the moment of enlightenment, there would be only one entity, Absolute Nothingness. The finite entity would be totally absorbed into the superordinate substantive reality of Absolute Nothingness even if here and now it appeared to exist apart or different from Absolute Nothingness. On the other hand, if Absolute Nothingness is akin to a transcendent activity which takes on determinate reality and form in and through the finite entity which it empowers to exist, then both Absolute Nothingness and the particular entity can in a sense "coexist," although only in dynamic interdependence. As Abe comments with respect to Ralph, an imaginary golden retriever, "Ralph, the concrete dog here and how, has his place in Absolute Nothingness, and at the same time, truly has his place in himself."[42] Ralph both is and is not Absolute Nothingness. Likewise, Absolute Nothingness both is and is not Ralph.

Awakening to the reality of Nobo's ontogenetic matrix (the conjoint activity of creativity and the extensive continuum in one's life) could also conceivably be a religious experience like Buddhist enlightenment. Within a theistic context, of course, the connection of this ontogenetic matrix with the reality of God would have to be spelled out as well. Here Whiteheadians such as Nobo and myself differ on how that is to be done. I will end this chapter with a brief description of our differences on this point and at the same time make clear how in either case my initial description of Whitehead's overall philosophical scheme as involving a logic of intersubjectivity still holds true.

In "Experience, Eternity, and Primordiality," Jorge Nobo distinguishes, first, between the eternal and non-eternal universes. Within the eternal universe there necessarily exists a single primordial entity. Within the non-eternal universe there exist God the Creator and a myriad number of finite contingent beings.[43] Within Nobo's

41. Cf. here Seiichi Yagi, "Buddhist-Christian Dialogue in Japan: Varieties of Immediate Experience," *Buddhist-Christian Studies* 14 (1994): 11-22. Yagi makes clear the different ways in which this total identification with Absolute Nothingness can take place.
42. Abe, "Nishida's Philosophy of 'Place,'" 368.
43. Nobo, "Experience, Eternity, and Primordiality," 180-84, 195-203.

scheme, in other words, the primordial entity becomes God the Creator within a non-eternal universe once it makes the decision to create finite entities. But this decision by the primordial actuality is merely enabled and not necessitated by the nature of the eternal universe or ontogenetic matrix. The primordial actuality could in principle choose simply to exist in and for itself. According to Nobo, therefore, the eternal universe together with its primordial actuality is thus characterized by four properties indissolubly linked with one another: creativeness, extensiveness, entensiveness (the way in which it "witnesses its own states"[44]), and determinativeness (the way in which it manifests structures of intelligibility or "eternal objects" [cf. Glossary]). Furthermore, all four of these properties are exhibited in every actuality within the non-eternal universe. Ultimate reality for Nobo, accordingly, is the eternal universe since it is (like Absolute Nothingness in Nishida's philosophy) the "place" or context within which all determinate entities, namely, God the Creator and all God's creatures, exist in dynamic interrelation. At the same time, the eternal universe enters into the self-constitution of all these entities. As Nobo comments, "the entire antecedent universe . . . functions in the becoming of every actuality, or what is the same, contributes to its determinacy. But each actuality also contributes its own determination; and this is possible because the begetting of each partially determinate actuality is the total universe incarnating and individualizing itself, and hence its eternal properties, in a new creation."[45]

My own account of this ontogenetic matrix is quite similar to that of Nobo in all respects save one. Whereas Nobo distinguishes between the eternal universe and its primordial actuality, I regard the eternal universe or ontogenetic matrix for all entities as the "nature" or internal principle of existence and activity for God as a personal being in the traditional sense, namely, someone who knows and loves both self and others. God in my scheme is thus a non-dual reality:

44. Nobo, "From Creativity to Ontogenetic Matrix: Learning from Whitehead's Account of the Ultimate," *Process Thought* 8 (1998): 90. N.B.: *Process Thought* is the journal of the Japan Society for Process Studies.
45. Nobo, "From Creativity to Ontogenetic Matrix," 90-89. N.B.: In *Process Thought*, as a Japanese journal, pages are numbered backwards by Western standards (from the last page to the first).

that is, both universal ground of being and a personal being at the same time. Furthermore, in my scheme, the ground of being for God's own existence and activity likewise serves as the ground of being or ultimate principle of existence and activity for all creatures. Thus, just as in Nobo's scheme, both God and all creatures exist in virtue of one and the same ontogenetic matrix or ground of being. But this matrix in my scheme is simply a dimension of the full reality of God rather than a reality distinct from God who is its primordial actualization.

The difference between Nobo and me thus basically reduces to differences in starting-points for our respective ontological schemes. Nobo's starting-point is purely philosophical. Ultimate Reality for him is an ontogenetic matrix which must have a primordial actuality as its necessary counterpart; otherwise, the ontogenetic matrix has no reason to exist. My starting-point is in Christian theology, in which the biblical revelation of God as Creator of heaven and earth is assumed. The primordial actuality is then for me the God of biblical revelation, and the ontogenetic matrix is the divine nature or divine principle of existence and activity which, as a result of a free decision by God, likewise is the principle of existence and activity for all creatures.

One further reason why I favor the understanding of the ontogenetic matrix as the nature of God rather than as a reality somehow distinct from God is that it thereby allows me to introduce the logic of intersubjectivity not only between God and creatures but even within the internal reality of God considered apart from creatures. That is, in line with classical Christian theology, I propose that God is not only personal but tripersonal. I interpret "tripersonal" in a strong sense to mean that there are three interrelated subjectivities within God who are governed by a logic of intersubjectivity in their relations with one another. Thus, in line with Nishida's explanation of "inverse correspondence" stated above, each of the divine persons has an "absolute contradictory self identity" in that each is its individual self by reason of its dynamic relation of opposition to the other two subjectivities. As Thomas Aquinas described it in his classical treatise on the Trinity in the *Summa Theologiae*, each of the divine persons is a "subsistent relation" defined in its own individual identity in virtue of its dynamic relation of opposition to the other two persons.[46] They have, in other words, nothing in common beyond their relations of opposition to one another; and yet, implicitly in line with Nishida's insight expressed above, they paradoxically possess a deeper identity; they are, in fact, one God, in virtue of those same relations of opposition.

Furthermore, in line with this scheme, one has at hand something of an explanation why Ultimate Reality, at least in part, should consist in an ontogenetic matrix. For, by their dynamic interrelation in virtue of the "logic of intersubjectivity," the divine persons sustain the ontogenetic matrix which is their common ground of being or conjoint field of activity. This is not to say, of course, that first the divine persons exist and then the ontogenetic matrix as their conjoint field of activity comes into existence. Rather, the divine persons coexist with the ontogenetic matrix as their ground of being or internal source of existence and activity. The divine persons, in other words, cannot exist except in virtue of their conjoint enabling principle of existence and activity, namely, the ontogenetic matrix. But the ontogenetic matrix, on the other hand, has no reason to be except as, in the first place, the principle of existence and activity for the divine persons. Subsequently, in virtue of a conjoint free decision of those same divine persons, the ontogenetic matrix has still further reason to be in that it now serves as likewise the ultimate principle of existence and activity for all creatures. But, as Nobo also maintains,[47] this ontogenetic matrix is not itself the cause of creation; it simply enables creatures to be once the decision is made by the primordial actuality (in Nobo's scheme) or the triune God (in my scheme) to create a temporal world.

To sum up, then, in this chapter I have tried to link Nishida's "logic of place" together with its companion notion of "inverse correspondence" or "absolute contradictory self identity" with a logic of intersubjectivity which I believe is implicit in the philosophy of Alfred North Whitehead. That is, as I see it, for both Nishida and Whitehead genuine subjects of experience are clearly distinct from the objects of thought represented as the "subjects" of sentences in the formal logic of Aristotle and Aquinas. They are, in other words,

46. Thomas Aquinas *Summa Theologiae* I, Q. 29, art. 4 resp.
47. Nobo, "Experience, Eternity, and Primordiality," 195.

dynamic self-constituting realities rather than fixed objects of thought. Furthermore, for both Nishida and Whitehead, the manner of self-constitution of these subjects of experience is basically the same: namely, self-affirmation through self-negation, an absolute contradictory self-identity in virtue of allowing oneself to be defined in one's own individual identity through relation to another independent subject of experience (or many such subjects of experience in combination).

Finally, for both Whitehead and Nishida this "inverse correspondence" between opposing subjectivities is paradoxically enabled by a dynamic relationship to a common transcendent reality: for Nishida, Absolute Nothingness; for Whitehead, creativity. As noted above, Jorge Nobo and I link Whitehead's category of creativity with the notion of the "extensive continuum" within Whitehead's metaphysical scheme so to constitute what Jorge Nobo labels the ontogenetic matrix of the universe and what I regard as the transcendent ground of being or principle of existence for the three divine persons and all their creatures. In both cases, however, the parallel with the notion of Absolute Nothingness in Nishida's philosophy is quite striking. That is, Absolute Nothingness for Nishida, the ontogenetic matrix for Nobo, and the nature of God or divine ground of being within my scheme, is not an actuality in the sense of some self-existing reality. Rather, it is an activity-oriented "field-being," so to speak, which achieves concrete actuality only in and through the particular entities which it empowers to exist.[48] Hence, it is both itself and yet not itself in each of the entities which it enables to exist. Thus, as Masao Abe noted above in connection with the notion of Absolute Nothingness for Nishida, this transcendent reality likewise is or has an absolute contradictory self-identity in that it both is and is not everything that can be said about it.

There is then an elusive vertical dimension in every instance of human intersubjectivity or, for that matter, in every instance of intersubjectivity anywhere (either among the three divine persons or

48. There is, to be sure, an International Institute for Field-Being under the direction of Professor Lik Kuen Tong at Fairfield University in Connecticut, which sponsors regular conferences on "field-being" as the postmodern alternative for "substance" in classical Western philosophy.

within the world of creation). It cannot be reified or in any way reduced to an object of thought since it is not an entity but rather the necessary context for the dynamic interrelationship of entities. The entities cannot exist without it as their immanent principle of existence and activity, but it has no reality apart from the entities which it empowers to exist. In the next chapter, I will outline what I call the horizontal dimension of a logic of intersubjectivity, that is, the way in which subjects of experience by their dynamic interrelation initially create and then sustain enduring patterns of interrelationship or objective structures of intelligibility within "the between" understood as this ontogenetic matrix for their interrelated existence and activity. For only as one combines the vertical dimension of intersubjectivity with the horizontal dimension, the transcendent with the immanent, does one come to grips with the inevitable product of sustained intersubjective activity, namely, a world-order in ongoing process of change and development.

5 Intersubjectivity: The Horizontal Dimension

As noted at the end of the preceding chapter, the vertical or transcendent dimension of a logic of intersubjectivity will not by itself account for the existence of a world-order or objective state of affairs characteristic of reality on a day-to-day basis for human beings. Above all, within a Whiteheadian context, where enduring subjects of experience are to be understood in terms of serially-ordered societies of actual occasions or strictly momentary subjects of experience, the transition to consideration of the horizontal dimension of a logic of intersubjectivity is absolutely imperative. For, as Whitehead himself comments, actual occasions literally come and go; societies of actual occasions alone perdure.[1] But even within a more common sense approach to reality, it is clear that intersubjective relationships between two or more human beings always arise within a given social context and somehow contribute to that same social context before they naturally end or are otherwise terminated. Hence a logic or philosophical analysis of human intersubjectivity must somehow take into account a broader social context, namely, the existence of specifically social entities such as local communities or environments which by their mutual interaction produce even broader social realities, that is, even bigger communities or environments where the component parts or mem-

1. Alfred North Whitehead, *Adventures of Ideas* (New York: The Free Press, 1967), 204.

bers are no longer individual entities but entire groups of entities in dynamic interrelation.

In this chapter, accordingly, I will initially attempt an integration of Whitehead's philosophy with a rival conceptual scheme, namely, systems philosophy, above all, as elaborated some years ago by Ervin Laszlo.[2] As I see it, only an adroit combination of these two metaphysical schemes will satisfy what I am calling the horizontal dimension of a projected philosophy of intersubjectivity. Then in the second part of the chapter I will make use of Jürgen Habermas's research in *The Theory of Communicative Action* to show how at least in principle such a dual-dimensional worldview might work out in practice.[3] For, as a philosopher as well as social scientist, Habermas is well-equipped to weigh the strengths and the weaknesses of both strictly interpersonal modes of thought and systems-oriented thinking for the analysis of concrete social problems. Finally, in the third part of the chapter I will indicate how the vertical dimension of a philosophy of intersubjectivity as described in the preceding chapter can be combined with the horizontal dimension as set forth in the present chapter so as to constitute a unified worldview grounded in the all-embracing reality of intersubjectivity.

A. Whitehead and Laszlo Compared

In contrast to the substance-oriented metaphysics of Aristotle and Thomas Aquinas, the philosophy of Alfred North Whitehead is usually set forth as a metaphysical scheme which recognizes the social character of this world, that is, the intrinsic interrelation of (actual) entities with one another from moment to moment.[4] While I certainly concede that Whitehead's philosophy with its doctrine of internal (as opposed to purely external) relations among actual occasions provides theoretical justification for the claim that every actual

2. Cf. Ervin Laszlo, *Introduction to Systems Philosophy: Toward a New Paradigm of Contemporary Thought* (London: Gordon and Breach, 1972).

3. Cf. Jürgen Habermas, *The Theory of Communicative Action*, trans. Thomas McCarthy, 2 vols. (Boston: Beacon Press, 1984 & 1987).

4. Ian G. Barbour, *Religion and Science: Historical and Contemporary Issues* (San Francisco: HarperCollins, 1997), 285.

entity is a microcosm of the entire past universe, I am not convinced that Whitehead's philosophy is for that reason a fully articulated social ontology (cf. Glossary). For, as I have made clear elsewhere,[5] there is an implicit tendency to atomism within Whitehead's thought which is at odds with the claim to be a truly social ontology. A social ontology, in other words, should begin with the premise that the "real things of which the world is made up"[6] are not simply actual entities but also the societies of which they are constituent parts. Societies, to be sure, cannot exist apart from a temporally-ordered series of actual entities, but actual entities are meaningless apart from the societies into which they aggregate. As Whitehead himself says in *Adventures of Ideas,* "[t]he real actual things that endure are all societies. They are not actual occasions."[7]

There is unquestionably an affinity here of my reinterpretation of Whitehead with the systems philosophy of Ervin Laszlo, since Laszlo also maintains that the basic components of the material universe are social realities or systems.[8] But there are also significant differences between myself and Laszlo. Laszlo, for example, distinguishes between natural and artificial (or humanly constructed) systems. A natural system he defines as a "nonrandom accumulation of matter-energy, in a region of physical space-time, which is nonrandomly organized into coacting interrelated subsystems or components."[9] In my judgment, this is roughly equivalent to Whitehead's notion of a society as a nexus with social order. That is, while for Whitehead there can exist aggregates or nexuses of actual entities which are purely coincidental and thus possess no principle of continuity or social order, the far more normal occurrence is that of aggregates or nexuses of actual entities both in space and over time which share what Whitehead calls a "common element of form" or defining characteristic.[10]

---

5. Joseph A. Bracken, "Proposals for Overcoming the Atomism within Process-Relational Metaphysics," *Process Studies* 23 (1994): 10-24.

6. Whitehead, *Process and Reality: An Essay in Cosmology,* corrected edition, ed. David Ray Griffin and Donald W. Sherburne (New York: The Free Press, 1978), 18.

7. Whitehead, *Adventures of Ideas,* 204.

8. Laszlo, *Introduction to Systems Philosophy,* 30.

9. Laszlo, *Introduction to Systems Philosophy,* 30.

10. Whitehead, *Process and Reality,* 34; cf. below, Glossary.

Furthermore, like Whitehead, Laszlo believes that natural systems (or, for Whitehead, societies) are organized hierarchically with more primitive systems such as atoms serving as component parts or members of more complex systems, e.g., molecules, organisms, etc.[11] But, whereas for Laszlo primitive natural systems possess "invariant properties" allowing them to become functioning parts of more sophisticated higher-level systems,[12] for Whitehead actual entities as momentary subjects of experience derive their internal structure and organization strictly from prehension of the external world out of which they are emerging. There is, in other words, no latent capacity for self-development within an actual occasion beyond what is needed for its self-constitution here and now. Since it only exists momentarily, there is no reason for an actual occasion to possess "invariant properties" for future self-development.

Here I follow Whitehead in maintaining that the ultimate components of natural systems are actual occasions or momentary subjects of experience which are context-dependent for their internal structure and organization. But I follow Laszlo in proposing that in the end only natural systems or Whiteheadian societies exist long enough to make a difference. As Whitehead himself notes in *Adventures of Ideas*, "[a] society . . . enjoys a history expressing its changing reactions to changing circumstances. But an actual occasion has no such history. It never changes. It only becomes and perishes."[13] Furthermore, with Laszlo I argue that natural systems or societies exercise agency, although I would disagree with him how that agency is effected. For Laszlo, natural systems exercise agency directly in virtue of their own internal structure and organization. I maintain that Whiteheadian societies exercise agency indirectly through the collective agency of their interrelated actual entities.[14] In this way, I preserve the validity of Whitehead's maxim that "agency belongs exclusively to actual occasions,"[15] even as I agree with Laszlo that complex natural systems or Whiteheadian structured societies exercise an

11. Laszlo, *Introduction to Systems Philosophy*, 47-53.
12. Laszlo, *Introduction to Systems Philosophy*, 49-53, 175.
13. Whitehead, *Adventures of Ideas*, 204.
14. Joseph A. Bracken, S.J., *Society and Spirit: A Trinitarian Cosmology* (Cranbury, N.J.: Associated University Presses, 1991), 39-56.
15. Whitehead, *Process and Reality*, 31.

agency proper to their own level of organization and activity. A human being, for example, exercises agency, not simply in virtue of her "soul" or dominant subsociety of actual occasions, but in virtue of the coordinated activity of all the subsocieties (with their constituent actual occasions) within her body.

I am carefully taking a position here midway between Whitehead and Laszlo on the nature of material reality because only thus in my judgment will the notion of a genuinely social ontology be internally consistent and broadly intelligible. For example, I find puzzling Laszlo's proposal that in the end only systems exist. For this begs the question of the ultimate constituents of those same systems. If the constituents of every system are themselves subsystems which in turn require still other subsystems as their constituent parts or members, then one is involved in a logical *regressus ad infinitum*. Much simpler, it seems to me, is Whitehead's proposal that the ultimate constituents of material reality are not themselves material entities but rather strictly immaterial subjects of experience which by their dynamic interrelation from moment to moment generate what common sense perceives as material reality but which on closer inspection turn out to be closely connected patterns of order or structures of intelligibility among successive energy-events (what Laszlo calls "natural systems"). Thus there is a clear distinction for Whitehead (and for me) between objective systems or societies within the world of nature and their ultimate subjective constituents.

On the other hand, Laszlo strikes me as more in tune with the different levels of the world in which we humans live. With his concept of natural system, he has a metaphysical category which applies equally well to the inorganic, organic, and supraorganic levels of reality.[16] Whitehead's notion of society is in principle equally comprehensive, if one allows for the existence of "structured societies" (cf. Glossary) which, even though democratically rather than monarchically organized, yet possess an ontological unity and exercise an agency appropriate to their own level of organization. But, as already noted in earlier chapters, here is where Whiteheadians generally follow the lead of Charles Hartshorne in privileging monarchically-organized structured

16. Cf. Ervin Laszlo, *The Systems View of the World: The Natural Philosophy of the New Developments in the Sciences* (New York: George Braziller, 1972), 30-33.

societies which possess ontological unity and exercise agency through their "regnant" subsociety of actual occasions or "soul" for the control and direction of the other subsocieties of actual occasions.[17] This ignores the fact, however, that the overwhelming majority of Whiteheadian structured societies are not monarchically organized. As either inorganic compounds or supraorganic organizations of individual entities in terms of environments or communities, they have no "soul" or dominant subsociety. Whiteheadians, therefore, are implicitly making the less common instance of societal organization into the standard or measure for all societies whatsoever.

One could indeed possibly argue that inorganic compounds are, as Hartshorne affirmed, nothing more than "composite individuals," that is, loosely connected aggregates of subsocieties with their constituent actual occasions. For, these inorganic compounds can often be taken apart and recombined in different ways much as one takes apart and rebuilds a machine. But can we realistically think of communities and environments in the same way, namely, as simply aggregates of subsocieties with their constituent actual occasions? Do not these supraorganic social realities possess an ontological unity in themselves and exercise a type of collective agency appropriate to their own level of organization? Laszlo's remarks on the subject of group identity are in my judgment quite perceptive:

> Since people behave differently in small intimate groups than in large public ones, there are some things we can say about the behavior of people in groups that refer to the structure of the group rather than to the individuality of its members. . . . The group manifests characteristics in virtue of being a group of a certain sort, and may maintain these properties even if all its individual members are replaced. Hence one might as well deal with the group *qua* group.[18]

Admittedly, if one were to explore exhaustively all the properties of the members of a group together with all their relationships to one

---

17. Charles Hartshorne, "The Compound Individual," in *Philosophical Essays for Alfred North Whitehead,* ed. F. S. C. Northrup (New York: Russell & Russell, 1936), 193-210.

18. Laszlo, *The Systems View of the World,* 29.

another, one could conceivably arrive at an understanding of the nature and structure of the group comparable to that achieved simply by studying the group as a corporate reality. But even in this extreme case it would not be clear whether one had thereby reduced a social totality to the sum of its member-parts or whether one had inadvertently stumbled upon the form or characteristic structure of the social totality precisely as such.

To sum up, then, in this first part of the chapter I have compared and contrasted Whitehead's metaphysical system with that of systems philosophy as elaborated by Ervin Laszlo. The result of my investigation has been the judgment that, while Whitehead's notion of actual occasions as momentary subjects of experience better accounts for the ultimate components of natural systems or societies, Laszlo's scheme provides an easier way for these natural systems or societies to be compared and evaluated with respect to one another. A fully articulated philosophy of intersubjectivity, accordingly, will have to incorporate within itself elements of both metaphysical schemes. In the second part of this chapter, I will take up once again Jürgen Habermas's celebrated theory of communicative action as the paradigm for rational human behavior in contemporary society. While I have certain reservations about the purely secular character of Habermas's project on which I will elaborate at the end of this section, I nevertheless agree with his endorsement of the idea that only a combination of systems theory and various interpersonal modes of social analysis adequately accounts for the complexity of life in society today.

B. Jürgen Habermas's *Theory of Communicative Action*

As already noted in chapter two, Habermas has three interrelated goals which he wishes to achieve in this work: "(1) to develop a concept of rationality that is no longer tied to, and limited by, the subjectivistic and individualistic premises of modern philosophy and social theory; (2) to construct a two-level concept of society that integrates the lifeworld and system paradigms; and, finally, (3) to sketch out against this background a critical theory of modernity which analyzes and accounts for its pathologies in a way that suggests a redirection rather than an abandonment of the project of enlightenment."[19] In this chapter I will be primarily interested in how Habermas achieves his second goal, namely, the construction of a two-level concept of society involving systems theory and the notion of a "lifeworld."

The latter term Habermas borrows from his predecessor in social theory, Alfred Schutz: "Phenomenologists like Alfred Schutz speak of the lifeworld as the unthematically given horizon within which participants in communication move in common when they refer thematically to something in the *world*."[20] The lifeworld, in other words, is what is created by human beings in their day-to-day contact with one another in the search for common meanings and values as the ongoing basis of their lives together. Once incorporated into the lifeworld, habits of thought and patterns of behavior are no longer consciously reflected upon but simply taken for granted by human beings as distinctive features of their communal way of life.

Thus understood, what Habermas and Schutz mean by a lifeworld bears in my judgment a distinct structural resemblance to a Whiteheadian "society" of actual occasions. For, as Whitehead comments in *Process and Reality*, "a set of entities is a society (i) in virtue of a 'defining characteristic' shared by its members, and (ii) in virtue of the presence of the defining characteristic being due to the environment provided by the society itself."[21] The defining characteristic, to be sure, can be relatively simple or quite complex, depending upon the degree of spontaneity present among the constituent actual occasions. The defining characteristic of the society of actual occasions constituting an atom or molecule, for example, is relatively simple since newly concrescing actual occasions basically just repeat the pattern of interrelation inherited from their predecessors. The defining characteristic for a higher-level living organism such as a human being must be significantly more complex, however, since a central nervous system and brain are needed to coordinate the diverse forms

19. Habermas, *Theory of Communicative Action*, I:vi.

20. Habermas, *Theory of Communicative Action*, 82. For a better understanding of Habermas's own understanding of the term "lifeworld," cf. II:119-52, esp. 135-40, where he indicates that a lifeworld has three interrelated structural components, namely culture, society, and person.

21. Whitehead, *Process and Reality*, 89.

of spontaneity emergent out of the various subsocieties of actual occasions within the organism as a whole. But the defining characteristic of a human lifeworld in which the community members are able to make conscious decisions either in line with or in opposition to the manifest will of the group is for that reason even more complex. The key point, however, is that in every instance the defining characteristic of the society in question is initially determined by the interrelated activity of its constituent occasions and is then sustained in existence by the society itself as the ongoing environment for successive generations of actual occasions.

Granted, therefore, that Whitehead's category of society is far more comprehensive in scope than Habermas's notion of a human lifeworld, structurally they are the same in that both a Whiteheadian society and a lifeworld for Habermas are the product of sustained intersubjective activity and both constitute an ongoing environment conditioning the further activity of their constituent parts or members. Yet for the same reason both suffer from a structural deficiency which can only be remedied by recourse to systems theory or some similarly-oriented metaphysical scheme. That is, what is further required for an adequate social ontology is some conceptual mechanism whereby one can interpret and evaluate the interplay of societies as such with one another rather than simply the relation of individual members of those societies to one another. Here someone might object that most Whiteheadian societies are "structured societies" in which the direct constituents are subsocieties, not actual occasions as such.[22] While this is certainly true, it is not clear to me how one analyzes the interplay of the various subsocieties within a Whiteheadian structured society except once more in terms of the constituent actual occasions for those same subsocieties.

As I noted in the first part of this chapter, Whiteheadians tend to follow the lead of Charles Hartshorne in giving priority among structured societies to those which are monarchically-organized in terms of a "regnant" subsociety over a large number of subordinate subsocieties. But this equivalently means that the latest actual occasion within the regnant subsociety exercises a controlling influence over all

22. Whitehead, *Process and Reality*, 99.

139

the other actual occasions within the structured society (much as the "soul" within classical metaphysics gives unity and order to the body as a whole). There is no sustained analysis of the interplay of the subsocieties as such with one another within a monarchically-organized structured society.[23] Likewise, within Whiteheadian structured societies which lack a regnant subsociety and thus are more democratically organized, the tendency among Whiteheadians, once again following the lead of Charles Hartshorne, is to regard these subsocieties as virtual aggregates of actual occasions and thus as lacking the unity and coherence necessary for direct exchange with one another precisely as subsocieties within a larger corporate reality. One must conclude, therefore, that, even though Whitehead was evidently aware of the "layered" character of structured societies in which subsocieties of actual occasions rather than the occasions themselves are the immediate members,[24] he lacks a conceptual mechanism for analyzing the relations of these subsocieties to one another except in terms of the interplay of their constituent actual occasions.

In any event, in the next few paragraphs I will summarize Habermas's own explanation of how systems theory can and should be integrated with the results of social analysis arising out of the investigation of human beings in dynamic interrelation within a given lifeworld. In chapter two, I focused attention on how the members of a given lifeworld use language to communicate with one another about shared meanings and values so as by degrees to build up such a lifeworld or shared culture. In this chapter I will indicate how in Habermas's judgment the use of systems theory becomes necessary as lifeworlds reach a certain stage of complexity and yet how care must nevertheless be taken not to allow systems analysis so to dominate reflection and action within a given social situation that the basic intersubjective meanings and values on which the lifeworld itself is based are jeopardized.

Habermas begins by noting that lifeworlds must reach a certain level of "rationalization" or systematization before systems analysis can come into play.[25] Primitive societies, in other words, in which the

---

23. Cf. on this point, Ian Barbour, *Religion and Science,* 290.
24. Cf. below, pp. 147-49.
25. Habermas, *Theory of Communicative Action,* II:156-72.

membership is modest and in which rules of behavior are set more by longstanding custom than by legal authority are not yet sufficiently institutionalized for the interplay of rival interest groups characteristic of systems analysis. Yet, as Habermas comments, to the extent that a given group of people begin to divide up tasks necessary for their communal well-being, "[t]here are inducements to regulate interaction in such a way that specialized activities can be *authoritatively joined together* and their different results (or products) *exchanged. . . .* The authoritative combination of specialized performances requires delegating the authority to direct, or *power,* to persons who take on the task of organization; the functional exchange of products calls for the establishment of *exchange relations.*"[26] Thus even within a relatively simple lifeworld a systems perspective begins to emerge in which attention is given primarily to objective results rather than to the intentions of community members at any given moment.

In the end, says Habermas, there is a gradual evolution from egalitarian tribal societies to hierarchically-organized tribal societies in which leadership roles become more evident: that is, to politically-stratified class societies with power operating as a "steering mechanism" and to economically-constituted class societies with money as a steering mechanism.[27] "But the mechanisms that serve to heighten system complexity are not a priori harmonized with the mechanisms that provide for the social cohesiveness of the collectivity via normative consensus and mutual understanding in language."[28] The price to be paid for the progressive systematization of life in society, therefore, is the "uncoupling" of systems and lifeworld: "The social system definitively bursts out of the horizon of the lifeworld, escapes from the intuitive knowledge of everyday communicative practice, and is henceforth accessible only to the counterintuitive knowledge of the social sciences developing since the eighteenth century."[29] But, as a result, ordinary people living in a given lifeworld understandably feel that they have lost control of their lives. They are no longer either in-

26. Habermas, *Theory of Communicative Action,* II:160.
27. Habermas, *Theory of Communicative Action,* II:165-67.
28. Habermas, *Theory of Communicative Action,* II:165.
29. Habermas, *Theory of Communicative Action,* II:173.

141

dividually or collectively making important decisions affecting their individual and communal well-being. Rather, economic and political forces beyond their understanding and control are dictating the character of their life together.

Granted its obvious advantages for objective social analysis, the uncritical use of systems theory, accordingly, poses certain real dangers to the proper functioning of the lifeworlds under investigation and the ultimate well-being of their members. For, as Habermas comments, "the more complex social systems become, the more provincial lifeworlds become. In a differentiated social system the lifeworld seems to shrink to a subsystem."[30] As noted above, what is valuable within the context of a lifeworld is that human beings are in a position directly to deal with one another and by rational argument gradually to come to a consensus position with respect to their most cherished meanings and values.[31] But the logic of the systems approach to life in society indirectly works to eliminate that kind of interpersonal communication. "Media such as money and power attach to empirical ties; they encode a purposive-rational attitude toward calculable amounts of value and make it possible to exert generalized, strategic influence on the decisions of other participants while *bypassing* processes of consensus-oriented communication."[32] Thus insofar as money and power with their own appeal in terms of concrete rewards and punishments equivalently replace the need for linguistic communication as to shared meanings and values among members of a given lifeworld, then the lifeworld is no longer needed for the coordination of action within society. As a result, what counts in the end is the survival of the economic or political system rather than the genuine well-being of the human beings it is intended to serve.

To counteract these dangers in the systematization or "rationalization" of contemporary society, Habermas urges the conscious use of both systems theory and the lifeworld paradigm for the analysis of contemporary social life. Neither can be dispensed with since each is dependent on the other to function properly. Systems thinking arises, as already indicated, only after a certain amount of sys-

30. Habermas, *Theory of Communicative Action*, II:173.
31. Cf. above, chapter two, pp. 65-68.
32. Habermas, *Theory of Communicative Action*, II:183.

tematization has already taken place in the lifeworld. On the other hand, the results of systems analysis are better accepted and implemented by those directly concerned if they have opportunities to express their views as to the practicality of what is thereby being proposed and together with their peers can make appropriate modifications in the governing theory in the light of their concrete needs and desires. Thus, as Jane Braaten points out, there are basically two different kinds of rationality at work in the smooth functioning of human relationships within society.[33] The first is the functional rationality involved in the reproduction of the goods and services required for the material well-being of the group. The various social systems thus set in place are best analyzed and evaluated in terms of systems theory or some similar conceptual scheme. The other ultimately more fundamental rationality at work in human society is what Habermas calls "communicative rationality" whereby human beings learn to deal equitably with one another in the achievement of both personal and communal goals and values.[34] Communicative rationality is more important than the functional or instrumental logic of systems theory because it sets the parameters or constraints within which the other more impersonal approach to human life can and should operate.

Here, of course, is where Habermas consciously differs from some of his illustrious predecessors in social theory, notably Max Weber, who believed that human beings are ultimately governed by a logic of self-interest in their dealings with one another and that systems theory is needed to keep them from consciously or unconsciously doing harm to one another in the pursuit of their own self-interest.[35] Habermas in that respect is more of an idealist in urging the ideal of communicative rationality in the light of which human beings gradually come to understand one another better and then to cooperate with one another in the achievement of commonly agreed upon goals and values. The whole purpose of human communication through language is to move toward rational consensus on the important is-

33. Cf. Jane Braaten, *Habermas's Critical Theory of Society* (Albany, N.Y.: State University of New York Press, 1991), 78.

34. Habermas, *Theory of Communicative Action,* I:94-101.

35. Habermas, *Theory of Communicative Action,* I:243-54, 279-86.

sues of life in community.[36] Precisely on this point, however, Habermas's theory of communicative action in my judgment is in need of supplementation from a traditional sphere of human life which he and Weber more or less set aside as something bypassed in the "modernization" of contemporary society.[37]

That is, to sustain this ideal of communicative rationality among contemporary human beings and thus to prevent them from resorting exclusively to a functional logic based on narrow self-interest in their dealings with one another, Habermas, it seems to me, should consciously make room for the influence of either institutional religions or of some other non-institutional but still religiously inspired worldview as a motivational factor in the behavior of human beings as they deal with one another on a day-to-day basis. Admittedly, within Habermas's scheme such forms of religiously-oriented "mythology," with their appeal either to divine revelation or to religious intuition, cannot be judged to be "true" since they are incapable of empirical verification. As a result, they are simply a matter of belief on the part of a minority of individuals involved in a discourse-situation in which all claims to truth and moral validity have to be argued out rationally.[38] At the same time, given Habermas's basically pragmatic orien-

36. Habermas, *Theory of Communicative Action,* I:94-101. Cf. also above, chapter two, pp. 65-67.

37. Habermas, *Theory of Communicative Action,* I:186-215. Cf. here also Helmut Peukert, *Science, Action, and Fundamental Theology: Toward a Theology of Communicative Action,* trans. James Bohman (Cambridge, Mass.: MIT Press, 1984), esp. 202-45. Peukert argues, first, that a theory of communicative action falls into self-contradiction unless justice is somehow done to the memory of victims of unjust suffering who witnessed by their tragic deaths to the ideal of free and unhindered communication, and, secondly, that this need of "anamnestic solidarity" with the victims of injustice with the past can only be satisfied by recourse to the biblical notion of the eschatological Kingdom of God in which all wrongs will be eventually righted. Below I make the more modest claim that belief in the definitive coming of the Kingdom of God may well serve as valuable supplementary motivation for many in striving to achieve the idealized community of discourse in which disagreements are settled by rational argument rather than by force. In any event, as I see it, Habermas should not dismiss such beliefs arising out of religious sources simply because they cannot be validated empirically and hence are not likely to be accepted by everyone in the community.

38. Habermas, *Theory of Communicative Action,* I:99: "The concept of communicative action presupposes language as the medium for a kind of reaching under-

tation to truth- and validity-claims in which practical agreement is prized higher than theoretical certitude, perhaps he should broaden his concept of what counts as evidence in favor of one course of action over another so as to include specifically religious experience, even though the latter is not universally accepted as true by all the participants. In other words, the fact that their religious beliefs motivate some members of the group to aspire to a pragmatic goal or value which all agree is worth attaining should be enough reason on pragmatic grounds to broaden the notion of pertinent evidence for the community deliberation. For at least some of the participants, religious beliefs and the worldview arising therefrom play a key role in the final decision.[39]

In any event, in the third and final section of this chapter, I will be setting forth a religiously inspired worldview which, as proposed above, will incorporate both the vertical and horizontal dimensions of a philosophy/theology of intersubjectivity as laid out in these last two chapters. For the moment, however, I will bring this part of the chapter to a close with the summary remark that in view of the careful analysis which Jürgen Habermas makes of the need for both systems theory and lifeworld paradigms in the analysis of human social behavior, and keeping in mind the close affinity between Whiteheadian societies and Habermas's notion of a lifeworld, one may suitably conclude that the horizontal dimension of this projected logic of intersubjectivity must include both systems theory and Whitehead's analysis of aggregates of actual occasions in terms of societies. For, as Anselm Min has pointed out recently in another context, purely intersubjective modes of social analysis tend to abstract

---

standing, in the course of which participants, through relating to a world, reciprocally raise validity claims that can be accepted or contested." Cf. also Braaten, *Habermas's Critical Theory of Society*, 22-23.

39. For a striking exemplification of how a religiously-inspired worldview can radically influence pragmatic decisions in the world of economics, politics, and jurisprudence, cf. Nancey Murphy and George F. R. Ellis, *On the Moral Nature of the Universe: Theology, Cosmology, and Ethics* (Minneapolis: Fortress, 1996). Likewise, cf. a hitherto unpublished paper written by Dr. Maeve Cooke of University College, Dublin, under the title "Critical Theory and Religion" and presented at a conference on contemporary philosophy of religion organized by Dr. D. Z. Phillips at Claremont Graduate University in Claremont, California, February 5-6, 1999.

from the complexity of human life in society while a systems approach to human social behavior runs the risk of thinking exclusively in terms of dehumanizing systems or "totalities" which pay little or no attention to the inevitable particularities of life in community. Only a triple dialectic based on the interplay of the notions of "infinity" (namely, the world of intersubjectivity), "totality" and the resultant "solidarity" of human beings with one another in community, as Min sees it, will prove adequate for the analysis of contemporary human life in society.[40]

C. Vertical and Horizontal Dimensions of Intersubjectivity

As I pointed out in chapter four, the vertical dimension of a logic of intersubjectivity involves the conscious acknowledgment of a transcendent context for the reciprocal relation of human beings and indeed all other subjects of experience within this world. Whether one contends, with Kitaro Nishida, that this transcendent context is to be understood as Absolute Nothingness or whether one understands, with Jorge Nobo and me, this transcendent context to be an ontogenetic matrix (cf. Glossary) empowering all concrete subjects of experience in their dynamic interrelations, one is naturally led to the conclusion, as I see it, that this context or "place" must be something like an all-encompassing energy-field. For, as noted in chapter four, Absolute Nothingness is not understood by Nishida and other Japanese Buddhists as a static but rather as a dynamic reality. It actively enters into the self-constitution of every entity in this world so that the entity in question is both itself and Absolute Nothingness at the same time.[41] Similarly, insofar as the ontogenetic matrix for Nobo and myself is constituted by the dynamic conjunction of "creativity" and "the extensive continuum" within Whitehead's metaphysical scheme,[42] the notion of an all-encompassing energy-field seems most

40. Cf. Anselm Min, "Toward a Dialectic of Totality and Infinity: Reflections on Emmanuel Levinas," *Journal of Religion* 78 (1998): 571-92.

41. Cf. above, chapter four, pp. 113-15.

42. *Ibid.*, pp. 123-25.

appropriate as explication of this presupposed transcendent context for the dynamic interplay of subjects of experience within this world. What has to be now further developed and explained is how Whiteheadian societies as aggregates of actual occasions with a "common element of form" fit into this all-embracing energy-field, equivalently "flesh it out" in terms of specific content and structure. Here I will rely upon a line of argument which I have pursued in the past with other Whiteheadians to the effect that societies within Whitehead's scheme are best understood as structured fields of activity for their constituent actual occasions. For if societies are best understood as fields, they very readily fit into a scheme in which Ultimate Reality is described as an all-encompassing energy-field. Whiteheadian societies are then simply further specifications of the one all-embracing primordial field. While actual occasions as momentary energy-events come into existence and then are gone, what remains as the enduring structure of reality are fields within fields, each with its own determinate structure which contributes to the overall structure of the primordial field.

Whitehead himself does not use the expression "field" in talking about societies as aggregates of actual occasions. But in *Process and Reality* he does describe societies in their dynamic interrelation as "environments" and "layers of social order":

> Thus a society is, for each of its members, an environment with some element of order in it, persisting by reason of the genetic relations between its own members. Such an element of order is the order prevalent in the society. But there is no society in isolation. Every society must be considered with its background of a wider environment of actual entities, which also contribute their objectifications to which the members of the society must conform. . . . Thus we arrive at the principle that every society requires a social background, of which it is itself a part. In reference to any given society the world of actual entities is to be conceived as forming a background in layers of social order, the defining characteristics becoming wider and more general as we widen the background.[43]

43. Whitehead, *Process and Reality*, 90. Cf. also 80 where he refers to the extensive continuum as the "physical field."

147

Thus understood, Whiteheadian societies seem to correspond to the conventional understanding of a field, namely, a context for the interaction of entities which is itself somehow structured by the interplay of those same entities. Fields, moreover, as the above-cited text also makes clear, can be readily seen as layered within one another so that the defining characteristics of the broader field of activity nevertheless influence and thereby condition the existence and behavior of entities located within a smaller, more sharply defined field of interaction.

Still another reason to think of Whiteheadian societies as fields rather than simply as aggregates of actual entities with an "element of order" existing between and among them is that the field, unlike an aggregate, can be said to perdure over time as successive generations of actual entities come and go. With each new generation of actual entities there must be a new aggregate. A field, on the other hand, as the context or "place" for the interplay of actual entities does not come and go with each new generation of actual entities. Rather, the field endures as the context out of which each new generation of entities arises and to which each generation contributes its own very modest modification of the pattern which it inherited from its predecessors. Whitehead's remarks in the same chapter of *Process and Reality* cited above are very telling in this regard:

> The causal laws which dominate a social environment [read, field] are the product of the defining characteristic of that society. But the society is only efficient through its individual members. Thus in a society, the members can only exist by reason of the laws which dominate the society, and the laws only come into being by reason of the analogous characters of the members of the society.[44]

A field, in other words, as simply a context for the interaction of entities has no reason to exist if it is totally empty, devoid of entities. But on the other hand, the entities, or more specifically Whiteheadian actual entities as momentary subjects of experience, need a structured or lawlike field of activity out of which to arise in order to pattern themselves in their individual self-constitution along the lines of

44. Whitehead, *Process and Reality*, 90-91.

predecessor actual entities in the same society.[45] Hence, there must be such a context or lawlike environment for successive generations of actual entities even though in and of itself apart from its constituent members the field is empty, a pure abstraction devoid of meaning and value.

In chapter four I argued, in agreement with Jorge Nobo, that the ultimate field of activity, namely the ontogenetic matrix for all concrete subjects of experience (even the three divine persons in my own scheme), is the effect of two conjoint principles within Whitehead's metaphysical scheme, namely, creativity and the extensive continuum.[46] Hence, the ontogenetic matrix as the ultimate field of activity is not just a spatial and temporal reality (that is, the extensive continuum) but a dynamic principle of activity (that is, creativity). Thus it may aptly be considered as an all-encompassing energy-field. But this would also seem to imply that individual societies within the neo-Whiteheadian scheme being presented here should likewise be considered not simply as spatial and temporal realities (as in the conventional Whiteheadian understanding of societies) but as subordinate energy-fields, further specifications of the ultimate energy-field, the ontogenetic matrix. Besides giving structure and order to successive generations of actual entities, societies in my scheme would then be equivalently the repository for the transmission of creativity from one set of actual entities to another.

---

45. A more orthodox Whiteheadian might counterargue that actual entities prehend the pattern exhibited by their predecessors through a process which Whitehead calls "objectification" (cf. Whitehead, *Process and Reality*, 23: "The term 'objectification' refers to the particular mode in which the potentiality of one actual entity is realized in another actual entity.") Physical feelings derived from antecedent actual entities are evaluated positively or negatively in terms of various conceptual feelings derived partly from those same antecedent actual entities and partly from other sources. Finally, there is a "transmutation" of these suitably modified physical feelings so as to attain a unified physical feeling of the "nexus" or aggregate of actual entities from which the original physical feelings in all their diversity were derived (cf. Whitehead, *Process and Reality*, 244-55). As I argued in a previous publication, however, it would be a much simpler process if newly concrescing actual entities directly prehended the basic structure of the field out of which they were originating (cf. Joseph A. Bracken, S.J., "Proposals for Overcoming the Atomism in Process-Relational Metaphysics," *Process Studies* 23 [1994]: 10-24, esp. 16-17).

46. Cf. above, chapter four, pp. 123-25.

Whitehead, for example, states clearly that creativity is transmitted from one set of actual occasions to another.[47] What is not so clear is how this transition takes place, since according to Whitehead a predecessor actual entity necessarily goes out of existence before its successor actual entity comes into being.[48] But then where does the creativity go if not into the society understood as an encompassing energy-field for both the antecedent and the subsequent actual occasion? Creativity, accordingly, does not come directly from the primordial ontogenetic matrix at every instant so as to energize the self-constitution of each new particular set of actual entities within a given society. Rather, it is habitually resident in the society when understood as a particular structured field of activity or lawlike context for the emergence of new generations of actual entities. Moreover, as thus situated within this structured field of activity, creativity acts in each instance to produce not just any nexus of actual occasions but only that nexus which more or less faithfully reproduces the pattern of interrelation present among the antecedent set of actual occasions within the field.

There are, to be sure, additional theoretical issues involved in the defense of my hypothesis that Whiteheadian societies are to be understood as structured fields of activity for their constituent actual occasions. But I have reserved discussion of them for a "concluding note" at the end of this chapter so that the main lines of my argument will not be obscured by attention to details which only an individual well-versed in Whiteheadian scholarship would be prepared to read and critique. To sum up, then, in this third part of chapter five I have tried to make clear how the horizontal dimension of a philosophy/theology based on a logic of intersubjectivity can be made compatible with the vertical dimension of such a theory as presented in

47. Whitehead, *Process and Reality*, 85: "The process of concrescence terminates with the attainment of a fully *determinate* 'satisfaction'; and the creativity thereby passes over into the 'given' primary phase for the concrescence of other actual entities." Cf. also 43: "The real internal constitution of an actual entity progressively constitutes a decision conditioning the creativity which *transcends* that actuality" (italics mine).

48. Whitehead, *Process and Reality*, 29: "Actual entities 'perpetually perish' subjectively, but are immortal objectively. Actuality in perishing acquires objectivity, while it loses subjective immediacy."

chapter four. In brief, my argument has been that, if the vertical dimension may be said to consist in an all-encompassing energy-field variously described as Absolute Nothingness by Buddhist philosophers like Kitaro Nishida and as an ontogenetic matrix by Western thinkers like Jorge Nobo and me, then the horizontal dimension of the theory stipulates that this all-encompassing energy-field is subdivided into a myriad number of subfields, and subfields within subfields. As I see it, this latter move is compatible with Whitehead's metaphysical scheme, provided that one interprets Whitehead's notion of societies of actual occasions as structured fields of activity for their constituent actual occasions. At the same time, in my judgment it is likewise compatible with the worldview of Ervin Laszlo and other systems-oriented thinkers in that they too envision a graded hierarchy of systems up to and including the all-embracing system of the universe (insofar as the latter can be known by human beings). Systems for Laszlo, in other words, are equivalently structured fields of activity for their constituent parts or members. Laszlo, to be sure, considers these constituent parts or members to be in each case subsystems or subordinate fields of activity, whereas for Whitehead the *ultimate* parts or members of the various fields of activity must always be actual occasions or momentary subjects of experience. But, as I tried to make clear in the middle section of this chapter through reference to Jürgen Habermas's theory of communicative action, an adroit combination of strictly intersubjective and systems-oriented paradigms carries with it many advantages for social analysis.

Concluding Note

Besides my own theory of Whiteheadian societies as ongoing structured fields of activity for their constituent actual occasions, there have been several other attempts made by Whiteheadian scholars to remedy the apparent lack of continuity between successive actual occasions within Whitehead's metaphysical scheme in virtue of his celebrated dictum that actual occasions are "the final real things of which the world is made up."[49] In a recent book-length publication,

49. Whitehead, *Process and Reality*, 18.

for example, Judith Jones argues persuasively that the functioning of an antecedent actual entity in a subsequent actual entity must be ascribed as much to the internal constitution of the first entity as to the process of self-constitution of the second entity: "The objective functioning of one thing in another, in other words, never completely loses the subjective, agentive quality of feeling that first brought it into being."[50] If I understand her rightly, Jones appears to be saying that, contrary to Whitehead's own dictum that actual entities must perish in their subjective immediacy before they can attain objective immortality in the self-constitution of subsequent actual entities,[51] a given actual entity retains at least some of its subjective immediacy as long as it continues to be prehended by subsequent actual entities. Furthermore, even in its subjective immediacy here and now, a concrescing actual entity experiences an increased intensity of feeling with respect to the impact which it anticipates it will have on its successors.[52]

I am sympathetic to Jones's proposal that concrescing actual entities experience further intensity of feeling in anticipation of their impact on subsequent actual entities. As Whitehead himself comments, this accounts for our feeling of moral obligation here and now toward the foreseeable future.[53] Likewise, I am favorably disposed toward the idea that subsequent actual entities somehow feel the subjective immediacy of their predecessors as an important factor in their own concrescence. When I feel myself becoming angry, for example, the intensity of the anger seems to build from moment to moment. I feel the feelings of past moments of anger in my present agitated state, and this adds to the feeling of anger here and now. But does this mean that those past angry moments are still present in their subjective im-

---

50. Judith A. Jones, *Intensity: An Essay in Whiteheadian Ontology* (Nashville: Vanderbilt University Press, 1998), 3.

51. Cf. above, n. 48. Jones, of course, cites still other passages from *Process and Reality* and still other works of Whitehead which seem to support her thesis: e.g., "An actual entity is at once the subject experiencing and the superject of its experiences. It is subject-superject, and neither half of this description can for a moment be lost sight of" (Whitehead, *Process and Reality*, 29).

52. Jones, *Intensity*, 8-10. Cf. also Whitehead, *Process and Reality*, 27: "The Category of Subjective Intensity."

53. Whitehead, *Process and Reality*, 27.

mediacy to me in a subsequent moment of experience or, to recall my own hypothesis set forth above, does it mean that, while the subjective immediacy of the past moment is gone, the feelings largely constitutive of that same moment are still present in the society understood as the encompassing energy-field for all those occasions?

There are, after all, conceptual problems connected with the retention of subjective immediacy within a society understood as an ongoing set of actual entities governed by a "common element of form." If a predecessor actual entity retains its full subjective immediacy in its successor, then the successor would be presumably identical with its predecessor and there would be at most a strictly numerical succession of actual entities. No change would have taken place; instead, much like the classical notion of substance, one and the same unchanging subject of experience would exist from moment to moment. On the other hand, if, as Jones proposes,[54] only some features of that original subjectivity pass over into the successor actual entity (entities), then is it still an integral subjectivity or is it a hybrid reality, in Whitehead's own language, a "subject-superject"? Jones maintains that this is what Whitehead must have had in mind with such a hyphenated expression. But at least an alternative possibility would be my proposal that the subjectivity as a power of self-constitution is indeed gone (as Whitehead likewise says)[55] but that the feelings remain as part of the encompassing energy-field and thus are available for prehension by subsequent actual entities occupying the same field. Those successor actual entities, accordingly, would prehend at the same time both the feelings emanating from their predecessors in the same society and their "common element of form" or intelligible pattern of interrelation.

Where Jones and I are in agreement, then, is in our mutual discomfort with the conventional understanding of the distinctness or lack of continuity between successive actual occasions within Whitehead's metaphysical scheme. Somehow this distinction between successive actual occasions has to be reconciled with Whitehead's other basic

54. Jones, *Intensity*, 3: "The objective functioning of one thing in another . . . never *completely* loses the subjective, agentive quality of feeling that first brought it into being" (italics mine).
55. Cf. above, n. 48.

premise that nothing exists in isolation, that everything in this world is intrinsically connected with everything else.[56] I work at this reconstructive task by rethinking the Whiteheadian notion of a society as more than an aggregate of actual occasions, namely, as an ongoing structured field of activity for successive generations of actual entities. Jones works at the same task by revising the notion of actual entity as superject so as to allow for past actual entities to be somehow present in their subjective immediacy within the self-constitution of subsequent actual entities.

Two other Whiteheadian scholars who have a similar project in mind may also be mentioned here briefly. Some years ago Bradford Wallack published a book in which she argued that every concrete actual existent, whether animate or inanimate, should be regarded at any given moment of its existence as an actual entity and that, if it perdures over time, it should be regarded as a society of such actual entities.[57] While I respect her basic insight that every concrete existent has an objective unity, I do not believe that it has the objective unity of an actual entity which is by definition a momentary *subject* of experience. Entities like the Castle Rock in Edinburgh, for example, despite what Whitehead seems to say to the contrary,[58] are not subjects of experience. What does enjoy objective unity, in my view, is a society as a structured field of activity for its constituent actual occasions. Thus, as I see it, Wallack mistook the reality of an actual entity as a constituent in a field for the reality of the field itself.

56. Whitehead, *Process and Reality*, 28: "For you cannot abstract the universe from any entity, actual or non-actual, so as to consider that entity in complete isolation. . . . In a sense, every entity pervades the whole world."

57. F. Bradford Wallack, *The Epochal Nature of Process in Whitehead's Metaphysics* (Albany, N.Y.: State University of New York Press, 1980), 7: "The actual entity is *any concrete existent whatsoever.*" Cf. also 28-29 for a list of Whiteheadian societies in line with this hypothesis.

58. Whitehead, *Process and Reality*, 43: "The real internal constitution of an actual entity progressively constitutes a decision conditioning the creativity which transcends that actuality. The Castle Rock at Edinburgh exists from moment to moment, and from century to century, by reason of the decision effected by its own historic route of antecedent occasions." But was the "route of antecedent occasions" constituting Castle Rock over the centuries the path of a series of single actual occasions or the path of a highly complex spatio-temporal society of such actual occasions? Whitehead's language is unquestionably ambiguous here.

Similarly, the noted Whiteheadian scholar Lewis Ford proposed some years ago that perhaps there are actual occasions of longer duration which are inclusive of other actual occasions of much shorter duration, in which case the longer-lasting actual occasion in its subjective aim would be affected by the subjective aims of the short-term occasions and vice versa.[59] Once again, this basically makes more sense to me in terms of my own field-oriented approach to Whiteheadian societies. Some actual occasions (e.g., the human mind at any given moment) are inclusive of other actual occasions (individual neurons in the brain at the same moment) only because the field over which the inclusive occasion here and now presides overlaps the fields of activity proper to the included actual occasions.[60] We are dealing, in other words, not with individual actual occasions as such but with actual occasions as the latest members of societies which in turn are to be understood as either superordinate or subordinate structured fields of activity vis-à-vis one another.

59. Lewis Ford, "Inclusive Occasions," in *Process in Context: Essays in Post-Whiteheadian Perspectives*, ed. Ernest Wolf-Gazo (Bern/Frankfurt: Peter Lang, 1988), 107-36.

60. Cf. Whitehead, *Process and Reality*, 106-9. Cf. also my article "Energy-Events and Fields," *Process Studies* 18 (1989): 153-65, esp. 159-63.

6 The Need for Common Ground in the Religion and Science Debate

Having presented a preliminary sketch of a metaphysics of inter-subjectivity in the preceding two chapters, I should now make clear how this new social ontology possesses advantages over more traditional metaphysical schemes for the solution of contemporary problems in theology. In one sense, I already began this task in chapter one with my critique of recent publications of various contemporary Roman Catholic systematic theologians. I pointed out that, while their work evidently moves in the direction of a fully intersubjective approach to the God-world relationship, they in different ways either still cling to some of the presuppositions of the older Thomistic metaphysics (e.g., LaCugna and Johnson) or reject outright any overt metaphysical approach to theology (e.g., Marion and Chauvet). But this is only to hint at what I view as the positive advantages of my own scheme for contemporary theological problems. What I wish to present in this chapter, accordingly, is a more explicit indication of how a metaphysics of intersubjectivity and, above all, a field-oriented interpretation of Whiteheadian "societies" as laid out in the preceding chapters can truly make a difference for a contemporary reinterpretation of the God-world relationship and other issues such as the mind-brain or soul-body interface. In effect, I hope to show how this neo-Whiteheadian approach to reality could provide much needed common ground, philosophically speaking, for contemporary theologians and natural scientists in their conjoint wrestling with the thorny issue of spiritual/personal agency in a world governed by material cau-

157

sality. For this issue, as I shall make clear below, is key to the religion-and-science debate at present.

My starting-point will be a recently published book, *God and Contemporary Science,* written by Philip Clayton. Therein he seeks to establish a dialogue between theologians, philosophers, and scientists with respect to the origin, the ongoing character, and the ultimate direction or finality of the cosmic process. His claim is that all three groups have something to contribute to this discussion. Theologians, for example, bring a long history of reflection on the Jewish and Christian Scriptures with their assertion that God is the Supreme Lord and Creator of the universe and, in the case of the Christian Scriptures, with the added belief that God the Father created the world through Christ (as the Incarnate Word of God) in the power of the Holy Spirit.[1] Many scientists, in turn, have come to see that their own investigations into the origin, current status, and possible destiny of the universe "plead for meta-physical, and ultimately theological, treatment and interpretation."[2] The data derived from science, in other words, underdetermine the theoretical conclusions that can be drawn from them. Hence, even though theologians should be "good listeners" when it comes to new scientific discoveries about the physical world, they have a right and even a duty to be "key players" when it comes to the interpretation of those scientific results.[3] Finally, philosophers likewise should be involved in this discussion since they are especially well-equipped to evaluate the various models for the understanding of the cosmic process, in particular for the understanding of the God-world relationship.

Clayton's own focus is primarily on the contribution of philosophy to the discussion of cosmology. For, as he notes after reviewing a variety of positions on the relation between theology and science, "what is required is a common framework for formulating agreements and disagreements — one within which common terms and definitions can be found for presenting the whole spectrum of views.

1. Philip D. Clayton, *God and Contemporary Science* (Edinburgh: Edinburgh University Press, 1997), 15-81.

2. Clayton, *God and Contemporary Science,* 161.

3. Clayton, *God and Contemporary Science,* 161.

Only then can their divergences (and the best arguments for and against each one) be clearly recognized."[4] But this is evidently the task of the philosopher who, on the one hand, constructs her theory primarily on the basis of reason rather than revelation; but who, on the other hand, likewise recognizes that scientific data, as noted above, are not to be understood simply as "facts" but inevitably require further interpretation in terms of a theory or speculative framework which is not in itself empirically verifiable.

Here I would argue that my own metaphysical scheme provides precisely that common ground, philosophically speaking, for theologians and scientists to continue their discussions on topics of mutual interest (e.g., the preexistence of God to the world of creation and the possibility of subjective immortality for a human being after the death of the body).[5] In particular, I will be offering a field-oriented understanding of the key notion of "supervenience" in Clayton's model both of the mind-body relationship and of the God-world relationship. Beforehand, however, it will be necessary to summarize briefly some of the key features of Clayton's own position in *God and Contemporary Science*.

In part three of that book, entitled "Towards a Theology of Divine Action," Clayton takes up the difficult issue of how God can unilaterally cause or at least strongly influence the outcome of particular events taking place within the cosmic process. For, if one wishes to avoid deism, namely, the belief that God plays no further role within the cosmic process after the initial act of creation, then one must find a way to show how God can be active within the world without disturbing the regularity of the laws of nature stipulated by modern natural science. Before setting forth his own position, Clayton first reviews the theories set forth by various other authors. Some have sought to find the "causal joint" for the action of God in the world within the realm of quantum mechanics since many scientists believe that nature itself is indeterminate at the quantum level. If God were silently at work to determine the course of billions of quantum events, then God could conceivably have an invisible but still very effective influence on the overall chain of events within the

4. Clayton, *God and Contemporary Science*, 156.
5. Clayton, *God and Contemporary Science*, 257-65.

cosmic process as a whole.[6] This presupposes, of course, that variations at the quantum level will not cancel one another out but will have significantly amplified effects on higher levels of existence and activity within the cosmic process. Here still other authors have appealed to contemporary chaos theory to support the idea that microscopic differences can sometimes result in unexpected macroscopic changes. But, as Clayton comments, it is still an open question within scientific circles whether the indeterminacy operative within chaos theory is due to human ignorance of initial conditions within a given system or to some ontological indeterminacy within nature itself.[7]

Aware of these apparent restraints on the action of God at the microscopic level of activity, John Polkinghorne advocates a "top-down" as well as a "bottom-up" approach to divine agency within the world. That is, God's role is to provide a steady stream of "information" to entities at both the microscopic and macroscopic levels of activity so as to influence the formation of "dynamic patterns" leading in one direction rather than in another.[8] As evidence for this mode of interaction between the physical and the mental or spiritual, Polkinghorne points to the way in which the human mind seems to influence what is happening in the body; the mind, in effect, directs the body by supplying "information" about ends and means, goals and values, otherwise unavailable to the organism as a whole. A similar model for the God-world relationship is advocated by both Nancey Murphy and Arthur Peacocke. That is, for both of them God directs the cosmic process by cooperating with various finite causal agencies

6. Clayton, *God and Contemporary Science*, 193-95.

7. Clayton, *God and Contemporary Science*, 195-96; cf. also 207, where Clayton makes reference to the work of Robert J. Russell and Wesley Wildman in "Chaos: A Mathematical Introduction with Philosophical Reflections," in *Chaos and Complexity*, ed. Robert John Russell, Nancey Murphy, and Arthur R. Peacocke (Berkeley, Calif.: Center for Theology and the Natural Sciences, 1995), 49-90.

8. Clayton, *God and Contemporary Science*, 204. Cf. also John Polkinghorne, *Belief in God in an Age of Science* (New Haven, Conn.: Yale University Press, 1998), 48-75, esp. 62-67; likewise, John F. Haught, *God After Darwin: A Theology of Evolution* (Boulder, Colo.: Westview, 2000), 57-80. Haught also uses the notion of "information" to indicate how God can influence the cosmic process without direct divine intervention. Moreover, one can thus allow for a hierarchical order within the physical universe without resorting to an ontological dualism.

even as God subtly influences the outcome of those same processes. Murphy, to be sure, like Polkinghorne, believes that God directly intervenes so as to determine quantum-level events even as God provides for the overall direction of the cosmic process from the "top-down."[9] Peacocke, on the other hand, is wary of any talk of direct divine intervention at the quantum level and prefers to think of God's holistic direction of the cosmic process exclusively from the "top-down." Thus God influences the individual entity in its activity only through the mediation of the myriad causal systems which make up the cosmic process as a whole.[10]

What Clayton borrows from Peacocke for elaboration of his own theory of divine agency in the natural world, however, is the notion of emergent properties or "supervenience." That is, with Peacocke, Clayton believes that higher-level systems within nature possess emergent properties which are distinct from the properties of their component parts or members. Water, for example, possesses properties (e.g., the ability to satisfy one's thirst) which are not possessed by hydrogen and oxygen molecules in isolation. In that sense, properties peculiar to water as a compound of hydrogen and oxygen molecules "supervene" on properties peculiar to hydrogen and oxygen atoms in isolation from one another. Carried over into the analysis of the mind-body relationship, mental or spiritual properties such as consciousness or acts of cognition can then be said to "supervene" on the physical properties of the neurons operative in the human brain. The mental is thus emergent out of the physical but still basically interactive with the physical for its own existence and activity as a higher-level system within nature as a whole.

There are, to be sure, two different explanations for this notion of supervenience. What Clayton calls "weak supervenience" is the position held by Jaegwon Kim and others to the effect that mental properties like consciousness are indeed supervenient upon the purely physical properties of the neurons in the human brain, but they are

9. Clayton, *God and Contemporary Science*, 217-19. Cf. also Nancey Murphy, *Beyond Liberalism and Fundamentalism: How Modern and Postmodern Philosophy Set the Theological Agenda* (Valley Forge, Pa.: Trinity Press International, 1996), 147-49.

10. Clayton, *God and Contemporary Science*, 224-25; cf. also Arthur Peacocke, *Theology for a Scientific Age* (Minneapolis: Fortress, 1993), 135-83, esp. 157-65.

ultimately to be explained in terms of neuronal interactions.[11] Consciousness has thus no ontological independence of the activity of neurons in the brain. What Clayton himself defends is what he calls "strong supervenience," namely, the belief, first, that one mental state can directly cause another mental state without the mediation of an antecedent change in neuronal states, and, secondly and much more importantly, that a mental state can itself effect a change in a subsequent neuronal state. Hence, causal activity can, at least in principle, take place primarily on the mental level with physical changes on the neuronal level as a by-product rather than the reverse, namely, that true causal activity is always operative on the physical level with changes in mental states simply as a by-product.

Yet, even granting the legitimacy of this notion of "strong supervenience," there are problems with its application to the explanation of two closely-related Christian beliefs, namely, the belief that God is transcendent of the world as well as immanent within it, and the belief that the human being somehow survives the death of the body. For, in making the mental or spiritual capacities of human beings supervenient upon the appropriate organization of neurons in the brain, one is likewise forced to conclude that those same mental capacities should disappear at death with the cessation of neuronal activity in the brain. Similarly, if one likens God's activity in the world of nature to the mind-body relationship within human beings, then the reality of God would not in any sense be independent of the cosmic process but rather emergent from it, namely, as an unintended by-product of enhanced neuronal organization within the human brain. Yet, argues Clayton, one cannot simply return to the postulates of classical metaphysics on the mind-body relationship and the God-world relationship without equally unhappy results. That is, one would not want to say that God and the human soul are spiritual substances totally different from the material world because one

---

11. Clayton, *God and Contemporary Science*, 253: " 'Mental properties are instantiated only by being realized by physical properties in physical systems.' " Reference is to Jaegwon Kim, " 'Downward Causation' in Emergentism and Non-Reductive Physicalism," in *Emergence or Reduction? Essays on the Prospects of Nonreductive Physicalism*, ed. Ansgar Beckermann, Hans Flohr, and Jaegwon Kim (Berlin: W. de Gruyter, 1992), 131-32. Cf. also Jaegwon Kim, *Supervenience and Mind* (Cambridge: Cambridge University Press, 1993).

could not then explain either how God as an independent spiritual reality can interact with the world of creation or how the mind as likewise a spiritual substance can interact with the body in which it is housed.[12]

Clayton's solution to this theological conundrum is to propose that, just as theologians should attend carefully to the results of scientific inquiry about the world of nature in the formulation of their hypotheses about the God-world relationship and related matters, so scientists should be willing to accept as plausible theological explanations of "trans-empirical" questions arising out of their research which resist determination by the scientific method alone. For example, with reference to the question whether God's existence is essentially dependent upon the world or in some sense independent of it, Clayton comments: "Nothing within the world could dictate the answer to this question, since nothing within the world could determine whether its source is essentially independent of it."[13] Hence, while some scientists might propose that the reality of God is nothing more than an emergent property of the human brain at a certain stage of its development, they can no more empirically verify this theory than the theologian can empirically verify her claim that God is the transcendent Creator of the world. In both cases, one is dealing with a truth-claim that is strictly trans-empirical and thus beyond scientific verification.

While I am in agreement with Clayton that theology should thus have an impact on the existential mind-set of scientists even as the results of natural science should not be overlooked by theologians in the formulation of their hypotheses about the God-world relationship, there is, I believe, a weakness in his argument at this point. Because he does not develop in his book an explicit philosophical conceptuality to serve as the common ground on which both theologians and scientists could possibly agree as the basis for their ongoing discussion on a given issue, his overall argument for such a com-

---

12. Clayton, *God and Contemporary Science*, 258: "One cannot return to a Cartesian dualism if it makes mind/body interaction more of a mystery than it was before. Nor can one break all links between human and divine agency, conceding the field to the philosophers of mind and simply insisting that God is an agent in a way that has no connection whatsoever with human agency."

13. Clayton, *God and Contemporary Science*, 260.

mon ground remains inevitably somewhat tentative. It is one thing, for example, for theologians to claim that there must be a subject underlying the mental properties to be found in scientific research on the workings of the human brain.[14] But how is this subject of mental properties to be distinguished from the "soul" or spiritual substance which was originally postulated by classical metaphysics but which has in subsequent centuries been radically called into question by empirical studies on the physiology of the human brain?[15] Similarly, while the concept of supervenience seems to allow for the emergence of higher-level wholes or dynamic systems within the natural order which have specific properties and functions that are not reducible to the properties and functions of their component parts or members, how is one, philosophically speaking, to distinguish this new type of organizational totality from the generally discredited notion of substance? Is not a substance by definition likewise a whole greater than the sum of its parts? Finally, if a theologian wishes to affirm the reality of God as a transcendent subject of experience who nevertheless interacts with the world of nature, how is this to be philosophically justified when one no longer feels comfortable with the notions of primary and secondary causality advanced by Thomistic metaphysics?

Here I propose, as noted above, that the metaphysical scheme of Alfred North Whitehead, albeit with the modifications developed in preceding chapters of this book, might well provide that philosophical common ground for theologians and natural scientists to talk

---

14. Clayton, *God and Contemporary Science*, 261-62.

15. Cf., e.g., *Whatever Happened to the Soul?* ed. Warren S. Brown, Nancey Murphy, and H. Newton Malony (Minneapolis: Fortress, 1998), esp. 127-48. The contributors to this volume all in different ways subscribe to a theory of "non-reductive physicalism" (as opposed to either a dualism of spirit and matter or reductive physicalism/ontological materialism) by way of explanation for the existence and function of consciousness and other mental operations within the human organism. As will become evident below, I, too, endorse a doctrine of non-reductive physicalism but give it a more overtly metaphysical orientation. That is, I use the Whiteheadian metaphysical categories of "actual occasion" and "society" (albeit in a somewhat revised form) to indicate how all of reality (including the reality of God) can be understood in terms of progressively more complex structured fields of activity with "top-down" as well as "bottom-up" causation at work between interrelated fields of activity (cf. also above, pp. 147-50).

more seriously with one another about the above-named issues. They would in effect have with Whitehead's metaphysical categories a common language with which to trade insights arising out of their separate disciplines and, as Clayton himself notes,[16] to see more clearly specific points of agreement and disagreement. Introducing a philosophical scheme into discussions between theologians and scientists, to be sure, initially complicates matters, for one then has to wrestle with still another trans-empirical hypothesis which cannot be settled by appeal either to common sense or to scientific data. But, once understood and basically accepted, a philosophical conceptuality is an invaluable tool for experts in different disciplines at least to communicate, if not always to agree, with one another.

As noted above, my focus with these remarks will be on a Whiteheadian, or more precisely a neo-Whiteheadian, explanation of the notion of supervenience, the way in which higher-level systems within nature seem to exhibit properties which are not reducible to the properties of their constituent parts or members. My argument, in brief, is that, if Whiteheadian "societies" are understood as enduring structured fields of activity for successive generations of dynamically interrelated "actual occasions" or momentary subjects of experience, then one has an analogy for the classical notion of substance without any of the theoretical difficulties attached to the latter concept in the modern era as a result of scientific research. Admittedly, there is no universal agreement among natural scientists about the nature and properties of fields, given the obvious discrepancies in the way fields function, first within classical physics and then within quantum theory.[17] On the other hand, given the inevitably metaphorical/analogical character of metaphysical language, "field" would still seem to be a better candidate than "substance" for the principle of continuity and ontological identity within contemporary philosophical cosmology, if only because it provides an appropriate philosophical explanation of the hitherto elusive concept of supervenience. As I shall explain below, there are properties characteristic of

16. Cf. above, 158-59.
17. Cf. John Polkinghorne, *Reason and Reality: The Relationship between Science and Theology* (Philadelphia: Trinity Press International, 1991), 85-98, esp. 92-94; cf. also Nick Herbert, *Quantum Reality: Beyond the New Physics* (New York: Doubleday, 1985), 31-53.

a field as such which are not immediately derivative from the properties of individual events within the field.

Let us begin, then, by reviewing briefly what Whitehead himself says about the nature of societies and then make clear how my own field-oriented approach to societies extends his remarks in a new direction which may be helpful for understanding the notion of supervenience. As already noted in preceding chapters, Whitehead proposes that a "society" is a set of actual occasions with "social order," that is, with a "common element of form" or defining characteristic analogously shared by each of the actual occasions constitutive of that society at any given moment (cf. also below, Glossary). What is important for our purposes here and now is to recognize that each of the actual occasions thus shares in that common element of form in a slightly different way from its contemporaries. Or, stated otherwise, each of the constituent actual occasions contributes to the maintenance of a common element of form for the society as a whole which the occasion by itself only imperfectly embodies. Thus there is from the beginning in this understanding of a Whiteheadian society an implicit distinction between the properties of the constituent parts or members (the actual occasions) and the properties of the society itself as that which is brought into being by the interplay of actual occasions but which enjoys its own ongoing identity precisely as a society.

Here I am possibly moving beyond what Whitehead himself and certainly beyond what many Whiteheadians think about the nature of societies as nexuses or sets of actual occasions. For these disciples of Whitehead (and possibly for Whitehead himself), there is no strictly defined form for the society as a whole but only a somewhat similar form shared by a group of actual occasions which is sufficient to link them together as an aggregate of individual entities but which in no way constitutes them as a higher-level organizational totality. If, then, a given set of actual occasions evidently achieves such a higher-level organization or ontological status, becoming what Whitehead calls a "structured society" or society made up of subsocieties of actual occasions (e.g., a physical organism with its different levels of internal organization), then the unity of this more complex society of actual occasions is provided from moment to moment by the latest member of the regnant subsociety of actual occasions within that overall group of sub-societies. As such, this regnant subsociety is equivalently the "soul" or unifying principle of the structured society. As already indicated in preceding chapters, this was in fact the line of thought proposed by Charles Hartshorne many years ago with his distinction be-tween "composite individuals" or mere aggregates of actual occa-sions with only an analogous common element of form and "com-pound individuals" which represent societies of actual occasions organized into a new higher-level totality in virtue of a regnant subsociety or "soul."[18]

My own argument both in this book and in previous publications has consistently been that all Whiteheadian societies, whether mo-narchically organized or not, constitute a higher-level ontological to-tality, namely, a structured field of activity which serves as the envi-ronment or ontological context for the interplay of its constituent actual occasions from moment to moment. Precisely as an enduring field of activity, however, rather than a momentary subject of experi-ence, a Whiteheadian society in its own structure and properties is distinct from the structure and properties of those same actual occa-sions.[19] A Whiteheadian society is thus necessarily a whole or total-ity which is greater than the sum of its parts or members. Admittedly, it initially came into existence and is here and now sustained in exis-tence only in virtue of the interrelated activity of successive genera-tions of actual occasions. But what these interrelated actual occa-sions are bringing into existence at every moment is an objective reality (namely, a field of activity) distinct from themselves as inter-related subjects of experience.

Furthermore, as I noted above, it is this admittedly somewhat un-orthodox understanding of Whiteheadian societies which provides a philosophical justification for the concept of supervenience used by many natural scientists to explain the emergent properties of higher-level systems within the world of nature and by theologians like Philip Clayton to explain first the mind-body relationship and then

18. Charles Hartshorne, "The Compound Individual," in *Philosophical Essays for Alfred North Whitehead,* ed. F. S. C. Northrup (New York: Russell & Russell, 1936), 193-220.

19. Cf., e.g., Joseph A. Bracken, S.J., *Society and Spirit: A Trinitarian Cosmology* (Cranbury, N.J.: Associated University Presses, 1991), 39-56.

by analogy the God-world relationship. Likewise, for those theologians like Clayton who support the notion of "strong supervenience" as opposed to the theory of "weak supervenience," this field-oriented approach to Whiteheadian societies underwrites their belief in the emergence not only of higher-level properties of basically lower-level entities but also of higher-level entities distinct from those same lower-level entities.

Within the conventional understanding of Whiteheadian societies, for example, the mind is a new set of actual occasions distinct from the actual occasions constituting the various subsocieties or subfields of activity within the human brain at any given moment.[20] Within my own field-oriented approach to Whiteheadian societies, the mind should be rather understood as an enduring intentional field of activity constituted by the ordered succession of those same mental actual occasions. In this way, the field provides the ongoing context or lawlike environment for the patterned succession of mental actual occasions, and the mental actual occasions by their regular succession sustain the existence of the field. This intentional field, moreover, overlaps the interrelated fields of activity proper to the various subsocieties of actual occasions within the brain as a physical organ. Each new actual occasion within the intentional field proper to the mind, therefore, "prehends" or mentally grasps both the structure already existent within its own field and also whatever structure may be emergent out of the lower-level fields of activity within the

---

20. Cf. Whitehead, *Process and Reality: An Essay in Cosmology,* corrected edition, ed. David Ray Griffin and Donald W. Sherburne (New York: The Free Press, 1978), 106-9. Cf. also Christine Hardy, *Networks of Meaning: A Bridge between Mind and Matter* (Westport, Conn.: Praeger, 1998), 60: "I propose a transversal network-type organization between semantic and neural levels of organization. This underlying, network-based level of semantic processes is hypothesized to interconnect with neuronal and subneuronal networks. . . . We thus have two interlaced and interwoven dynamical-network systems. Each system's configuration, and their common interlacing, are both products of self-organizing dynamics." As I see it, Hardy's explanation of mental activity in terms of self-organizing "semantic constellations" or clusters of concepts, beliefs, feelings, and behaviors within an individual's "semantic field" (p. 3) bears a strong resemblance to Whitehead's description of the mind-body relation (noted above), especially if one thinks of Whiteheadian societies as structured fields of activity for their constituent actual occasions.

brain in terms of neuronal organization. All that information is incorporated into its own self-constituting decision as the latest member of the mind's intentional field. Finally, this decision of the presiding occasion within the mind is then transmitted first to the subfields of activity within the brain and then in various ways to all the other fields of activity within the human being as a complex physical organism.[21]

Not every supervenient field, to be sure, is, like the human mind, presided over by a single "personally ordered" actual occasion from moment to moment (cf. Glossary). Most Whiteheadian societies and therefore most supervenient fields of activity are constituted by a number of actual occasions at any given moment which are both spatially and temporally ordered. The key point here for our purposes, however, is that as soon as a new field of activity with unexpected emergent properties is spontaneously generated by the interrelated activity of lower-level actual occasions, then higher-level actual occasions concomitantly emerge to populate and sustain that new field of activity. Atomic actual occasions thus give rise to molecular actual occasions as soon as conditions are ripe for the emergence of those higher-level actual occasions, that is, as soon as a field of activity suitable for the ongoing existence and activity of molecular actual occasions is available. Thus new forms of subjectivity are emergent out of lower forms of subjectivity through the medium of progressively

---

21. Whitehead, *Process and Reality*, 108-9. Cf. here James B. Ashbrook and Carol Rausch Albright, *The Humanizing Brain: Where Religion and Neuroscience Meet* (Cleveland: Pilgrim Press, 1997). Ashbrook and Albright postulate a "triune" brain with different functions in the mental life of individuals. In my judgment, their notion of a "triune brain" could be readily transposed into my metaphysical scheme with its interrelated, hierarchically-ordered fields of activity as constitutive of brain function. Simply put, I would propose that the intentional field proper to the mind or soul might well be centered in the frontal lobes of the neocortex but likewise overlap the fields of activity proper to the so-called reptilian brain, the paleomammalian brain or limbic system, and the rest of the neocortex or neomammalian brain (52-55). Ashbrook and Albright themselves comment on the special importance of the frontal lobes within the human brain (as opposed to the brain of other primates): "More than the rest of the neocortex, the frontal lobes receive direct input from other parts of the brain. . . . In addition, the frontal lobes have valuable input from the body itself" (134).

more organized fields of activity.[22] In this way, as I see it, the notion of strong supervenience (as opposed to weak supervenience) is justified in that one has a philosophical explanation not only for the emergence of higher-level properties among lower-level entities but for the emergence of higher-level entities which can exert "top-down" causation on those lower-level entities. The mind, for example, in this way affects neuronal activity in the brain and through the central nervous system likewise affects activity in all other parts of the human body as well.

Here I find myself differing from the point of view expressed by Warren Brown, Nancey Murphy, H. Newton Malony, and their collaborators in *Whatever Happened to the Soul?* For, while I agree with them that the classical dualism of spirit versus matter must be overcome, I do not think it necessary to conclude that "the human nervous system, operating in concert with the rest of the body in its environment, is the seat of consciousness (and also of human spiritual or religious capacities)."[23] In effect, then, for Brown, Murphy, and Malony there is no "mind" over and above the brain or nervous system within the body but only higher-level functions of the brain in virtue of an expanded context or environment. On the other hand, as noted above, in terms of my own neo-Whiteheadian theory there is a distinct set of personally-ordered actual occasions proper to the mind as opposed to the various subsets of actual occasions proper to the brain. The mind, accordingly, when understood as an ongoing intentional field of activity for its constituent mental occasions, is indeed

22. Cf. here Niels Henrik Gregersen, "The Idea of Creation and the Theory of Autopoietic Processes," *Zygon* 33 (1998): 333-67, esp. 335-39; also by the same author, "Autopoiesis: Less than Self-Constitution, More than Self-Organization: Reply to Gilkey, McClelland and Deltete, and Brun," *Zygon* 34 (1999): 117-38. As indicated by the title of his second article, Gregersen regards autopoietic processes as more than the self-organizing of pre-existent elements into new systematic configurations, but likewise as less than self-constituting, i.e., as requiring an antecedent substructure out of which to emerge: "Autopoiesis is a prolific self-development of systems already at play" (118). As I see it, my field-oriented understanding of progressively more complex Whiteheadian societies provides a philosophical explanation of the notion of autopoiesis. Cf. also on this point, chapter five, pp. 132-37, where I compare and contrast Whitehead's metaphysical scheme with that of Ervin Laszlo, one of the early proponents of systems theory.

23. Brown, Murphy, and Malony, *Whatever Happened to the Soul?* 131.

an entity and not just a higher-level activity of the brain in a new context as in the theory of Brown, Murphy, and Malony. But it is a field-based entity which is structurally akin to the lower-level fields of activity out of which it emerged and on the basis of which it is constituted. Hence, it is not separate from the brain and the rest of the body as "spirit" in classical philosophy and theology was separate from "matter."

Brown, Murphy, and Malony, to be sure, in virtue of their theory of "non-reductive physicalism" do not wish to cast into doubt traditional Christian belief in the resurrection of the body and life after death. As they make clear elsewhere in their book, they argue for the continuance of personal identity or life after death as a result of the power of God: "The identity for self as a body/soul unity is now dependent upon a source and power beyond its own capacity for survival."[24] But my counter-argument to them is basically the same as my argument earlier against the position of Philip Clayton, namely, that theological trans-empirical hypotheses in the religion-and-science debate are certainly legitimate in terms of one's antecedent belief in the truth-claims of Christian revelation. But there is as a result no philosophical common ground with nonbelievers, whether they be agnostic scientists or the adherents of rival faith-traditions. As I will make clear shortly, however, there is in my judgment a plausible philosophical explanation of how the human person can be incorporated into the communitarian life of the triune God at the moment of death, one that is, moreover, consistent with my overall metaphysical scheme for the nature of reality.

Turning then to my exposition of the God-world relationship, I note, first of all, that the notion of supervenience does not seem to work in this context. The reality of God, in other words, cannot be supervenient upon the evolution of the human brain in the same way that the mind with its distinct field of activity is supervenient upon the development of the field (or fields) of activity proper to the brain. God as Creator of the cosmic process according to orthodox Jewish-Christian-Islamic belief must antedate the gradual evolutionary development of the cosmic process, including the evolution of the human brain. Yet here, too, my field-oriented approach to

24. Brown, Murphy, and Malony, *Whatever Happened to the Soul?* 189.

171

Whiteheadian societies might well provide an answer for this theological conundrum. The notion of elementary fields of activity which over time coalesce so as to form more complex, highly-structured fields of activity would seem to imply the concomitant existence of an antecedent all-encompassing field of activity as the necessary ontological context for their interrelated growth and development. This was basically my contention in chapter four when I compared and contrasted Kitaro Nishida's notion of Absolute Nothingness and Jorge Nobo's and my own postulate of an "ontogenetic matrix" as the necessary "vertical" dimension for a world populated by subjects of experience in dynamic interrelation. Furthermore, as I see it, this is a presupposition which is basically consistent with both Whitehead's and Hartshorne's metaphysical schemes even though not explicitly developed by either one of them.

In *Process and Reality,* for example, Whitehead lists as one of the "givens" of his metaphysical system what he calls "the extensive continuum," namely, "one relational complex in which all potential objectifications [of actual occasions] find their niche. It underlies the whole world, past, present, and future."[25] He also refers to it as the "physical field" for the actual world.[26] Whitehead, to be sure, makes no explicit connection between this extensive continuum and the activity of God in the world, perhaps because he only developed the notion of God as personally interactive with the world in the final pages of *Process and Reality* when he introduced the notion of the "consequent nature" of God.[27] In recent issues of *Process Studies,* the official journal for process philosophy and theology, there has been a lively exchange among Whiteheadians about the nature of the God-world relationship from a Whiteheadian perspective with my own field-oriented approach to the issue included among them.[28] Here it

25. Whitehead, *Process and Reality,* 66.
26. Whitehead, *Process and Reality,* 80.
27. Cf. on this point Lewis S. Ford, *The Emergence of Whitehead's Metaphysics 1925-1929* (Albany: State University of New York Press, 1984), 227-29.
28. Cf., e.g., Denis Hurtubise, "The Enigmatic 'Passage of the Consequent Nature to the Temporal World' in *Process and Reality,*" *Process Studies* 27 (1998): 93-107; Palmyre M. F. Oomen, "The Prehensibility of God's Consequent Nature," *Process Studies* 27 (1998): 108-33; Lewis S. Ford, "The Consequences of Prehending the Consequent Nature," *Process Studies* 27 (1998): 134-46; Palmyre

suffices to say that, while Whitehead evidently did not conceive the God-world relationship in terms of a joint field of activity for God and creatures, in my judgment with the category of the extensive continuum he could readily have been thinking along those lines.

Likewise, Charles Hartshorne does not make explicit use of the image of a common field of activity for God and the world in his analysis of the God-world relationship. But, insofar as he conceives God not as a single nontemporal actual entity like Whitehead but as a "personally-ordered" society of actual occasions much like the mind or the "soul" within human beings, and insofar as he considers God as thus understood to be the "soul" of the world and the world to be the "body" of God,[29] the notion of a common field of activity for God and the world is an easy inference. That is, in line with my explanation for the mind-body relationship given above, the field proper to God as a personally-ordered society of actual occasions thus coincides with the extensive continuum as the all-encompassing field of activity for the societies of actual occasions in the world, both past, present, and future. At the same time, in line with Hartshorne's belief that God is the life-principle or "soul" not only of this world but of any and all other worlds, possible or actual,[30] one may likewise claim that for Hartshorne God is not emergent out of the world but always ontologically prior to it. Unlike the human mind or soul, which in line with the notion of strong supervenience is said to be emergent out of the activity of neurons in the human brain, God as the "soul" of the physical universe is indeed never without a "body," a world with which to interact, but is in no sense dependent upon precisely this body, this world, for God's own existence.

This notion of God's ontological independence of the world is

---

M. F. Oomen, "Consequences of Prehending God's Consequent Nature in a Different Key," *Process Studies* 27 (1998): 329-31; Duane Voskuil, "Discussion of Palmyre M. F. Oomen's Recent Essays in *Process Studies,*" *Process Studies* 28 (1999): 130-36; Joseph A. Bracken, S.J., "Prehending God in and through the World," *Process Studies* 29 (2000): 4-15.

29. Hartshorne, "The Compound Individual," 218-20; cf. also by the same author, *Man's Vision of God and the Logic of Theism* (Hamden, Conn.: Archon Books, 1964), 174-211.

30. Hartshorne, *Man's Vision of God,* 230-32.

even more strikingly confirmed in my own trinitarian reinterpretation of Whitehead's and Hartshorne's understanding of the God-world relationship. As I have made clear in previous publications,[31] the triune reality of God should be understood in Whiteheadian terms as a "structured society" (cf. Glossary) composed of three personally-ordered societies of actual occasions corresponding to the three divine persons of orthodox Christian belief. They are one God rather than three gods in close interrelationship because they preside over a single all-comprehensive field of activity proper to themselves in their own divine being. That is, instead of presiding over separate fields of activity proper to themselves as individual persons, they preside over this single all-encompassing field of activity which constitutes their common nature or essence as one God. Furthermore, this divine field of activity has no necessary connection either with the field of activity proper to this world or with the field of activity proper to any other world, possible or actual. In this way, the reality of God is not in any sense emergent out of the field of activity proper to the world; quite the contrary, the reality of this world is necessarily emergent out of the field of activity proper to the three divine persons in their dynamic interrelation.[32]

31. Cf., e.g., Bracken, *Society and Spirit*, 123-39.

32. My conclusions here bear some resemblance to the cosmological speculations of the celebrated philosopher/anthropologist Pierre Teilhard de Chardin. Cf. here Donald P. Gray, *The One and the Many: Teilhard de Chardin's Vision of Unity* (New York: Herder & Herder, 1969), 21: "For Teilhard the whole of reality is a process involving the unification of the multiple, and this process in its entirety springs from God, is patterned upon his own life, and is destined to participate in that trinitarian life from which it has come." Gray bases his argument on a hitherto unpublished manuscript of Teilhard de Chardin, *Comment je vois* (1948), in which Teilhard describes the origin and development of the physical universe from the realm of "pure multiplicity" as the mirror image of the "process of self-unification" already taking place within the divine life among the three divine persons (Gray, *The One and the Many*, 17). Hence, somewhat akin to my own hypothesis of an all-encompassing field of activity for the divine persons which likewise serves as the "matrix" or field of activity for all finite entities, creation for Teilhard is not primarily a centrifugal movement outward from an infinitesimal point as in the conventional understanding of the "Big Bang" theory for the origin of the universe, but rather a centripetal movement inward from pure extension or virtual nothingness to more and more complex forms of unification of creatures both with one another and with the divine persons within the all-

That is, if this world originated in a "Big Bang," as many cosmologists believe, then this "Big Bang" necessarily took place within the "divine matrix" or divine field of activity. As Charles Hartshorne pointed out many years ago,[33] this is the logic of the notion of panentheism. All things other than God must exist in God and yet be themselves at the same time. For, as Hartshorne comments, "[t]he superrelative or reflexively transcendent perfection of God is the fullness of his being, his wholeness as always self-identical, but self-identical as self-enriched, influenced but never fully determined by (and never fully determining) others — in short, a living, sensitive, free personality, preserving all actual events with impartial care and forever adding new events to his experience."[34] What Hartshorne excludes from this conception of the God-world relationship, of course, is the possibility of subjective immortality at least for human beings, if not for all finite entities, as a result of their coming to be and continuing to exist within God. And yet, as Clayton points out, this is another crucial Christian belief which must be somehow vindicated in the ongoing dialogue between religion and science. My own conviction is that a field-oriented approach to the God-world relationship such as I have laid out here could likewise contribute significantly to a philosophical justification of this traditional Christian belief.

In a previous publication, I took note of my basic agreement with the hypothesis of Marjorie Suchocki that God "prehends" or mentally grasps human beings at the moment of death in their subjective immediacy as they complete their lifelong process of self-constitution.[35] Thus God incorporates them into the divine consequent nature or the fullness of divine life in such a way that they are not only objectively

---

encompassing divine matrix. Given the empirical evidence for an expanding universe, however, one might be obliged to say that the process of creation is simultaneously a movement outwards and inwards, albeit from different perspectives.

33. Cf. Charles Hartshorne, "The Logic of Panentheism," in *Philosophers Speak of God*, ed. Charles Hartshorne and William L. Reese (Chicago: University of Chicago Press, 1963), 499-514.

34. Hartshorne, "The Logic of Panentheism," 514.

35. Cf. Bracken, *Society and Spirit*, 143-47; cf. also Marjorie Suchocki, *The End of Evil: Process Eschatology in Historical Context* (Albany, N.Y.: State University of New York Press, 1988), 81-96.

immortal (as Hartshorne and presumably Whitehead himself believed) but subjectively immortal, experiencing themselves for the first time as a unitary reality before God. This full self-awareness before God, to be sure, may be initially painful since one thus has to come to terms with the full consequences of one's life both for oneself and others. But in the end, the individual will presumably come to terms with his inevitable limitations and peacefully take his place within the overall cosmic drama of creation, thus enjoying eternal life with a loving God.[36]

At the same time, in that earlier publication I proposed that a field-oriented approach to the God-world relationship might help to resolve some of the residual ambiguities in Suchocki's proposal. First of all, the idea that God and all of creation occupy a common field of activity helps to explain how creatures, above all human beings, can begin to live the divine life more fully at the moment of death. They have been, in other words, unconsciously participant in the divine life during their earthly existence; at the moment of death they are consciously assumed into this transcendent matrix of divine life. One has to remember here that in terms of Whitehead's metaphysical scheme a human life (and, indeed, the finite existence of all creatures) is a moment-by-moment affair, an ongoing series of actual occasions rapidly succeeding one another. Once these occasions of experience achieve "satisfaction," that is, complete their momentary process of self-constitution, they equivalently leave their mark on the society or field of activity of which they were a member and pass out of existence, at least as a subject of experience. But if the society or field of activity to which they belong is integrated with the divine field of activity, then one can readily conjecture with Suchocki that in becoming more fully part of the divine field of activity they take on the subjective immortality proper to God in God's own being.[37] They contribute to the subjective immortality of God not simply as an objective fact of past experience for God but as a conscious co-participant with God in the ongoing divine field of existence and activity.

36. Suchocki, *The End of Evil*, 109: "The judgment that flows from the [actual] occasion's relation to the whole is finally, then, a knowledge of one's participation and belonging within the completed whole: judgment is transformation, redemption, and peace."
37. Suchocki, *The End of Evil*, 91-96.

Furthermore, this field-oriented approach to the God-world relationship likewise resolves the speculative issue of how one at the moment of death is reunited with all one's past moments of experience without having to experience them serially all over again. In terms of my field-oriented approach to Whiteheadian societies, what exists at any given moment is not so much the single actual occasion but the field of which the occasion is the latest member. Thus, if the intentional field of activity which constitutes the mind or soul of a human being in all the conscious moments of his life until death is preserved as part of the divine field of activity, then the actual occasion which is operative at the moment of death will be consciously reunited not with all its predecessor actual occasions, taken individually, but with the field to which they all belong in God. In and through becoming fully aware of itself as the focus of an individualized field of activity within the divine being, this surviving actual occasion within the human mind can both take possession of itself as a unitary reality and at the same time experience its participation in the divine being. That is, once the limiting conditions of life in the body are removed at the moment of death, then in and through its first moment of conscious experience after death each human subject should be able to experience herself or himself in a new way as a unitary reality within the divine life.[38]

To sum up, then, in this chapter I have tried to show the applicability and usefulness of the metaphysical scheme developed in previous chapters for the solution of contemporary philosophical and theological issues. The focus of my remarks was on two of the key issues in the contemporary religion-and-science debate, namely, different understandings of the mind-brain and God-world relationship. To that end, I first summarized the argument of Philip Clayton that theologians, philosophers, and natural scientists should all have something to contribute in any discussion of the origin, ongoing existence, and ultimate destiny of the cosmic process. In particular, I noted his own use of the philosophical concept of strong supervenience to explain so-called "top-down" causation, above all, in terms of the mind-brain relationship. But I also called attention to the fact that he did not provide an explicit philosophical concep-

38. Bracken, *Society and Spirit,* 150.

tuality for theologians and scientists to use in exchanging rival trans-empirical explanations of the mind-brain relationship.

My own contribution lay precisely in providing that philosophical grounding for the notion of supervenience in the mind-brain relationship. That is, I proposed that my own rethinking of the White-headian category of society as a structured field of activity for its constituent actual occasions would provide a common conceptual scheme for use by theologians and scientists in their discussion of the mind-brain relationship. Likewise, I indicated how in virtue of this modest reinterpretation of Whitehead's own scheme one would be able to affirm (a) the reality of the mind or soul as the ongoing subject of mental experiences not reducible to the activity of neurons in the brain, (b) the reality of God as transcendent of as well as immanent within the cosmic process, and (c) the possibility of subjective immortality for human beings after death. All of these are key Christian beliefs which, as Clayton says, must somehow be affirmed in the ongoing dialogue with natural scientists. My purpose in this chapter was simply to provide a philosophical rationale for making those same truth-claims and thereby to vindicate the legitimacy of my metaphysical scheme as a logical tool in the ongoing discussion between theologians and scientists. Still other areas of application for my metaphysical scheme, of course, will have to be explored before I can consider my project in any sense completed. But, at least for the moment, I hope to have made clear my basic presupposition in this entire book, namely, that metaphysics is not dead as many contemporary deconstructionists have claimed, but only in need of reconstruction along the lines of a viable social ontology or metaphysics of universal intersubjectivity.

Appendix: A Research
Program for the Future

In his overview of what is meant by the term "postmodernity" and his own critical response to it, Paul Lakeland asserts that there are three major schools of thought associated with this complex cultural phenomenon of the late twentieth century. Defining postmodern thought in general as "a series of attitudes struck in face of questions bequeathed by modernity about the character of rationality, the nature of subjectivity, issues of rights and responsibility, and the constitution of the political community,"[1] he continues:

> Some thinkers — let us call them, for now, *late moderns* — find the project of modernity unfinished, and wish to carry it forward, albeit in the vastly changed world of cultural postmodernity. Others — the *true postmoderns* — see in the exhaustion of modernity and its unmasking as simply the latest in a long line of totalizing discourses the chance to move forward into a radical historicism. Still others — let us call them the *countermoderns* — celebrate the demise of modernity as an opportunity to return to the securities of an earlier age.[2]

Lakeland counts himself as a "late modern," as do I and, as far as I can judge, the authors whose thought will be compared and contrasted with my own in this appendix. That is, all of us believe that there are

1. Paul Lakeland, *Christian Identity in a Fragmented Age* (Minneapolis: Fortress Press, 1997), 12.
2. Lakeland, *Christian Identity,* 12.

179

resources available in the Western philosophical tradition for coping with the issues raised by the "true postmoderns" in the matter of truth and objectivity, totalizing modes of thought, etc. Likewise, perhaps even more than Lakeland, these other authors and I believe that metaphysics, albeit a metaphysics based on principles of becoming rather than principles of being, is integral to the project of "late modernism." The appeal to metaphysics and cosmology, in other words, is not by itself symptomatic of the nostalgic yearning for "the securities of an earlier age" so characteristic of the "countermoderns" in Lakeland's scheme. Everything, after all, depends on whether one uses metaphysics to understand why things change rather than why they remain basically the same with the passage of time. If the *telos* of the metaphysical system is open-ended so that it does not specify the contents but only the basic pattern of things to come, then one cannot reasonably object that metaphysics is inevitably a totalizing discourse. For, thus employing metaphysics, one cannot predict the future with any measure of certainty; one merely has the mental tools to understand in some measure what is happening here and now and to deal responsibly with the various possibilities which the present situation seems to offer.

A. Critique and Comparison of Other Theories

1. Colin Gunton

In *The One, The Three and the Many,* Colin Gunton offers a probing critique of modernity and postmodernity in the light of philosophical issues which originated in antiquity but which were never properly addressed in subsequent centuries. What he especially has in mind is the underlying relationship between the One and the Many both in academic discourse and in the popular mind-set. As he sees it, from Plato onwards Western thought has favored the primacy of the One over the Many, with the One being characteristically understood as undifferentiated unity and the Many as pure diversity.[3] This, however, has the unintended negative consequence of a "totalitarianism"

3. Colin E. Gunton, *The One, the Three and the Many: God, Creation and the Culture of Modernity* (Cambridge: Cambridge University Press, 1993), 20-21.

of the One over the Many: "Both the ancient and the modern eras . . . share in a tendency to elevate the one over the many: to enslave the many to the heteronomous rule of the one."[4]

Within antiquity, to be sure, the One was generally conceived to be God as the transcendent source of the unity and rational order of the world. Within modernity, on the other hand, says Gunton, God as the source of rationality and meaning has been displaced by the "unifying rational mind" of the human being which becomes then equivalently the center of its own subjective world.[5] But in both cases the unity of the One is simple and undifferentiated, standing over against the sheer multiplicity and diversity of the Many. Hence, the One (either God or the ordering mind of the individual human being) has to impose an extrinsic order on the Many in order to bring this chaotic mass of individuals into proper relation with itself. Gunton labels this purely heteronomous relation of the One to the Many a "false universal," because "it does not encompass the realities of human relations and of our placing in the world, and so operates deceptively or oppressively."[6] The attempt to throw off the tyranny of the One over the Many in favor of the opposite priority of the Many over the One, moreover, has likewise tended to end in failure: "Either the many become an aggregate of ones, each attempting to dominate the world, the outcome being those regimes now labelled fascist, in which the strongest survives and dominates; or the many become homogenized, contrary to their true being, into the mass (Kierkegaard's 'public')."[7] Individualism thus metamorphoses into collectivism as its *alter ego*.[8]

What is needed, therefore, is a new understanding of the relationship between the One and the Many whereby the Many are related to one another as well as to the One and the One is internally differentiated in virtue of its intrinsic (as opposed to purely extrinsic) relation to the Many. Precisely here is where, in Gunton's view, the doctrine of the Trinity can and should play a key role in rethinking the classical understanding of the God-world relationship. For even

4. Gunton, *The One, the Three and the Many*, 34.
5. Gunton, *The One, the Three and the Many*, 28.
6. Gunton, *The One, the Three and the Many*, 31.
7. Gunton, *The One, the Three and the Many*, 33.
8. Gunton, *The One, the Three and the Many*, 42.

181

though Thomas Aquinas, for example, developed a trinitarian understanding of God in his *Summa Theologiae,* he did not employ it in his scheme for the God-world relationship. Rather, in line with the philosophy of antiquity as carried forward by Origen and Augustine, he conceived God as the transcendent Creator of the world to be utterly simple and thus lacking in any intrinsic relationship to creation.[9] What must be recovered, therefore, is a specifically trinitarian understanding of God's relation to creation, something which was inchoatively present in Irenaeus's depiction of Christ and the Spirit as the "two hands" of God the Father in dealing with creation, but which was lost sight of in subsequent development of the God-world relationship among both the Greek and Latin Fathers.[10]

In particular, what Gunton wishes to draw from renewed focus on the classical doctrine of the Trinity are what he calls "transcendentals" for the understanding of the relationship of creatures, above all, human beings, both to one another and to God. In the classical sense, the transcendentals were Unity, Truth, Goodness, and Beauty and they applied to God as utterly simple being. Gunton's transcendentals, on the contrary, take into account God as triune and thus as internally differentiated. The trinitarian transcendentals which characterize the reality both of the divine persons and of their creatures, accordingly, are *perichoresis,* substantiality or particularity, and relatedness. Among the Greek Fathers, the term *perichoresis* was used to indicate the dynamic unity in plurality of the divine persons, their ontological interdependence and reciprocal interrelatedness: "God is not simply shapeless, a negatively conceived monad, but eternal interpersonal life."[11] Applied transcendentally to creation, it implies that the world is "an order of things, dynamically related to each other in time and space. It is perichoretic in that everything in it contributes to the being of everything else, enabling everything to be what it distinctively is."[12]

9. Gunton, *The One, the Three and the Many,* 137-41. Cf. also Thomas Aquinas *Summa Theologiae* I, Q. 3, art. 7 resp.

10. Gunton, *The One, the Three and the Many,* 53-54, 81. Cf. also Gunton's later work, *The Triune Creation: A Historical and Systematic Study* (Grand Rapids: Eerdmans, 1998), 52-56, 61-64.

11. Gunton, *The One, the Three and the Many,* 164.

12. Gunton, *The One, the Three and the Many,* 166.

This leads into the discussion of the second transcendental notion, namely particularity or substantiality. In contrast to the modern and postmodern tendency to treat individual entities as homogeneous units, particularity or substantiality insists that each individual entity in its material concreteness is unique. Just as "the *substantiality* of God resides not in his abstract being, but in the concrete particulars that we call the divine persons and in the relations by which they mutually constitute one another,"[13] so individual material things are paradoxically constituted in their particularity not by what they are in themselves apart from other entities but by what they are in terms of their multiple relations to one another: "Something is real — what it is and not another thing — by virtue of the way it is held in being not only by God but also by other things in the particular configurations of space and time in which its being is constituted; that is to say, in its createdness."[14] Furthermore, just as the Holy Spirit's function within the Godhead is to particularize the *hypostases* or persons of the Father and the Son,[15] so it is peculiarly the work of the Spirit within creation to relate to one another individual beings and realms of being that are opposed or separate: "That which is or has spirit is able to be open to that which is other than itself, to move into relation with the other."[16]

The third transcendental Gunton labels relationality as opposed to sociality. For, while all entities are relationally ordered to one another for their existence and activity, only persons can be freely related to one another as members of a covenantal society or community.[17] The logic of sociality (as opposed to mere relationality) is then one of gift and reception: "What we receive from and give to others is constitutive: not self-fulfilment but relation to the other as other is key to human being, universally."[18] As such, human sociality mirrors the sociality of the divine persons, that is, the self-gift of the Father to the Son, the Son's giving of himself to the Father, and the Spirit's enabling of created participation in this dynamic of giving and re-

13. Gunton, *The One, the Three and the Many*, 191.
14. Gunton, *The One, the Three and the Many*, 200.
15. Gunton, *The One, the Three and the Many*, 190.
16. Gunton, *The One, the Three and the Many*, 181.
17. Gunton, *The One, the Three and the Many*, 229.
18. Gunton, *The One, the Three and the Many*, 227.

ceiving.[19] Non-personal creation, which is characterized simply by relationality rather than sociality, achieves its intended perfection through the mediation of human beings and their special participation in the dynamic of gift and reception characteristic of the divine persons in their dynamic sociality.

Reviewing Gunton's scheme, I would have very few negative comments since my own project, as noted above in chapters four and five, is likewise heavily trinitarian in its orientation to the God-world relationship. Hence, I applaud his efforts to use the notion of *perichoresis* derived from the classical doctrine of the Trinity as a way to rethink the contemporary philosophical approach to the relationship of the One and the Many. Likewise, I agree with much of his analysis of the problems of modernity and postmodernity with respect to this same philosophical issue. As noted above in chapter three, simple emphasis on otherness for its own sake does not solve the problems associated with identity and difference in the modern world. For differences to make a difference, there must paradoxically be a sameness connecting those things which are said to be different from one another.

What I would recommend to Gunton, however, would be a much more careful study of the potentialities of Whitehead's process-relational metaphysics for further articulation of his own cosmological scheme. For, as Whitehead himself commented in *Adventures of Ideas,* the notion of *perichoresis* represented a singular advance of the early Greek Fathers of the Church over the philosophy of Plato. That is, *perichoresis* involves "a doctrine of mutual immanence in the divine nature" whereby the divine persons are intrinsically constituted in their individual being or particularity by their mutual relations to one another.[20] Unhappily, says Whitehead, the Greek Fathers never generalized this doctrine of mutual immanence or internal relations among the divine persons into an overall metaphysical scheme: "They made no effort to conceive the World in terms of the metaphysical categories by means of which they interpreted God, and they made no effort to conceive God in terms of the metaphysical categories which they applied to the World."[21] The same, of course, was partially true

19. Gunton, *The One, the Three and the Many,* 225n. 19.
20. Whitehead, *Adventures of Ideas* (New York: The Free Press, 1967), 168.
21. Whitehead, *Adventures of Ideas,* 169.

of Whitehead in his own metaphysical scheme. That is, even though the notion of mutual immanence or internal relations among actual entities might in principle have allowed him to develop a specifically trinitarian understanding of God as a community of divine persons, he set that possibility aside in favor of a unipersonal God who is immanent in the self-constitution of each finite actual entity even as that same entity is immanent in God's ongoing self-constitution. Thereby, however, as I indicated above in chapter five, he missed an opportunity to set forth a much more consistent social ontology in which "societies" or groups of interrelated actual entities rather than the individual actual entities themselves would be "the final real things of which the world is made up."[22]

Gunton's reproach to process-relational metaphysics is that it tends to deny the transcendence of God in favor of a God purely immanent within the cosmic process.[23] This, of course, could be remedied by a specifically trinitarian understanding of God within Whitehead's metaphysical scheme.[24] That is, if the three divine persons exist in their perichoretic interrelatedness even apart from creation, and if, as Gunton maintains, they are at the same time active in the cosmic process precisely as a community of divine persons, then in line with orthodox Christian belief God is both transcendent of and immanent within the world of creation. In any event, the modest revision of Whitehead's metaphysical scheme in terms of a metaphysics of universal intersubjectivity, which I have proposed in this book, would seem admirably suited to accommodate Gunton's three transcendentals: *perichoresis,* substantiality or particularity, and relatedness.

2. Nancey Murphy

Turning now to Nancey Murphy's recent book, *Anglo-American Postmodernity,* we find a similar discussion of the proper relationship be-

22. Whitehead, *Process and Reality: An Essay in Cosmology,* corrected edition, ed. David Ray Griffin and Donald W. Sherburne (New York: The Free Press, 1978), 18

23. Gunton, *The One, the Three and the Many,* 145.

24. Cf., e.g., my book *Society and Spirit: A Trinitarian Cosmology* (Cranbury, N.J.: Associated University Presses, 1991), 123-60.

tween the One and the Many as in Gunton's work but in a somewhat different context. Murphy's claim is that the modern era was initially characterized by methodological reductionism in the natural sciences, that is, the belief "that the proper approach to scientific investigation is analysis of entities into their parts and that the laws governing the behavior of higher-level entities should be reducible to (shown to be special instances of) the laws of the lower levels."[25] The unexpected success of that methodology in the natural sciences subsequently led to the widespread acceptance of philosophical or ontological reductionism not only in the natural sciences but also in various social sciences, namely, the belief that, in opposition to the tenets of vitalism or any other form of mind-body dualism, higher-level entities are nothing but complex organizations of simpler entities.[26] Likewise, in line with Gunton's remarks on the loss of a sense of genuine particularity among individuals within the modern world, Murphy believes that "generic individualism" reigns supreme among many natural and social scientists, namely, the belief that "the whole is a mere collectivity of identical and interchangeable parts rather than an interaction of parts with different characteristics and complementary functions."[27]

Murphy's solution to this stumbling-block for the modern mind is not to appeal like Gunton to the classical doctrine of the Trinity as a theoretical model for a new understanding of the relationship between the One and the Many in a postmodern era. Rather, one should first look to new forms of holistic thinking which seem to be emergent within the natural and social sciences, contemporary language analysis and, finally, ethical theory; then one should investigate whether these new paradigms for thought and activity together might not constitute what she regards as specifically Anglo-American postmodernity (in distinction from deconstructionism and other forms of postmodernity in Europe). She believes, for example, that "emergent order" or "top-down causation" is gaining ground in scientific circles as a way to explain "the appearance of properties and processes that

---

25. Nancey Murphy, *Anglo-American Postmodernity: Philosophical Perspectives on Science, Religion and Ethics* (Boulder, Colo.: Westview Press, 1997), 14.
26. Murphy, *Anglo-American Postmodernity*, 14.
27. Murphy, *Anglo-American Postmodernity*, 16.

are describable only by means of concepts pertaining to a higher level of analysis. New levels of order appear that require new levels of description."[28] Similarly, she claims that within language analysis a shift has taken place "from a focus on meaning as reference to a focus on meaning as use," as in the philosophies of J. L. Austin and the later Wittgenstein.[29] Thus language can only be understood in terms of an overall social context or "form of life" rather than simply in terms of an external reference for individual words, phrases, and sentences. Furthermore, in epistemology foundationalism, the belief that knowledge must be grounded in something indubitable (either sense experience or a priori certain truths) is gradually being replaced by a new sense of the necessary interconnectedness of beliefs (both basic and non-basic) so as to constitute a "web" or internally consistent pattern of beliefs.[30] Finally, in ethical theory she follows Alasdair MacIntyre in looking to the traditions of a community and its social practices as the basis for the understanding of virtue in the life of the individual. Virtues equip one to perform properly those social practices which are consistent with one's own life-history and are approved by the ongoing traditions of the community.[31]

Key to Murphy's analysis in all these cases is the notion of "supervenience," that is, the way in which the laws appropriate to isolated lower-level systems of explanation have to be subtly modified in order to account for new circumstances involved in the working of higher-level systems of explanation in which the lower-level systems have become a functioning part.[32] The move from a lower-level system of explanation (e.g., physics) to a higher-level system (e.g., organic chemistry) inevitably carries with it an alteration of meaning and value for those terms (e.g., atoms and molecules) involved in both systems. In this way, ontological reductionism is avoided, since one cannot explain simply in terms of the laws of

---

28. Murphy, *Anglo-American Postmodernity,* 20.
29. Murphy, *Anglo-American Postmodernity,* 23.
30. Murphy, *Anglo-American Postmodernity,* 27.
31. Murphy, *Anglo-American Postmodernity,* 28-30.
32. Murphy, *Anglo-American Postmodernity,* 22: "Thus, I define supervenience as follows: for any two properties A and B, where B is a higher-level property than A, B supervenes on A if and only if something's being A in circumstance c constitutes its being B."

physics, for example, the behavior of atoms and molecules active within organisms. Ontological reductionists, to be sure, have likewise conceded that individual entities sometimes behave differently in new environments, but they argue that this happens in virtue of properties already inherent in the individual entity, not as a result of the environment. Murphy's argument, on the contrary, is that at least in certain cases the new environment itself makes the decisive difference in the behavior of the individual entity.[33]

Among the many ways in which Murphy illustrates her thesis of an emergent Anglo-American postmodernity, I will comment on only two as pertinent to my own project in the present book: namely, her critique of the appeal to religious experience on the part of many "liberals" in theology at present as a way to ground their theoretical reflections in something self-evident and, by way of contrast, Murphy's own reliance on careful integration of one's project into established intellectual traditions or "research programs" in theology. With respect to the first item, Murphy in my judgment makes a valid point in saying that liberals who appeal to religious experience are just as fundamentalist in their thinking as conservatives who appeal to texts of Scripture in support of their own positions.[34] For just as conservatives generally appeal to the inerrancy of the Bible as the foundation for their reconstruction of Christian belief and practice, so liberals frequently appeal to (presumably) universal religious experience as the touchstone for their rival interpretation of those same beliefs and practices. In neither case, however, does the alleged foundation for the truth and objectivity of one's assertions hold up under scrutiny. How can one prove, for example, that the Bible is the Word of God in a way that evidently surpasses the scriptures of the other world religions which likewise claim to be based on divine revelation? Likewise, how can one know with certitude that one's religious experience is revelatory of the objective reality of God and not just "a symbolic expression of humankind's

---

33. Murphy, *Anglo-American Postmodernity*, 32-34. Cf. above, however, chapter six, pp. 170-71, where I question whether Murphy's understanding of supervenience is adequate to account for the existence of the "soul" as the underlying subject of consciousness and other mental activities.

34. Murphy, *Anglo-American Postmodernity*, 87-112, esp. 94-97.

highest aspirations or basic life attitudes, as Ludwig Feuerbach suggested already in Schleiermacher's day"?[35]

Murphy's own "postmodernist" solution to this problem is to generalize on Alasdair MacIntyre's vindication of his approach to virtue theory in terms of an accompanying survey of competing intellectual traditions or "research programs" within the history of Western philosophy or, more specifically, within the history of moral inquiry in the West. MacIntyre's criterion for the truth and objectivity of his understanding of virtue theory is then that it is both internally consistent and, more to the point, entirely consonant with an overarching intellectual tradition (Aristotelian-Thomistic metaphysics) which itself has stood the test of time in terms of both "diachronic" and "synchronic" justification. That is, an intellectual tradition like Aristotelian-Thomistic metaphysics "is to be called true if it has proved itself better than its competitors in terms of its ability to overcome its own problems and even, in some cases, the problems of its rivals that cannot be solved using the rivals' own resources and, furthermore, is able to explain why things must have appeared as they did to its predecessors and contemporary rivals from their more limited or defective perspectives."[36] Since, in MacIntyre's opinion, Aristotelian-Thomistic philosophy meets that criterion for justification in competition with its rivals, then his own version of virtue theory, which is a legitimate extension and application of that same system of metaphysics, should be regarded as true, until significant evidence to the contrary arises either that his own approach to virtue theory lacks internal consistency or that Aristotelian-Thomistic metaphysics is itself deficient vis-à-vis one or other of its major competitors.

Murphy thus concludes:

MacIntyre's is far from an absolutist account of knowledge and truth. In the best of cases, one can claim only that a given tradition at a given stage of its development is the best so far. "No one at any stage can ever rule out the future possibility of their present beliefs and judgments being shown to be inadequate in a variety of ways."

---

35. Murphy, *Anglo-American Postmodernity*, 111.
36. Murphy, *Anglo-American Postmodernity*, 125.

So whereas the meaning of 'truth' is unsurpassability, *claims* to truth are always fallible.[37]

I find myself agreeing with Murphy on this point for two reasons. First of all, the simple appeal to religious experience for validation of one's beliefs ignores the fact that such experience is inevitably perspectival and for that same reason frequently distorted. Careful reflection on one's religious experience and, above all, communication with others who have had somewhat similar experiences is necessary to be sure that one is not deceiving oneself with respect to the contents of one's own experience. Thus intersubjectivity, not subjectivity, is the key to truth and objectivity in a postmodern world.

Secondly, Murphy's reliance on established intellectual traditions as the basis for the claim of truth and objectivity for one's own theory appeals to me because it in principle vindicates an explicitly metaphysical approach to theology against its contemporary detractors. For, metaphysical systems that outlast the lifetime of their authors (e.g., Thomism, Kantianism, Hegelianism) are in effect research programs or intellectual traditions that are being carried forward by other individuals who remain strongly attracted by the imaginative power of the author's original synthesis. Once again, therefore, intersubjectivity plays a key role in deciding what is objective and true in both philosophy and theology. If the disciples of the original thinker cannot develop his or her thought to meet the challenge of new and unexpected historical circumstances or, even more, if they cannot adequately defend the master's thought against the claims of competing contemporary thought-systems, then that intellectual tradition or research program in philosophy or theology is doomed to eventual extinction, quite irrespective of the high regard in which it is held on purely historical grounds. Needless to say, my own efforts in this book to rethink Whitehead's metaphysical system in terms of a logic of intersubjectivity which is itself grounded in an explicitly trinitarian understanding of God are consciously designed to keep that intellectual tradition competitive with still other meta-

---

37. Murphy, *Anglo-American Postmodernity,* 128. Reference is to Alasdair MacIntyre, *Whose Justice? Whose Rationality?* (Notre Dame, Ind.: University of Notre Dame Press, 1988), 361.

physical schemes in the contemporary search for an adequate under-standing of the God-world relationship.

3. Calvin Schrag

In the introduction to his recent book, *The Self after Postmodernity*, Calvin Schrag first notes how the classical notion of the self as un-changing substance and the modern construal of the self as transpar-ent mind have been radically called into question by contemporary postmodernists. He then adds: "In the aftermath of the deconstruc-tion of traditional metaphysics and epistemology, a new self emerges, like the phoenix arising from its ashes — a praxis-oriented self, de-fined by its communicative practices, oriented toward an under-standing of itself in its discourse, its action, its being with others, and its experience of transcendence."[38] In following out Schrag's rethink-ing of a postmodern understanding of self in the next few para-graphs, we will see how he seems to be setting forth an implicit meta-physics of intersubjectivity which is very much akin to what I have proposed in chapters four and five of this book.

In the opening chapter entitled "The Self in Discourse," for exam-ple, Schrag suggests that the appropriate question to pose with respect to human self-identity is not "What am I?" but rather "Who am I?"[39] Descartes, to be sure, answered the first question by declaring the self to be a thinking or mental substance. But Schrag, quoting Jacques Derrida, thinks that the second question is far more appropriate for a contemporary understanding of the self: " 'The singularity of the "who" is not the individuality of a thing that would be identical with itself, it is not an atom. It is a singularity that dislocates or divides itself in gather-ing itself together to answer to the other, whose call somehow precedes its own identification with itself.' "[40] Subjectivity, in other words, is to

38. Calvin O. Schrag, *The Self after Postmodernity* (New Haven, Conn.: Yale University Press, 1997), 8.

39. Schrag, *The Self after Postmodernity*, 12.

40. Schrag, *The Self after Postmodernity*, 14. Reference is to Jacques Derrida, "Eating Well, or the Calculation of the Subject," in *Who Comes after the Subject?* ed. Eduardo Cadava, Peter Connor, and Jean-Luc Nancy (New York: Routledge, 1991), 100.

be defined in terms of intersubjectivity and not vice versa.[41] Schrag makes basically the same point when he says: "Speaking is a creative act, at once a discovery of self and a self-constitution, but a creative act that takes place only against the background of a language already spoken, which has both a history and a formal structure, a language ensconced in the tradition, operating behind our backs, as Hans-Georg Gadamer would be wont to say."[42]

Elaborating on how the self gradually builds a stable self-identity in and through participation in various forms of discourse, Schrag points to the key role which narrative or story plays in this effort at self-constitution: "Narrative supplies the horizon of possible meanings that stimulate the economy of discourse. Some of these meanings have been articulated in stories already told; others are potential meanings yet to be unfolded in the emplotment of future narratives."[43] Hence, while linguistics is interested in the interplay of the elementary units of discourse (e.g., individual words, phrases, and sentences), narrative, understood as "someone saying something to someone,"[44] is indispensable for answering the question, "Who am I?": "To be a self is to be able to render an account of oneself, to be able to tell the story of one's life."[45] Schrag makes reference to a distinction employed originally by Paul Ricoeur between "*idem*-identity" and "*ipse*-identity." "*Idem*-identity" has to do with numerical identity or permanence in time of a thing or object of thought. "*Ipse*-identity, in contrast, is the identity of selfhood, . . . the sense of identity applicable to a person's character, which for Ricoeur finds its direct analogue in 'character' as a protagonist in a story."[46] The identity of the self is thus bound up with temporality in such wise that with the passage of time one understands one's identity, the story of one's life, differently and is able to express it to others in new ways.

In his second chapter, "The Self in Action," Schrag notes, quoting Kerby, that human action is likewise best understood in a narrative context: " 'The actions of human agents, to be intelligible, must be

41. Cf. above, chapter one, pp. 17-18.
42. Schrag, *The Self after Postmodernity*, 16.
43. Schrag, *The Self after Postmodernity*, 19-20.
44. Schrag, *The Self after Postmodernity*, 22.
45. Schrag, *The Self after Postmodernity*, 26-27.
46. Schrag, *The Self after Postmodernity*, 35.

seen against the background of a history, a history of causes and goals, of failure, achievements, and aspirations.' "[47] Moreover, it is the *embodied* self which thus participates both in its own personal history and in the history of the community (communities) to which it belongs. Thus embodied in space and time, the human self inevitably finds its deeper meaning and value within an intersubjective context, for the decision to do *x* or *y* is almost invariably a response to a prior action. The individual is thus at the same time both active and passive in everything he or she does. Furthermore, as Schrag makes clear in chapter three on the self in community, this response to prior action is most often a response to the action of another human being toward oneself. Thus the other is not present to me as an extension of myself, an *alter ego;* but, as Levinas made clear in *Totality and Infinity,* I am there so as to respond to the other in his or her antecedent appeal to me.[48] Moreover, the other is not simply the individual other, as in an I-Thou relationship. Equally important is the institutional other as represented by the various communities to which one belongs and whose collective history and future destiny deeply affect one's own sense of self-identity. Schrag comments: "Any philosophy of the self will at the same time be a philosophy of society and community."[49] From the perspective of this book, one could further argue that an adequate philosophy of the self should likewise broaden out into a cosmology or metaphysical scheme based on the principle of universal intersubjectivity.

In the fourth and final chapter of his book, Schrag addresses the issue of the self in transcendence. By transcendence he has in mind here not primarily the relative transcendence of the other person to the self as suggested by Levinas or the relative transcendence of the community and the common good to the individual as he/she makes

47. Schrag, *The Self after Postmodernity,* 43. Reference is to Anthony Paul Kerby, *Narrative and the Self* (Bloomington, Ind.: Indiana University Press, 1991), 40.

48. Schrag, *The Self after Postmodernity,* 84-85; cf. also Emmanuel Levinas, *Totality and Infinity: An Essay on Exteriority,* trans. Alphonso Lingis (Pittsburgh: Duquesne University Press, 1969), 194-201; Marie Baird, "Divinity and the Other: The Ethical Relation as Revelatory of God," *Eglise et Theologie* 30 (1999): 93-109.

49. Schrag, *The Self after Postmodernity,* 90. Cf. also Charles Taylor, *Sources of the Self: The Making of Modern Identity* (Cambridge, Mass.: Harvard University Press, 1989), 25-52.

an ethical decision. Rather, he is thinking of an absolute transcendence of the Infinite to the finite in the metaphysical and mystical sense, namely, the Infinite as that which is all-encompassing but which for that same reason cannot be grasped in human concepts. As I shall indicate below, he seems to be arguing here for the existence of what I have called the "vertical" dimension of a logic of intersubjectivity in chapter four, that is, the reality of an ultimate context or "place" for the dynamic interaction of subjects of experience.

Schrag's way to address this issue is through a comparison of Søren Kierkegaard's distinction between "religiousness A" (religion as an institutional reality) and "religiousness B" (religion as the encounter with a radically transcendent Other).[50] Religiousness A is a culturally-conditioned sphere of human activity somewhat on a par with science, morality, and art as the three spheres of human existence demarcated by Immanuel Kant in his *Critique of Pure Reason, Critique of Practical Reason,* and *Critique of Judgment* respectively.[51] Whereas Jürgen Habermas sought to link the validity claims of science, morality, and art within his theory of communicative rationality, Schrag claims that these three spheres of human activity plus the fourth sphere of institutional religion can be dynamically interrelated in terms of what he calls "transversality": "convergence without coincidence, conjuncture without concordance, overlapping without assimilation, and union without absorption."[52] As such, tranversality is a process or an activity rather than a product or a determinate entity. Thereby it stands in sharp contrast to the notion of God or any other conventional conception of Ultimate Reality in classical Western metaphysics.[53]

Schrag's understanding of "transversality" has thus, in my opinion, a clear affinity with what Jorge Nobo and I have described as the ontogenetic matrix for the existence and activity of interrelated subjects of experience.[54] That is, the ontogenetic matrix is an all-

---

50. Schrag, *The Self after Postmodernity,* 119-20. Cf. also Søren Kierkegaard, *Concluding Unscientific Postscript,* trans. David F. Swenson (Princeton, N.J.: Princeton University Press, 1941), 493-98.

51. Schrag, *The Self after Postmodernity,* 120.

52. Schrag, *The Self after Postmodernity,* 128.

53. Schrag, *The Self after Postmodernity,* 129.

54. Cf. above, chapter four, pp. 123-28.

encompassing place or context within which the Whiteheadian principle of creativity links actual entities with one another in a pattern of mutual interdependence. Within this ontogenetic matrix, accordingly, there is a balancing-off of particularity or individuality, on the one hand, and relationality on the other hand, much akin to what Colin Gunton referred to as *perichoresis* in his book *The One, the Three and the Many*.[55] That is, each entity is both itself and part of an encompassing network of other entities at the same time. What is at stake in Schrag's description of "transversality" is in any case a new understanding of the relationship between the One and the Many whereby the One is understood not as a transcendent entity but rather as a transcendent principle of unification at work within an all-encompassing "horizon of possibilities."[56]

Schrag, to be sure, distances himself from what he calls the "theo-metaphysical" approach to transcendence in terms of a "quasi-scientific" cosmology or all-encompassing worldview. His approach is rather to see transcendence as "a transforming dynamics that breaks into the economy of the four culture-spheres and transfigures their intramundane intentionalities."[57] But, in my judgment, one can, so to speak, have it both ways. One can, in other words, properly include such a "transforming dynamics" or principle of creativity within the context of a metaphysical cosmology based on the principle of universal intersubjectivity. As I indicated above, much of what Schrag envisions as the self in discourse, the self in action, and the self in community fits readily into the metaphysical scheme which I have elaborated in chapters four and five. Even the paradox of "gift-giving"[58] on which Schrag relies so heavily in the concluding pages of his book to exemplify the new notion of the self in transcendence can be assimilated into a metaphysics of intersubjectivity (as I have indicated in reviewing the thought of Jean-Luc Marion in chapter one). Hence, one does not have to resort to a "grammar of paradox" as opposed to a more conventional philosophical logic in order to reshape or "refigure" the classical God-world relationship.[59]

55. Cf. above in the present chapter, p. 182.
56. Schrag, *The Self after Postmodernity*, 133.
57. Schrag, *The Self after Postmodernity*, 134-35.
58. Schrag, *The Self after Postmodernity*, 139-41.
59. Schrag, *The Self after Postmodernity*, 135.

For while specific metaphysical schemes evidently come and go, metaphysical thinking as such would seem to be a constant in human experience.

4. David Griffin

The last three authors to be included in this overview of contemporary responses to the philosophical problems posed by deconstructionism, one and all, echo those last sentiments about the enduring need for metaphysical reflection in human life. David Griffin, for example, as noted in my introductory chapter, is the editor of a series in "constructive postmodern thought" published by the State University of New York Press. As he comments in the general introduction to the series, constructive postmodernism (as opposed to deconstructive or eliminative postmodernism) "seeks to overcome the modern worldview not by eliminating the possibility of worldviews as such, but by constructing a postmodern worldview through a revision of modern premises and traditional concepts. This constructive or revisionary postmodernism involves a new unity of scientific, ethical, aesthetic, and religious intuitions."[60] Griffin illustrates what he has in mind here with an essay critiquing the deconstructive approach to theology in *Erring: A Postmodern A/theology* by Mark C. Taylor.[61] Griffin's essay is divided into four parts which I will briefly summarize, after which I will offer comments on where the two of us as mutual students of Whitehead agree and disagree with respect to an appropriate postmodern theology.

In part one of his essay, Griffin sets forth points of agreement with Mark Taylor in the latter's assessment of the failures of modernity. The first such point of agreement is what Griffin calls "the death of the supernatural God, that is, the God of traditional West-

60. David Ray Griffin, "Introduction to SUNY Series in Constructive Postmodern Thought," in *Varieties of Postmodern Theology*, ed. David Ray Griffin, William A. Beardslee, and Joe Holland (Albany, N.Y.: State University of New York Press, 1989), xii.

61. David Ray Griffin, "Postmodern Theology and A/theology: A Response to Mark C. Taylor," in *Varieties of Postmodern Theology*, 29-52. Cf. also Mark C. Taylor, *Erring: A Postmodern A/theology* (Chicago: University of Chicago Press, 1984).

ern (Augustinian) Christian theology."[62] According to Griffin, "[t]hat God was the model of solitary, isolated selfhood. The idea that God (and God alone) was *causa sui* meant that God was totally independent of the world: relationship to the world was not constitutive of God's selfhood."[63] From this understanding of God's strictly unilateral relation to the world followed, moreover, the classical attributes of divine immutability vis-à-vis what happens in the world, likewise divine omniscience and divine omnipotence with respect to those same events. In Griffin's view, modernity rightly rejected this belief in a "supernatural God" but retained the notion of self-sufficiency or isolated selfhood as the implicit goal of human self-realization. Thus modernity unconsciously promoted excessive competition and strife among human beings and fostered a strictly utilitarian attitude toward non-human nature. Likewise, modernity retained the premodern understanding of human history as moving toward an ultimate goal, but redefined the goal in terms of economic and technological progress rather than as union with God, thus opening the door to consumerism and the systematic exploitation of the poor by more affluent members of society.[64]

In the second part of his essay Griffin asserts that Taylor's critique of the failures of modernity overshoots the mark in that it eliminates altogether the notion of a personal God with a providential care for the world and calls into question the notion of the self as distinct from " 'the forces that play through it.' "[65] As a Whiteheadian, Griffin does not complain about Taylor's understanding of the self as primarily constituted by its relations to other entities, but he does object to the further implication that the self is nothing but the passive result of the interplay of these causal forces. Likewise, Griffin objects to Taylor's questioning of a translinguistic referent for language, in which case one cannot distinguish what is true from what is false, and to Taylor's denial of an immanent end or goal for human history, in which case objective judgments about good and evil become impossible.[66]

---

62. Griffin, "Postmodern Theology and A/theology," 31.
63. Griffin, "Postmodern Theology and A/theology," 31.
64. Griffin, "Postmodern Theology and A/theology," 31-32.
65. Griffin, "Postmodern Theology and A/theology," 33. Cf. also Taylor, *Erring*, 136.
66. Griffin, "Postmodern Theology and A/theology," 33-34.

In part three of his essay, accordingly, Griffin proposes certain "hard-core" commonsense notions which cannot be denied in theory without self-contradiction in practice, among which are the following:

> (1) that the person has *freedom*, in the sense of some power for self-determination; (2) that there is an *actual world* beyond the person's present experience which exists independently of and exerts causal efficacy upon that person's interpretive perception of it; (3) that one's interpretive ideas are *true* to the degree that they correspond to that independently existing world; and (4) that, for at least some events, a distinction exists between what happened and *better and/or worse* things that could have happened.[67]

Employing these "hard-core" commonsense notions in the fourth and final section of his essay, Griffin sets forth his own scheme for a constructive or revisionary postmodernism based on the philosophy of Whitehead. He rejects, for example, the classical notion of God as omnipotent and of creatures as totally lacking in power; instead, he proposes in line with Whitehead's scheme that finite actual occasions also possess creativity as a power of self-constitution independently of God. Thus the power of God is seen to be a power of persuasion, not coercion. God, in other words, has no detailed plan for the unfolding of human history and the cosmic process. Rather, in virtue of God's all-encompassing vision of possibilities contained in the "divine primordial nature," God lures actual occasions in their self-constitution to the attainment of a harmony consistent with their own existence and the future development of the societies to which they belong.[68] There is, moreover, an objective difference between good and evil, based on God's evaluation of possibilities in terms of the divine primordial nature and mediated to the concrescent actual occasion through a divine "initial aim" for its self-constitution. Likewise, the notion of factual truth is tied to the divine consequent nature whereby God "prehends" everything that happens and gives it its place within the divine scheme of things. Our human sense of what is true and false is thus an imperfect reflection of what is known to be such within the divine mind.[69]

---

67. Griffin, "Postmodern Theology and A/theology," 36.
68. Griffin, "Postmodern Theology and A/theology," 49.
69. Griffin, "Postmodern Theology and A/theology," 50.

Here deconstructionists like Taylor might well object that there is a subtle logocentrism at work in Griffin's conception of the God-world relationship if all truth and value in this world are legitimated only with reference to God as the principle of unity and order for the cosmic process. I tend to agree with them on this point since, as I noted above in chapter three, Griffin and other Whiteheadians who follow the lead of Charles Hartshorne on this matter picture the world as the body of God and God as the soul of the world. As I see it, this is an implicit form of logocentrism since the meaning and value of the world is then strictly derivative from its meaning and value for God as the "transcendental signified" (cf. Glossary). On the other hand, as I also argued in chapter three, my reconception of the Whiteheadian category of "society" allows one to affirm the objective unity of the world from moment to moment even apart from God's prehension of it. That is, the world as an enormous "structured society" of subsocieties and their constituent actual occasions achieves its own objective unity from moment to moment in and through the interrelated activity of those same actual occasions. This is not to imply that God has no influence on the cosmic process in its ongoing development, but only that the world possesses an ontological unity from moment to moment in virtue of immanent processes which are truly self-determining, though always under divine inspiration and guidance.

Furthermore, I likewise take issue with Griffin in his rejection of two classical Christian beliefs, namely, the belief in God as tripersonal instead of unipersonal and the belief in God's creation of the world out of nothingness. Admittedly, both of these beliefs are inconsistent with the "naturalistic theism" which Griffin sees as foundational for a constructive postmodern worldview. That is, as he points out elsewhere, a *tri-dimensional* understanding of God may well be consistent with a naturalistic theism derived from rational reflection on the God-world relationship; but a *tripersonal* understanding of God presupposes some form of divine revelation which cannot be empirically established. Furthermore, belief in divine creation of the world out of nothingness is clearly a regression to a premodern mythological understanding of the God-world relationship.[70] Several

70. Cf. David Ray Griffin, "A Naturalistic Trinity," in *Trinity in Process: A Rela-*

points are worthy of comment here. First of all, Griffin by his own admission is working with a "generic idea of God" which prescinds from any form of divine revelation to a special group.[71] While this may be suitable for some people in terms of the debate between religion and science, it is offensive to others since it explicitly sets aside what they regard as pivotal religious beliefs for themselves. Scholars like Colin Gunton, for example, are quite critical of Whitehead's process-relational metaphysics because it makes no reference to God as tripersonal and, even more importantly, because it seems to undercut the traditional transcendence of God to creation. In Gunton's view, for process theologians God seems to be reduced to a function within the cosmic process rather than portrayed as its creator.[72]

My own position for many years now has been to mediate between Whiteheadians like David Griffin and more traditional theologians like Colin Gunton by affirming the legitimacy of a trinitarian understanding of God within Whitehead's overall metaphysical scheme. For this trinitarian understanding of God within a process-oriented worldview should both provide for the classical emphasis on God's transcendence of creation and respond to Griffin's critique of the classical doctrine of divine creation of the world out of nothingness. That is, if the divine persons constitute a community of life and love even apart from creation, then their decision to create can be said to be motivated by love, namely, an unselfish desire to share the riches of their communitarian life with creatures, above all with their rational creatures. This does not mean, of course, that creation had a beginning in time; but only that, however long it has existed or will exist, creation is grounded in a free decision on the part of the divine persons rather than a necessity of nature (as in Whitehead's scheme).[73] Furthermore, the classical doctrine of God's creation of the world out of nothingness can thus be understood more as a manifestation of God's gratuitous

tional Theology of God, ed. Joseph A. Bracken, S.J., and Marjorie Hewitt Suchocki (New York: Continuum, 1997), 23-40.

71. Cf. David Ray Griffin, *God and Religion in the Postmodern World: Essays in Postmodern Theology* (Albany, N.Y.: State University of New York Press, 1989), 51-67.

72. Gunton, *The One, the Three and the Many*, 145.

73. Whitehead, *Process and Reality*, 348: "It is as true to say that God creates the World, as that the World creates God."

love rather than of God's absolute power. As Griffin himself notes, the notion of God's absolute power (and, therefore, the powerlessness of creatures to resist the divine will) is not characteristic of medieval scholasticism. Rather, it represents an earlier Augustinian line of thought which was carried over into the modern era first by Luther and Calvin and then by Descartes, Boyle, Newton, and others. In any event, within the context of a metaphysics of universal intersubjectivity such as I have proposed in these pages, the act of creation makes much more sense as a sharing of God's own life with creatures (including the power of self-constitution) rather than as an exercise in unilateral power and control on God's part.[74]

5. Robert Neville

Like Griffin, Robert Neville, in his book *The Highroad Around Modernism*, believes that many postmodernists are implicitly guilty of self-contradiction in that they affirm in practice what they deny in theory. That is, in interpreting the history of Western philosophy as guilty of "logocentrism," they inadvertently oversimplify that same tradition in terms of some totalizing scheme and thus are themselves guilty of a new form of "logocentrism."[75] Neville's strategy, however,

74. Cf. here Clayton, *God and Contemporary Science* (Edinburgh: Edinburgh University Press, 1997), 82-124. Clayton argues for a panentheistic understanding of the God-world relationship along the lines of an analogy with the soul-body relationship in human experience. While I have reservations about the appropriateness of the soul-body analogy for the God-world relationship and would much prefer the more explicitly trinitarian understanding of the God-world relationship in which the divine persons share their communitarian life with their (rational) creatures (cf. above, chapter six), I fully concur with Clayton that panentheism effectively does away with the classical understanding of God who by an exercise of divine power creates the world out of nothingness as an entity separate from God's own being (cf. also *ibid.*, p. 65, where, in conscious reliance on the theology of Karl Barth, Clayton claims that divine "omnipotence must be conceived as the omnipotence of love").

75. Neville, *The Highroad Around Modernism* (Albany, N.Y.: State University of New York Press, 1992), xi. He uses as an example Heidegger's interpretation of the history of Western philosophy as the progressive "forgetfulness of Being." But this, Neville argues, is a totalizing scheme which effectively ignores much of what is valuable in the history of Western philosophy (cf. 8).

is basically not to "deconstruct" postmodernism in terms of its questionable presuppositions but to present a metaphysical alternative to it as a better way to deal with foundationalism and an ahistorical approach to reality characteristic of philosophical modernism.[76] The metaphysical tradition which he has in mind is American pragmatism, broadly conceived so as to include Whitehead as well as Peirce, James, and Dewey. In my comments here I will focus primarily on Neville's evaluation of Whitehead's contribution to that metaphysical tradition, but I will first take note of his introductory remarks on Peirce's philosophy and its affinity to Whitehead's cosmological scheme.

Long before the postmodernists, says Neville, Peirce argued that all thinking takes place by means of signs.[77] But whereas for the postmodernists signs refer only to other signs so as to set up a closed system of signs, for Peirce signs have meaning and value only with respect to an external world and one's activity within it: "Learning is the modification of one's signs and interpretations so as to correct deficiencies in the guidance of one's activities."[78] Because knowledge is bound up with signs and their interpretations, all knowledge is hypothetical. The real, accordingly, is the object of a well-founded hypothesis, but for the same reason the real is never definitively known.[79] At the same time, there are the equivalent of Colin Gunton's three "transcendentals" in dealing with reality, namely, Firstness, Secondness,

---

76. Neville, *The Highroad Around Modernism*, 5-6: "The historical thesis of this book . . . is that Peirce is not postmodern. Nor is Whitehead (or Griffin). They are, rather, late modern thinkers building upon and correcting the modern tradition in exactly the modes of critical and experimental argument at the heart of modernity."

77. Neville, *The Highroad Around Modernism*, 26. Cf. also *The Collected Papers of Charles Sanders Peirce*, vol. 5, ed. Charles Hartshorne and Paul Weiss (Cambridge, Mass.: Harvard University Press, 1934), par. 283: "Whenever we think, we have present to the consciousness some feeling, image, conception, or other representation, which serves as a sign. . . . Now a sign has, as such, three references: first, it is a sign *to* some thought that interprets it; second, it is a sign *for* some object to which in that thought it is equivalent; third, it is a sign, *in* some respect of quality, which brings it in connection with its object."

78. Neville, *The Highroad Around Modernism*, 29; cf. also *The Collected Papers of Charles Sanders Peirce*, vol. 5, par. 9, 19.

79. Neville, *The Highroad Around Modernism*, 31.

and Thirdness. Firstness has to do with sameness, that which makes a thing to be what it is in and of itself; Secondness has to do with otherness, that which makes a thing to be different from other things; Thirdness has to do with relationality, that which makes a thing to be with respect to something else.[80]

Here Whitehead's Category of the Ultimate comes to mind: "The ultimate metaphysical principle is the advance from disjunction to conjunction, creating a novel entity other than the entities given in disjunction. The novel entity is at once the togetherness of the 'many' which it finds, and also it is one among the disjunctive 'many' which it leaves. . . . The many become one, and are increased by one."[81] As I see it, both Peirce and Whitehead are herewith describing the same principle of creative advance, albeit from different perspectives. Whitehead is typically concerned with the unity to be found within an actual occasion, the final real thing of which the world is made up.[82] Peirce is more concerned with the larger social configuration or (in Whitehead's terms) society of which the new actual occasion is the latest member. But both Whitehead and Peirce are in their own way developing an evolutionary logic of becoming or creative advance as opposed to the formal logic of fixed relations among entities within classical metaphysics.

Neville argues, to be sure, that Whitehead is inconsistent in his explanation of the Category of the Ultimate. On the one hand, in virtue of Whitehead's Ontological Principle, the reason why things are the way they are is to be found in actual entities (either in the self-constituting decision of a concrescing actual entity or in the self-constitution of an already existing actual entity).[83] But Whitehead also claims that God is a "creature" of creativity, subject to its workings like any other actual entity.[84] Yet, says Neville, God cannot be the reason or ultimate explanation for a metaphysical category to

---

80. Neville, *The Highroad Around Modernism*, 32. Cf. also *The Collected Papers of Charles Sanders Peirce*, vol. 1, ed. Charles Hartshorne and Paul Weiss (Cambridge, Mass.: Harvard University Press, 1931), par. 302-53.

81. Whitehead, *Process and Reality*, 21.

82. Whitehead, *Process and Reality*, 18.

83. Whitehead, *Process and Reality*, 24. Cf. also Neville, *The Highroad Around Modernism*, 94-95.

84. Whitehead, *Process and Reality*, 88.

which God is also subject. Hence, the Category of the Ultimate within Whitehead's scheme has no explanation; it is simply a metaphysical given.[85] Peirce, on the other hand, according to Neville, does not have the same problem since in his scheme God is acknowledged to be the creator of whatever metaphysical principles are used to describe the world. But within a given metaphysical scheme whatever is said about God must be consistent with the metaphysical principles used for the world of creation.[86]

Here I find myself midway between Whitehead, on the one hand, and Neville (and Peirce) on the other hand, for I agree with all three thinkers that whatever metaphysical categories apply to creation should likewise apply to God as Creator so that the resulting system of thought will be all-inclusive.[87] The deeper question raised by Neville, however, is whether Ultimate Reality (as opposed to a specific notion of God the Creator within a given metaphysical system) is totally beyond metaphysical description and thus purely indeterminate.[88] Neville's argument is to the effect that God cannot be the transcendent Creator of everything determinate in this world and at the same time be in God's own being a determinate reality; for everything determinate is caused by creativity as a transcendent activity

---

85. Neville, *The Highroad Around Modernism*, 95.

86. Neville, *The Highroad Around Modernism*, 48-49. Cf. also *The Collected Papers of Charles Sanders Peirce*, vol. 6, ed. Charles Hartshorne and Paul Weiss (Cambridge, Mass.: Harvard University Press, 1935), n. 491: "The hypothesis of God's Reality is logically not so isolated a conclusion as it may seem. On the contrary, it is connected so with a theory of the nature of thinking that if this be proved so is that."

87. This is also my reason for urging Elizabeth Johnson and other contemporary Roman Catholic theologians to make their concept of God consistent with the rest of their metaphysical scheme for the interpretation of reality (cf. above, chapter one, n. 80). Admittedly, the entire metaphysical scheme is as such an illustration of the doctrine of the analogy of being since it only models in a tentative and imperfect way the suprasensible reality of the universe as a whole. But within a given theoretical scheme, the concept of God (as opposed to the extramental reality of God) should be understood univocally, that is, in terms of the same metaphysical categories as are applicable to all other entities thus described.

88. Neville, *The Highroad Around Modernism*, 287n. 6. Cf. also Neville's other work *Eternity and Time's Flow* (Albany, N.Y.: State University of New York Press, 1993), 153-58.

which is in itself indeterminate and determinate only in those entities which it determines to be what they are. Thus even the reality of God as Creator is an effect of the operation of creativity in this world. Moreover, creativity itself proceeds from a necessarily indeterminate ontological source: "The source would be nothing at all, not even source, if there were no creation. Apart from creation, it would be wholly indeterminate, indistinguishable from nothing."[89]

My counterargument, as laid out in my earlier book *The Divine Matrix*,[90] is, on the one hand, to concede to Neville that everything determinate is indeed grounded in creativity as a transcendent activity which is in itself indeterminate and determinate only in its instantiations; but, on the other hand, to contend that creativity thus understood is the nature of God, the transcendent ground of existence and activity for the three divine persons of the Christian doctrine of the Trinity in their dynamic interrelation. Thus creativity is not ontologically prior to the existence of the three divine persons, but rather coexistent with them as the conjoint principle of their existence and activity even as they by their dynamic interrelation provide a reason for creativity itself to exist.[91] Whitehead, accordingly, in my judgment erred in calling God a "creature" of creativity since creativity is the very nature of God. But Neville likewise erred in urging that creativity proceeds from a totally indeterminate and unknowable source.

---

89. Neville, *Eternity and Time's Flow*, 155.

90. Bracken, *The Divine Matrix: Creativity as Link between East and West* (Maryknoll, N.Y.: Orbis Books, 1995), 56-57, 138-40.

91. Cf. also above, chapter four, pp. 126-28, where I take note of the fact that my starting-point in postulating an antecedent "ontogenetic matrix" for the world of finite entities is theological rather than strictly philosophical. That is, unlike Nobo, who from a strictly philosophical viewpoint stipulates that there must be a "primordial actuality" to justify the existence of this ontological matrix as an eternal reality apart from the world, I propose, in line with Christian belief in the doctrine of the Trinity, that this ontological matrix is, in the first place, the nature or source of being for the three divine persons in their existence apart from the world, and, in the second place, the source of existence and activity for the world of creation. At the same time, my proposal that the generic "primordial actuality" to which Nobo refers is in fact a community of divine persons fits very well with my overall project in this book, namely, the creation of a metaphysics of universal intersubjectivity in which all realities, even the reality of God, are intrinsically social, that is, ontological wholes made up of interacting parts or members.

In subsequent chapters of his book, Neville expresses further reservations about Whitehead's metaphysical system even as he applauds the originality and insight of the latter's thought in general. I will single out only one for comment here. In a chapter entitled "Hegel and Whitehead on Totality," he points out that Whitehead confused the (presumed) objective totality of the cosmic process with the subjective unification of that process within the divine consequent nature.[92] I agree with Neville on this point on the grounds that the world as a complex structured society possesses its own objective unity quite apart from God's prehension of it.[93] But for the same reason I disagree with Neville in his further contention that the world in all likelihood is not an objective totality or universe but fragmented into "pockets of order" which are "sometimes interrelated, sometimes not, often irrelevant and indeterminate with respect to each other, passing with tangential connections, partially overlapping, sometimes in conflict but even then not in coherent agreement concerning what the fight is about."[94] For if the world can be said to possess an objective unity quite apart from its "prehension" into the divine consequent nature, still less can one say that the world is divided into "pockets of order" simply because human beings with their inevitably perspectival understandings of the world process cannot fully agree about the basic features of that objective state of affairs.[95]

92. Neville, *The Highroad Around Modernism*, 123-25.
93. Cf. above, chapter three, pp. 100-101.
94. Neville, *The Highroad Around Modernism*, 119.
95. One could, of course, counterargue that the physical universe is so huge that the different galaxies cannot be causally linked together into a unified whole because of the limitations of the speed of light in causal transmission. On the other hand, as I pointed out in chapter three, n. 61, it is a controversial issue in subatomic physics whether the principle of locality still holds in the wake of Bell's Theorem and its experimental testing by Alain Aspect and others. It may be possible, in other words, to distinguish between causal interactions traveling at the speed of light and "influences" on a given field of activity as a result of widely separated events happening therein which have the effect of instantly reconfiguring the basic structure of the field. If such non-local "influences" can be said to exist, then the sheer expanse of the physical universe is not in itself an impediment to its being at the same time conceived as a unified whole, a single all-comprehensive field of activity. Cf. on this point Henry Stapp, "Einstein Time and Process Time," in *Physics and the Ultimate Significance of Time*, ed. David Ray Griffin (Albany, N.Y.: State University of New York Press, 1986), 264-69.

Ironically, of course, the varied ways in which human beings conceive the unity of the world process each and all contribute to the de facto unity of the world process here and now as something that in principle they can never comprehend. Whitehead's dictum, in other words, that no actual entity can be conscious of its own satisfaction[96] implicitly distinguishes between how an actual entity views itself and the world to which it belongs and what it de facto accomplishes with its contemporaries in bringing about an objective state of affairs through their mutual interrelation. This, as I see it, is the revolutionary character of Whitehead's notion of society when properly understood. From one perspective, objectivity is the result of sustained intersubjectivity, that is, an intensive interplay of related actual entities over an extended period of time.[97] But from another perspective, the operation of intersubjectivity at any given moment always presupposes an established objective state of affairs created by the interplay of earlier actual entities. Intersubjectivity and objectivity thus mutually condition one another, with each serving as the ground for the other from a different perspective.[98]

6. William Desmond

Finally, William Desmond, in his recently published book *Being and the Between,* likewise deals with the philosophical issues attending a metaphysics of intersubjectivity, albeit from a different perspective than that taken by myself and the various authors cited above. He begins with the classical question: "What is being? What does it mean to be?"[99] His response is that there are four "senses" of being: univocal, equivocal, dialectical, and metaxological. The last of these best corresponds in his mind to "the between," that is, both the tran-

96. Whitehead, *Process and Reality,* 85: "No actual entity can be conscious of its own satisfaction; for such knowledge would be a component in the process, and would thereby alter the satisfaction."
97. Whitehead, *Process and Reality,* 34.
98. Cf. my article, "Authentic Subjectivity and Genuine Objectivity," *Horizons* 11 (1984): 290-303.
99. William Desmond, *Being and the Between* (Albany, N.Y.: State University of New York Press, 1995), 3.

scendent source and the immanent context for the dynamic interplay of finite entities in this world (somewhat akin, therefore, to the "vertical" dimension of my own metaphysics of universal intersubjectivity). In the following paragraphs I will first elaborate on the different senses of being according to Desmond and then briefly sketch the basic features of his metaxological metaphysics, indicating points of agreement and disagreement with my own system of thought in chapters four and five of this book.

The univocal sense of being, says Desmond, has a long history, dating back to the philosophies of Plato and Aristotle. Plato, for example, saw that Becoming is intelligible provided that the things that become participate in their ideal forms.[100] Similarly, Aristotle stipulated that to be is to be a determinate reality.[101] The inherent weakness of this approach to being, of course, is that it ignores the fullness of being, specifically, the residual indeterminacy and latent equivocality within and among beings. Nature, for example, as a process of becoming is in itself indeterminate and therefore equivocal: "For becoming to be becoming, there is an indeterminacy at work in the between, in the interstices between fixed determinations."[102] Especially is this true of human beings as, in Desmond's words, "the acme of equivocity."[103] Even to ourselves we are a mystery, as is manifest in the phenomenon of self-deception where we implicitly know and yet refuse to admit that we are deceiving ourselves.[104]

If, then, subjectivity is in large measure the reason for the existence of ambiguity and equivocity in human life, then subjectivity in another guise should provide the answer to the problem. Here Desmond introduces the dialectical sense of being. After acknowledging that the notion of dialectic has a long history, dating back to Zeno and Plato, he focuses primarily on the speculative dialectic of Hegel, wherein transcendental subjectivity, namely, thought thinking itself, overcomes ambiguity and equivocity through a dialectical process of self-mediation. Every living being, to be sure, undergoes this dialectic of self-mediation in a practical way through interaction with its envi-

100. Desmond, *Being and the Between*, 51.
101. Desmond, *Being and the Between*, 52.
102. Desmond, *Being and the Between*, 90.
103. Desmond, *Being and the Between*, 106.
104. Desmond, *Being and the Between*, 109.

ronment.[105] But in a human being this process of self-mediation can and should take place, above all, in the self-transcending activity of thought as it comes to terms with the world around it. Other human beings, however, are likewise engaged in their own processes of mediated self-identity and thus cannot be reduced to logical moments in one's own search. Thus the dialectical sense of being inevitably gives way to the metaxological. Seeking to pin down the elusive reality of the between, Desmond comments: "It is a being mindfully there for the other as other, and not for the self itself. It goes toward the other, it delivers itself to the other; and this making itself available for the other is its communication of itself to the other."[106] Such an "agapeic" mindset is ultimately derivative from the transcendent reality which is the origin of being and the between but it is effective only insofar as it is mediated to all finite entities within the between.

With these four "senses" of being in hand, Desmond then in the second part of his book sets forth the rudiments of his new metaphysics. The first two topics to be considered are "origin" and "creation." With the term "origin" he makes reference to the transcendent reality noted above. The origin is the One, but not in the univocal sense of an "inert self-sameness" since it must have "the power to originate beyond itself."[107] It is likewise a process of becoming, a creative indeterminacy giving rise to a community of determinate finite beings to which it stands in relation. In the metaxological sense of being, the One is agapeic being: "A movement of creative origination that goes forth from itself, from its own surplus, but it does not go forth for the sake of itself; it offers the other being, for the sake of the other."[108] "Creation," on the other hand, is the collective Other which thus has being for itself apart from the One.[109] Creation is "a middle world between the origin and the nothingness out of which it has been brought into being; a middle world that lacks absolute being, yet is not nothing."[110]

105. Desmond, *Being and the Between*, 147.
106. Desmond, *Being and the Between*, 197.
107. Desmond, *Being and the Between*, 236.
108. Desmond, *Being and the Between*, 261.
109. Desmond, *Being and the Between*, 269.
110. Desmond, *Being and the Between*, 293. Cf. above, chapter four, Kitaro Nishida's description of Absolute Nothingness and Jorge Nobo's and my own de-

The next two topics for consideration are "things" and "intelligibilities." Things, says Desmond, are "certain determinate happenings of the power of being" that come to be for themselves.[111] Hence, they owe their existence both to the power of being and to their own self-determining activity.[112] The question of intelligibility arises as one probes the relations between things. Here Desmond makes clear that he is opposed to intelligibility understood as a human construct, an expression of the will to power on the part of human beings; rather, intelligibility is ultimately derivative from the One as the transcendent ground of both possibility and actuality in the world of creation. This is, however, not another instance of "logocentrism," since the One as primordial source of possibility, for example, merely sets forth the contours for the concrete realization of possibilities by things themselves.[113]

The next two topics, "selves" and "communities," further specify what Desmond means by the metaxological sense of being. For while the self regularly expresses itself in what is other than itself (e.g., in various forms of work or artistic production),[114] it ultimately finds its fulfillment in the other-seeking of the metaxological self. Such a call to agapeic self-giving is enabled, of course, only in virtue of the self's relation to the One as the transcendent ground of its existence and activity. Community, on the other hand, "is the very milieu in which self-surpassing and transcendence come to form and fruit."[115] Personal growth for human beings thus involves a gradual progression from purely self-interested participation in community to unselfish service of others in community. "This agapeic self-transcendence into the between is not a de-centering so much as an *excentering* of self. For the self is still a cen-

---

scription of the all-encompassing ontogenetic matrix as operative within the world of creation.

111. Desmond, *Being and the Between*, 299.

112. Desmond, *Being and the Between*, 307.

113. Desmond, *Being and the Between*, 341: "Intelligibility is not incompatible with a certain openness in creation. We find a togetherness of structure and free indeterminacy; and as things become more ontologically complex, their intelligibility lets open a greater play of free indeterminacy."

114. Desmond, *Being and the Between*, 398-400.

115. Desmond, *Being and the Between*, 417.

ter, even when it makes its original energy of being available for the other; it is centered eccentrically."[116]

The final two topics addressed by Desmond are the traditional metaphysical transcendentals: truth and goodness. They, too, attain their ultimate meaning and value in the metaxological sense of being. Truth, for example, is conventionally understood in terms of the correspondence of the mind to reality.[117] But in the end one must move to the metaxological understanding of truth in which individuals through ongoing dialogue share their separate understandings of the truth in question and acknowledge the One as the transcendent source and ground of truth.[118] Similarly, evil as "the equivocality of the good,"[119] is ultimately overcome only when we reflect on the transcendent origin of good, the patience of the One (or God) to bear with the presence of evil out of respect for the freedom of the evildoer.[120] Agapeic love or self-sacrificing service of the other in the midst of real or apparent evil is thus the metaxological form of the good which is available to human beings only when it is gratefully received as a gift from the transcendent source of goodness, agapeic being itself.[121]

A critique of Desmond's scheme should first acknowledge its imaginative scope and depth of insight. But, insofar as he writes largely from a phenomenological perspective, using examples out of ordinary life to make his point, one could object that his scheme would be even more persuasive if it were more firmly anchored in an already existing metaphysical tradition. Like myself, he clearly has a high regard for the classical metaphysical tradition, above all, with its focus on the transcendence of God to creation. At the same time,

116. Desmond, *Being and the Between,* 453.
117. Desmond, *Being and the Between,* 467.
118. Desmond, *Being and the Between,* 494: "The call of truth is emergent in dialogue. It comes to pass in a plurivocal process. There is more than one voice seeking and speaking; the truth pluralizes itself in these many voices. . . . Truth pluralizes itself, not because it is the fragmentation of a one into a dispersed many, but because there is transcendence to it that can never be exhausted by any finite one or determinate unity." Cf. also 501: "The ultimate metaphysical truth is in the agapeic origin that opens up the promise of truth in the difference between itself and creation."
119. Desmond, *Being and the Between,* 520.
120. Desmond, *Being and the Between,* 538.
121. Desmond, *Being and the Between,* 540-46.

with his insistence on things as "open wholes" engaged in a process of "selving" and on communities as open-ended processes for the dynamic interrelation of human "selves," he is implicitly at work on a metaphysics of becoming, possibly even a metaphysics of universal intersubjectivity such as I have proposed in this book, without explicitly admitting this to be the case. His principal dialogue-partner is clearly Hegel because of the latter's mastery of the dialectical approach to being. While Desmond makes numerous positive references to Whitehead's metaphysics, he does not declare himself a student of Whitehead even though so much of the latter's thought is quite congenial to what he himself says about becoming and relationality. I suspect that his reserve here is due to the purely immanent function of the concept of God in Whitehead's metaphysics; by Whitehead's own admission, God needs the world for the divine becoming as much as the world needs God for its becoming.[122] A trinitarian reconception of Whitehead's God, such as I have attempted in these pages and in earlier publications, however, should restore the transcendence of the triune God to creation and make room for Desmond's conception of God as the agapeic servant of being.[123] The Thomistic doctrine of the three divine persons as "subsistent relations" vis-à-vis one another,[124] for example, could easily be reinterpreted to mean that those same persons exercise perfect self-giving or agapeic love first toward one another and then conjointly toward all their creatures so as to incorporate the latter, wherever possible, into their own divine communitarian life. This would seem to be an even richer possible explanation of the notion of the between than Desmond himself provides.

B. Concluding Remarks

Almost inevitably, a survey of different authors on a given topic will tend to focus on relatively minor points of difference instead of the

122. Whitehead, *Process and Reality*, 348.

123. Desmond, *Being and the Between*, 537. N.B.: Here, too, Desmond's obvious reference with the term "erotic sovereign" is to God in Hegel's philosophy rather than in Whitehead's.

124. Thomas Aquinas *Summa Theologiae* I, Q. 29, art. 4, resp.

broad areas of agreement which link them in a common intellectual enterprise. In these concluding paragraphs, I will try to address that potential deficiency. As I see it, all of the authors surveyed respect the metaphysical tradition of the West even as they see the need to rethink that tradition in the light of problems raised by modernity. In that sense, they are one and all, myself included, "late moderns" rather than "postmoderns" in the sense specified by Paul Lakeland at the beginning of this chapter. That is, they wish to correct the tradition, not to reject it altogether. One way in which that tradition should be corrected is, in the view of most of them, a careful rethinking of the classical approach to the relationship of the One and the Many. Where classical and early modern metaphysics took it for granted that the One is to be understood univocally as either God in relation to creation or the individual self in relation to the objects of experience, each of the authors cited above made clear in his or her own way that the One must be an internally differentiated reality composed of interrelated parts or members. This is not to imply that all of them endorse a trinitarian understanding of God and the God-world relationship like Colin Gunton and myself. But they all agree that relationality is key to the new understanding of the One. For some (e.g., Schrag and Neville), this means that the One is a transcendent activity linking individual finite entities to one another within the cosmos. For others (Desmond, Griffin, Gunton, and I), the One is both unifying cosmic activity and transcendent individual entity, albeit from different perspectives.

For that same reason, in my judgment all the authors cited above share with me the conviction that Being is intrinsically social, that is, that individual entities exist only in virtue of their dynamic interrelation with other individual entities. One of my major differences with David Griffin as a fellow Whiteheadian, to be sure, is that societies of actual occasions as well as the actual occasions themselves should be counted among the final real things of which the world is made up, hence that societies possess an ontological unity proper to themselves, even if that unity is mediated through the interrelated agencies of their constituent actual occasions. But he and I both agree with the other authors cited above that the meaning and value of the individual entity can only be properly understood if account is taken of its social context and its dynamic relation to other individual entities.

Still another point on which we all agree is that Becoming is equiprimordial with Being; neither holds an ontological priority over the other. One cannot understand Being apart from a process of Becoming, and one cannot understand Becoming except in terms of successive stages of Being. Even the being of God, therefore, has to be understood dynamically, at least in terms of an ongoing relation with creation, itself understood as a cosmic process. Furthermore, for those of us who embrace a trinitarian understanding of God, the strictly intradivine reality of God can and should be understood dynamically in terms of the unchanging but still continuous relations of the three divine persons to one another even apart from the reality of creation. God as agapeic being *par excellence* is thus manifest in the total self-giving of the divine persons to one another as well as in their conjoint self-giving to their creatures in and through the cosmic process.

Given such a broad range of agreement on basic metaphysical issues with these other authors, what I have tried to do in this book is to use a somewhat modified understanding of Whitehead's process-relational metaphysics as a way to systematize and further organize these same controlling insights into the nature of reality. In that respect, I have been guided by Nancey Murphy's proposal, mentioned earlier in this chapter, that the truth and objectivity of theories in both the sciences and humanities are best assessed in a postmodern context in terms of their relation to major intellectual traditions, especially when the latter are understood to be "research programs" jointly undertaken by many individuals over an extended period of time. As a result, in addressing what I saw as an implicit paradigm shift in contemporary Roman Catholic theology toward inter-subjectivity as a model for understanding the Trinity and the God-world relationship, I consciously tried to rethink Whitehead's process-relational metaphysics so as to present it as a metaphysics of universal intersubjectivity which could support and further specify similar efforts at an intersubjective model for the God-world relationship as laid out by Karl Rahner and other Roman Catholic theologians with a background in trinitarian theology. Moreover, this did not demand a major rethinking of Whitehead's intellectual legacy, but only, as noted above, a modification or expansion of his own thinking on the nature of societies as aggregates of actual occasions controlled by a "common element of form."

Chapters two and three of the book were dedicated to the task of dealing with potential objections to such a metaphysical scheme even before its actual presentation in chapters four and five. For if there are good reasons to think that language (above all, metaphorical language) can liberate human beings to see the world differently and to express these new insights to one another with some measure of self-confidence, and if even Jacques Derrida as the foremost deconstructionist of the late twentieth century can be said to be implicitly "doing metaphysics" in his own unconventional way, then a modest sketch or bare outline of a metaphysics of universal intersubjectivity would seem to be a risk worth taking. I presented it in terms of contrasting dimensions (vertical and horizontal) for two reasons. First of all, with reference to the horizontal dimension of a metaphysics of intersubjectivity, I thought it necessary to point out that intersubjectivity is not exhausted by a vast network of I-Thou relationships. For not only do individuals have impact on other individuals, but groups *qua* groups impact on one another, sometimes positively, but other times negatively. Hence, some form of systems theory seemed to be necessary to supplement what Whitehead himself said about the interaction of societies of actual occasions on one another in *Process and Reality* and elsewhere. The reasons for inclusion of a vertical dimension to a metaphysics of universal intersubjectivity were more subtle. Among contemporary Western philosophers, only William Desmond with his extended reflection on being and the between seemed in my judgment to grasp the significance of the ontological "place" or context for exchange between different subjects of experience. I chose the Japanese Buddhist philosopher Kitaro Nishida, however, partly out of a desire to introduce an interreligious, transcultural dimension into the discussion, and partly because Nishida's analysis of "the place of Absolute Nothingness" lent itself so easily to comparison with what Jorge Nobo and I refer to as the ontogenetic matrix for the existence and activity of actual entities within a modified version of Whitehead's metaphysics. In any event, the vertical dimension of a metaphysics of intersubjectivity is in my judgment at least as important, if not even more important, than the horizontal dimension in gradually working out the details of such a scheme.

Finally, in the present chapter I once again heeded the admonition of Nancey Murphy that theories in philosophy and theology should be considered as extensions or further developments of already existing intellectual traditions or research programs; hence, that one should present one's theory in full awareness of other alternatives as presented either by colleagues in the same intellectual tradition or by colleagues in rival traditions which address the same basic issues. One has to legitimate, in other words, one's novel interpretation of an existing tradition in the light of what one perceives to be changing circumstances and then indicate how with such a change one's own tradition fares better than its rivals in meeting the demands of the new situation. Yet, as Murphy, quoting Alasdair MacIntyre, comments, "[n]o one at any stage can ever rule out the future possibility of their present beliefs and judgments being shown to be inadequate in a variety of ways."[125] Above all, in speculative theology where imagination (rather than factual evidence) plays such a key role, one should never forget that all such claims to superiority or "unsurpassability" on the part of individuals for their theories are eminently fallible and thus almost certainly will be set aside with the ongoing development of the discipline in question.

Certainly I myself am fully aware of the fallibility of the metaphysical scheme which I have presented in these pages. Yet I offer it to the broader academic community both because I am relatively confident of its internal consistency and coherence as a response to the problems posed by contemporary postmodernism and because in my judgment it meets a need for a rethinking of the metaphysical presuppositions of their religious beliefs about God and the God-world relationship on the part of many Roman Catholics and like-minded Protestants. As I mentioned in chapter one, I do not believe that the otherwise very impressive work of intellectual giants like Karl Rahner and Bernard Lonergan within the Roman Catholic community goes far enough in working out a full-scale metaphysics or cosmology as opposed to a theological anthropology for addressing the theoretical issues raised by the current understanding of the God-world relationship. Here, as I see it, is where Whitehead's process-relational metaphysics could be invaluable in helping Roman Catholics and Protestants alike to make that paradigm shift to a new

125. Cf. above, n. 37.

metaphysics based on principles of becoming and relationality rather than to rely on the classical metaphysics of being with its more "timeless" approach to reality.

In any event, what I have presented above should be seen as a research program for the future which is itself grounded in the more comprehensive intellectual tradition of process-relational metaphysics. My hope is that others will see fit to develop further the project of a metaphysics of universal intersubjectivity, above all in connection with the problematic of the God-world relationship. In that sense, I would be honored to see my own theory surpassed by someone who took it seriously enough to work out its implications for a future, even more articulate system of metaphysics.

Glossary of Technical Terms

Actual Entity: A submicroscopic subject of experience which exists only for an instant but in that interval makes a self-constituting *decision* as to what it is to be. Gathered into *societies* of varying degrees of complexity (see below), actual entities constitute the macroscopic world of inanimate things, plants, animals (including human beings), even communities and entire environments.

Actual Occasion: Another term for an *actual entity* but with emphasis on its event-like character. Whitehead and Hartshorne differ on whether God should be conceived as a single ever-developing actual entity or a *society* of *personally-ordered* actual occasions (see below).

Causal Efficacy: In Whitehead's philosophy, the more primitive and fundamental mode of perception in which data from past actual occasions are transmitted on a feeling-level to a *concrescing actual occasion* in a massive but nevertheless vague and inarticulate manner.

Common Element of Form: An objective pattern of intelligibility simultaneously present in the self-constitution of all the member *actual occasions* of a given *society* and thus constituting them as this macroscopic reality rather than that.

Consequent Nature of God: God's *prehension* of everything that has happened thus far within the cosmic process. Within a trinitarian understanding of God, the three divine persons' prehension of what has just

218

come into existence both in terms of their own interrelatedness as a divine community and with respect to events taking place in creation.

Concrescence of an Actual Entity: The unitary process of self-constitution for an *actual entity* whereby it synthesizes multiple data from the external world so as to come to a *decision* with respect to its own self-constitution as an entity emergent out of that world and yet participant in it.

Creativity: The ultimate principle of existence and activity both for the self-constitution of *actual occasions* (including the divine persons at any given moment) and for the co-constitution of the various *societies* to which they belong (up to and including the *society* of the divine persons as one God).

Decision: Literally a "cutting away" of irrelevant possibilities for the self-constitution of a given *actual entity* so that it becomes this rather than that entity. It is not simply to be equated with conscious human choices since normally an entire series of subconscious *decisions* is involved in making a single conscious human choice. Moreover, all *actual entities* whatsoever, even those making up inanimate objects, make *decisions* with respect to their self-constitution unconsciously.

Eternal Objects: Objective possibilities of existence and activity for *actual entities* which are to be found in their fullness (as conceptually ordered to one another) within the *primordial nature* of God and in a more limited though concrete way within the world of past *actual entities*.

Initial aim: The initial phase of the *subjective aim* governing the *concrescence* of an *actual entity*; within the trinitarian context of this book, a vital impulse from God the "Father" empowering a finite *actual entity* both to exist as an individual subject of experience and, together with its contemporaries, to co-constitute a *society* according to a given *common element of form*.

Logocentrism: As understood by Jacques Derrida and other contemporary philosophers, the tendency within classical metaphysics to locate the order and intelligibility for a given set of terms (or "signifiers") in a "transcendental signified," i.e., in an object of thought which stands outside the system of terms to be thus defined as their *"Logos"* or objective principle of intelligibility.

Ontogenetic Matrix: In simplest terms, a matrix is something within which

219

something else originates or develops; an ontogenetic matrix is that ultimate context or field within which everything determinate (even the divine persons of the Christian doctrine of the Trinity, as I see it) originates and is sustained in existence. On the other hand, as a context or field for the interrelation of *actual entities*, the ontogenetic matrix has no independent reality or reason to exist apart from those same *actual entities*.

Prehension: Literally, the grasping by a *concrescing actual entity* of data (both physical and conceptual) outside itself in view of its own self-constitution. Physical prehensions have to do with physical data, i.e., past actual entities in their concreteness; conceptual prehensions, with conceptual data, i.e., *eternal objects* either embodied in past actual entities or mediated to the *actual entity* by God the "Father" through an *initial aim.* Intellectual prehensions or "intellectual feelings" are only available to those higher-level *actual occasions* which can prehend the difference between settled fact and imaginative possibility and thereby attain some measure of (self-)consciousness.

Presentational Immediacy: The more sophisticated and complex of the two modes of perception for Whitehead in which data from past actual occasions are presented as spatially located in the imagination with sharp and precise features but without affect, i.e., feeling-tone or emotion.

Primordial Nature of God: The ordered relevance of all *eternal objects* to one another as grasped by God (in this book, the three divine persons) in a comprehensive vision and progressively employed by God (the divine persons) in guiding the world of creation in its ongoing development.

Process: A dynamic unity in totality of functioning parts or members such that the whole is more than the sum of its parts and yet does not exist except in and through those same parts or members; moreover, a temporally successive totality wherein all past moments of the reality in question are effectively recapitulated in each new moment here and now coming into being. As such, this term applies to the community of the three divine persons of Christian belief, the created universe as a whole, and likewise all its member *societies* and subsocieties.

Social Ontology: A metaphysical vision of reality in which *societies* or *structured fields of activity* are the conventional units of reality (the equivalent of "substances" in classical metaphysics). Within this metaphysical vision, to be sure, *actual entities* are the ultimate constituents of these *societies* or *structured fields of activity*. But, inasmuch as *actual entities* by definition so rapidly come and go, *societies* or *structured fields of activity* are viewed as the "building blocks" or enduring constituents of reality (both physical and spiritual).

Society: Any non-random grouping or "nexus" of actual entities which perdures through time and is governed by a *common element of form;* in this sense, a *process* as defined above. Corpuscular societies exist as extended both in space and time (material realities); personally-ordered societies exist in time alone (the soul or unifying principle in human beings and other living beings).

Structured field of activity: In this book, the model for *societies,* both corpuscular and personally ordered; thus, that which is extended through space and over time as the process-relational equivalent of the classical notion of "substance."

Structured Society: A *society* constituted, not by *actual entities* directly, but by subsocieties; frequently governed by one subsociety which is "regnant" over all the others (e.g., the soul within human beings and other higher-level organisms), but sometimes the result of the interrelationship of coequal subsocieties (as in human communities or natural environments and in the divine community).

Subjective Aim: The teleological principle operative within each *actual entity* which governs its process of *concrescence.* Though set in motion by the *initial aim* of God, it nevertheless represents the element of spontaneity or freedom within the *actual entity* which allows it to be itself through its own *decision.*

Superject: Whitehead's term for an *actual entity* which has completed its process of *concrescence* or self-constitution and is now available for *prehension* by subsequent actual entities. As such it has lost subjectivity, understood as the power of internal self-constitution, but gained objectivity in that it can now be prehended in terms of both the formal structure and intensive feeling which it generated through its antecedent process of self-constitution.

Bibliography

A. Books

Aquinas, Thomas. *Summa Theologiae.* Translated from the Latin by the Fathers of the English Dominican Province. New York: Benziger Brothers, 1947.

Aristotle. *The Basic Works of Aristotle.* Edited by Richard McKeon. New York: Random House, 1941.

Ashbrook, James B., and Carol Rausch Albright. *The Humanizing Brain: Where Religion and Science Meet.* Cleveland: Pilgrim Press, 1997.

Barbour, Ian. *Religion and Science: Historical and Contemporary Issues.* San Francisco: HarperCollins, 1997.

Bernstein, Richard. *Beyond Objectivism and Relativism: Science, Hermeneutics, and Praxis.* Philadelphia: University of Pennsylvania Press, 1983.

Braaten, Jane. *Habermas's Critical Theory of Society.* Albany, N.Y.: State University of New York Press, 1991.

Bracken, Joseph A., S.J. *Society and Spirit: A Trinitarian Cosmology.* Cranbury, N.J.: Associated University Presses, 1991.

————. *The Divine Matrix: Creativity as Link between East and West.* Maryknoll, N.Y.: Orbis Books, 1995.

Bracken, Joseph A., S.J., and Marjorie Hewitt Suchocki, eds. *Trinity in Process: A Relational Theology of God.* New York: Continuum, 1997.

Brown, Warren S., Nancey Murphy, and H. Newton Malony, eds. *Whatever Happened to the Soul?* Minneapolis: Fortress, 1998.

Buber, Martin. *I and Thou.* Translated by Walter Kaufmann. New York: Scribner's, 1970.

Caputo, John D. *The Prayers and Tears of Jacques Derrida: Religion without Religion.* Bloomington, Ind.: Indiana University Press, 1997.
———, ed. *Deconstruction in a Nutshell.* New York: Fordham University Press, 1997.
Carter, Robert E. *The Nothingness Beyond God: An Introduction to the Philosophy of Kitaro Nishida.* 2nd ed. St. Paul, Minn.: Paragon House, 1997.
Chauvet, Louis-Marie. *Symbol and Sacrament: A Sacramental Reinterpretation of Christian Existence.* Translated by Patrick Madigan, S.J., and Madeleine Beaumont. Collegeville, Minn.: Liturgical Press, 1995.
Clayton, Philip D. *God and Contemporary Science.* Edinburgh: Edinburgh University Press, 1997.
Copleston, Frederick. *A History of Philosophy.* Vol. 2. Garden City, N.Y.: Doubleday Image Book, 1962.
Derrida, Jacques. *Of Grammatology.* Translated by G. C. Spivak. Baltimore: Johns Hopkins University Press, 1976.
Desmond, William. *Being and the Between.* Albany, N.Y.: State University of New York Press, 1995.
Fagg, Lawrence. *Electromagnetism and the Sacred: At the Frontier of Spirit and Matter.* New York: Continuum, 1999.
Farmer, Ronald L. *Beyond the Impasse: The Promise of a Process Hermeneutic.* Macon, Ga.: Mercer University Press, 1997.
Ford, Lewis S. *The Emergence of Whitehead's Metaphysics 1925-1929.* Albany, N.Y.: State University of New York Press, 1984.
Franklin, Stephen. *Speaking from the Depths: A Hermeneutical Metaphysics of Propositions, Experience, Symbolism, Language and Religion.* Grand Rapids: Eerdmans, 1990.
Gadamer, Hans-Georg. *Truth and Method.* Translated by Joel Weinsheimer and Donald G. Marshall. Second revised edition. New York: Crossroad, 1992.
Gelpi, Donald L., S.J. *Varieties of Transcendental Experience: A Study in Constructive Postmodernism.* Collegeville, Minn.: Liturgical Press, 2000.
Gilson, Etienne. *The Unity of Philosophical Experience.* Westminster, Md.: Four Courts Press, 1982.
Gray, Donald P. *The One and the Many: Teilhard de Chardin's Vision of Unity.* New York: Herder & Herder, 1969.
Griffin, David Ray, William A. Beardslee, and Joe Holland. *Varieties of Postmodern Theology.* Albany, N.Y.: State University of New York Press, 1989.
Griffin, David Ray. *God and Religion in the Postmodern World: Essays in Postmodern Theology.* Albany, N.Y.: State University of New York Press, 1989.
Gunton, Colin E. *The One, the Three and the Many: God, Creation and the Culture of Modernity.* Cambridge: Cambridge University Press, 1993.

223

———. *The Triune Creation: A Historical and Systematic Study.* Grand Rapids: Eerdmans, 1998.

Habermas, Jürgen. *The Theory of Communicative Action.* Translated by Thomas McCarthy. 2 vols. Boston: Beacon Press, 1984 & 1987.

Hardy, Christine. *Networks of Meaning: A Bridge between Mind and Matter.* Westport, Conn.: Praeger, 1998.

Hartshorne, Charles. *Man's Vision of God and the Logic of Theism.* Hamden, Conn.: Archon Books, 1964.

Haught, John. *God After Darwin: A Theology of Evolution.* Boulder, Colo.: Westview, 2000.

Heidegger, Martin. *The End of Philosophy.* Translated by Joan Stambaugh. New York: Harper & Row, 1973.

Herbert, Nick. *Quantum Reality: Beyond the New Physics.* New York: Doubleday, 1985.

Johnson, Elizabeth A. *She Who Is: The Mystery of God in Feminist Theological Discourse.* New York: Crossroad, 1992.

———. *Friends of God and Prophets: A Feminist Theological Reading of the Communion of Saints.* New York: Continuum, 1998.

Jones, Judith A. *Intensity: An Essay in Whiteheadian Ontology.* Nashville: Vanderbilt University Press, 1998.

Kant, Immanuel. *Critique of Pure Reason.* Translated by Norman Kemp Smith. New York: St. Martin's Press, 1965.

Kerby, Anthony Paul. *Narrative and the Self.* Bloomington, Ind.: Indiana University Press, 1991.

Kierkegaard, Søren. *Concluding Unscientific Postscript.* Translated by David F. Swenson. Princeton, N.J.: Princeton University Press, 1941.

Kim, Jaegwon. *Supervenience and Mind.* Cambridge: Cambridge University Press, 1993.

Komonchak, Joseph A. *Foundations in Ecclesiology* (Supplementary Issue of the *Lonergan Workshop Journal,* vol. 11). Edited by Fred Lawrence. Chestnut Hill, Mass.: Boston College, 1995.

LaCugna, Catherine Mowry. *God for Us: The Trinity and Christian Life.* San Francisco: Harper, 1991.

Lakeland, Paul. *Christian Identity in a Fragmented Age.* Minneapolis: Fortress, 1997.

Laszlo, Ervin. *Introduction to Systems Philosophy: Toward a New Paradigm of Contemporary Thought.* London: Gordon and Breach, 1972.

———. *The Systems View of the World: The Natural Philosophy of the New Developments in the Sciences.* New York: George Braziller, 1972.

Levinas, Emmanuel. *Totality and Infinity: An Essay on Exteriority.* Translated by Alphonso Lingis. Pittsburgh: Duquesne University Press, 1969.

———. *Otherwise than Being, or Beyond Essence.* Translated by Alphonso Lingis. The Hague: Martinus Nijhoff, 1981.

Lonergan, Bernard J. F. *Insight: A Study of Human Understanding.* London: Longmans, Green & Co., 1957.

———. *Method in Theology.* New York: Herder & Herder, 1972.

MacIntyre, Alasdair. *Whose Justice? Whose Rationality?* Notre Dame, Ind.: University of Notre Dame Press, 1988.

Magliola, Robert. *Derrida on the Mend.* West Lafayette, Ind.: Purdue University Press, 1984.

Marion, Jean-Luc. *God Without Being.* Translated by Thomas A. Carlson. Chicago: University of Chicago Press, 1995.

Murphy, Nancey. *Beyond Liberalism and Fundamentalism: How Modern and Postmodern Philosophy Set the Theological Agenda.* Valley Forge, Pa.: Trinity Press International, 1996.

———. *Anglo-American Postmodernity: Philosophical Perspectives on Science, Religion and Ethics.* Boulder, Colo.: Westview Press, 1997.

Murphy, Nancey, and George F. R. Ellis. *On the Moral Nature of the Universe: Theology, Cosmology, and Ethics.* Minneapolis: Fortress, 1996.

Neville, Robert C. *Creativity and God: A Challenge to Process Theology.* New York: Seabury, 1980.

———. *The Highroad Around Modernism.* Albany, N.Y.: State University of New York Press, 1992.

———. *Eternity and Time's Flow.* Albany, N.Y.: State University of New York Press, 1993.

Nishida, Kitaro. *Last Writings: Nothingness and the Religious World View.* Translated by David A. Dilworth. Honolulu: University of Hawaii Press, 1987.

———. *An Inquiry into the Good.* Translated by M. Abe and C. Ives. New Haven, Conn.: Yale University Press, 1990.

Nobo, Jorge. *Whitehead's Metaphysics of Extension and Solidarity.* Albany, N.Y.: State University of New York Press, 1986.

Peirce, Charles Sanders. *Collected Papers of Charles Sanders Peirce.* Edited by Charles Hartshorne and Paul Weiss. Vol. 1. Cambridge, Mass.: Harvard University Press, 1931; Vol. 5. Cambridge, Mass.: Harvard University Press, 1934; Vol. 6. Cambridge, Mass.: Harvard University Press, 1935.

Peukert, Helmut. *Science, Action, and Fundamental Theology: Toward a Theology of Communicative Action.* Translated by James Bohman. Cambridge, Mass.: MIT Press, 1984.

Polkinghorne, John. *Reason and Reality: The Relationship between Science and Theology.* Philadelphia: Trinity Press International, 1991.

———. *Belief in God in an Age of Science.* New Haven, Conn.: Yale University Press, 1998.

225

Power, David N. *Sacrament: The Language of God's Giving.* New York: Crossroad, 1999.

Purcell, Michael. *Mystery and Method: The Other in Rahner and Levinas.* Milwaukee: Marquette University Press, 1998.

Quine, Willard Van Orman. *From a Logical Point of View: Nine Logico-Philosophical Essays.* 2nd ed. New York: Harper Torchbook, 1963.

Rahner, Karl. *The Trinity.* Translated by Joseph Donceel. New York: Herder & Herder, 1970.

Ricoeur, Paul. *Interpretation Theory: Discourse and the Surplus of Meaning.* Fort Worth: Texas Christian University Press, 1976.

Rorty, Richard. *Philosophy and the Mirror of Nature.* Princeton, N.J.: Princeton University Press, 1979.

Royce, Josiah. *The Problem of Christianity.* Chicago: University of Chicago Press, 1968.

Schrag, Calvin. *The Self after Postmodernity.* New Haven, Conn.: Yale University Press, 1997.

Sellars, Wilfrid. *Science, Perception and Reality.* London: Routledge & Kegan Paul, 1963.

Suchocki, Marjorie Hewitt. *The End of Evil: Process Eschatology in Historical Context.* Albany, N.Y.: State University of New York Press, 1988.

Tallon, Andrew. *Personal Becoming.* Milwaukee: Marquette University Press, 1982.

Taylor, Charles. *Sources of the Self: The Making of Modern Identity.* Cambridge, Mass.: Harvard University Press, 1989.

Taylor, Mark C. *Deconstructing Theology.* New York: Crossroad, 1982.

———. *Erring: A Postmodern A/theology.* Chicago: University of Chicago Press, 1984.

———, ed. *Deconstruction in Context: Literature and Philosophy.* Chicago: University of Chicago Press, 1986.

Taylor, Mark Lloyd. *God Is Love: A Study in the Theology of Karl Rahner.* Missoula, Mont.: Scholars Press, 1986.

Wallack, Bradford. *The Epochal Nature of Process in Whitehead's Metaphysics.* Albany, N.Y.: State University of New York Press, 1980.

Whitehead, Alfred North. *Symbolism: Its Meaning and Effect.* New York: G. P. Putnam's Sons, 1959.

———. *Science and the Modern World.* New York: The Free Press, 1967.

———. *Adventures of Ideas.* New York: The Free Press, 1967.

———. *Process and Reality: An Essay in Cosmology.* Corrected edition edited by David Ray Griffin and Donald W. Sherburne. New York: The Free Press, 1978.

Zizioulas, John. *Being as Communion.* Crestwood, N.Y.: St. Vladimir's Seminary Press, 1985.

B. Articles

Abe, Masao. " 'Inverse Correspondence' in the Philosophy of Nishida: The Emergence of the Notion." Translated by James L. Fredericks. *International Philosophical Quarterly* 32 (1992): 325-44.

———. "Nishida's Philosophy of 'Place.' " Translated by Christopher Ives. *International Philosophical Quarterly* 28 (1988): 355-71.

———. "The Problem of 'Inverse Correspondence' in the Philosophy of Nishida: Comparing Nishida with Tanabe." Translated by James L. Fredericks. *International Philosophical Quarterly* 39 (1999): 59-76.

Baird, Marie. "Divinity and the Other: The Ethical Relation as Revelatory of God." *Église et Théologie* 30 (1999): 93-109.

Bracken, Joseph A., S.J. "Authentic Subjectivity and Genuine Objectivity." *Horizons* 11 (1984): 290-303.

———. "Energy-Events and Fields." *Process Studies* 18 (1989): 153-65.

———. "Proposals for Overcoming the Atomism within Process-Relational Metaphysics." *Process Studies* 23 (1994): 10-24.

———. "Trinity: Economic and Immanent." *Horizons* 25 (1998): 7-22.

———. "The Theology of God of Elizabeth Johnson." In *Things New and Old: Essays on the Theology of Elizabeth Johnson.* New York: Crossroad, 1999.

———. "Prehending God in and through the World." *Process Studies* 29 (2000): 4-15.

Derrida, Jacques. "Différance." In *Margins of Philosophy,* trans. by Alan Bass. Chicago: University of Chicago Press, 1982.

———. "Eating Well, or the Calculation of the Subject: An Interview with Jacques Derrida." In *Who Comes after the Subject?* edited by Eduardo Cadava, Peter Connor, and Jean-Luc Nancy, 96-119. New York: Routledge, 1991.

———. "Khora." In *On the Name,* trans. by Ian McLeod, edited by Thomas Dutoit. Stanford, Calif.: Stanford University Press, 1995.

———. "A Conversation with Jacques Derrida." In *Deconstruction in a Nutshell,* edited by John D. Caputo. New York: Fordham University Press, 1997.

Ebert, Howard. "Immutability of God: Metaphysical Inconsistency or Essential Grounding for Human Transcendence." *Philosophy and Theology* 8 (1993): 41-61.

Faber, Roland. "Trinity, Analogy, and Coherence." In *Trinity in Process: A Rela-*

tional Theology of God, edited by Joseph A. Bracken, S.J., and Marjorie Hewitt Suchocki. New York: Continuum, 1997.

Ford, Lewis. "Inclusive Occasions." In *Process in Context: Essays in Post-Whiteheadian Perspectives,* edited by Ernst Wolf-Gazo. Bern/Frankfurt: Peter Lang, 1988.

―――. "The Consequences of Prehending the Consequent Nature." *Process Studies* 27 (1998): 134-46.

Gregersen, Neils Henrik. "The Idea of Creation and the Theory of Autopoietic Processes." *Zygon* 33 (1998): 333-67.

―――. "Autopoiesis: Less than Self-Constitution, More than Self-Organization: Reply to Gilkey, McClelland and Deltete, and Brun." *Zygon* 34 (1999): 117-38.

Griffin, David Ray. "Introduction to SUNY Series in Constructive Postmodern Thought." In *Varieties of Postmodern Theology,* edited by David Ray Griffin, William A. Beardslee, and Joe Holland, xi-xiv. Albany, N.Y.: State University of New York Press, 1989.

―――. "Postmodern Theology and A/theology: A Response to Mark C. Taylor." In *Varieties of Postmodern Theology,* edited by David Ray Griffin, William A. Beardslee, and Joe Holland, 29-52. Albany, N.Y.: State University of New York Press, 1989.

―――. "A Naturalistic Trinity." In *Trinity in Process: A Relational Theology of God,* edited by Joseph A. Bracken, S.J., and Marjorie Hewitt Suchocki, 23-40. New York: Continuum, 1997.

Hartshorne, Charles. "The Compound Individual." In *Philosophical Essays for Alfred North Whitehead,* edited by F. S. C. Northrup. New York: Russell & Russell, 1936.

―――. "The Logic of Panentheism." In *Philosophers Speak of God,* edited by Charles Hartshorne and William L. Reese, 499-514. Chicago: University of Chicago Press, 1963.

Heisig, James. "Non-I and Thou: Nishida, Buber, and the Moral Consequences of Self-Actualization." *Philosophy East and West* 50 (2000): 179-207.

Hogan, Kevin. "Entering into Otherness: The Postmodern Critique of the Subject and Karl Rahner's Theological Anthropology." *Horizons* 25 (1998): 181-202.

Hurtubise, Denis. "The Enigmatic 'Passage of the Consequent Nature to the Temporal World' in *Process and Reality.*" *Process Studies* 27 (1998): 93-107.

Johnson, Elizabeth A. "Does God Play Dice? Divine Providence and Chance." *Theological Studies* 57 (1996): 3-18.

―――. "Forging Theology: A Conversation with Colleagues." In *Things New and Old: Essays on the Theology of Elizabeth A. Johnson.* New York: Cross-road, 1999.

Kim, Jaegwon. " 'Downward Causation' in Emergentism and Non-reductive Physicalism." In *Emergence or Reduction? Essays on the Prospects of Non-reductive Physicalism,* edited by Ansgar Beckermann, Hans Flohr, and Jaegwon Kim. Berlin: W. de Gruyter, 1992.

Marion, Jean-Luc. "Saint Thomas d'Aquin et l'onto-théo-logie." *Revue Thomiste* 95 (1995): 31-66.

Min, Anselm Kyonsuk. "Solidarity of Others in the Body of Christ: A New Theological Paradigm." *Toronto Journal of Theology* 14 (1998): 239-54.

―――. "Toward a Dialectic of Totality and Infinity: Reflections on Emmanuel Levinas." *Journal of Religion* 78 (1998): 571-92.

Nagami, Isamu. "Whitehead's Thought and Metaphoric Language." Paper delivered at International Whitehead Conference, Claremont, Calif., August, 1998.

Nobo, Jorge. "Experience, Eternity, and Primordiality: Steps Towards a Metaphysics of Creative Solidarity." *Process Studies* 26 (1997): 171-204.

―――. "From Creativity to Ontogenetic Matrix." *Process Thought* 8 (1998): 90-79. (In *Process Thought,* a Japanese journal, pages are numbered backwards by Western standards.)

Oomen, Palmyre M. F. "The Prehensibility of God's Consequent Nature." *Process Studies* 27 (1998): 108-33.

―――. "Consequences of Prehending God's Consequent Nature in a Different Key." *Process Studies* 27 (1998): 329-31.

Pedraja, Luis. "Whitehead, Deconstructionism and Postmodernism." *Process Studies* 28 (1999): 68-84.

Russell, Robert J., and Wesley Wildman. "Chaos: A Mathematical Introduction with Philosophical Reflections." In *Chaos and Complexity,* edited by Robert John Russell, Nancey Murphy, and Arthur R. Peacocke. Berkeley, Calif.: Center for Theology and the Natural Sciences, 1995.

Stapp, Henry. "Einstein Time and Process Time." In *Physics and the Ultimate Significance of Time,* edited by David Ray Griffin, 264-69. Albany, N.Y.: State University of New York Press, 1986.

Voskuil, Duane. "Discussion of Palmyre M. F. Oomen's Recent Essays in *Process Studies.*" *Process Studies* 28 (1999): 130-36.

Yagi, Seiichi. "Buddhist-Christian Dialogue in Japan: Varieties of Immediate Experience." *Buddhist-Christian Studies* 14 (1994): 11-22.

Wright, John H., S.J. "Divine Knowledge and Human Freedom: The God Who Dialogues." *Theological Studies* 38 (1977): 450-77.

Index

180-85, 186, 195, 200, 202, 213

Habermas, Jürgen, 11, 47, 50, 53, 64-68, 71-73, 132, 137-46, 151, 194
Hardy, Christine, 59n.34, 168n.20
Hartshorne, Charles, 7, 47, 94, 99-100, 101, 104, 135-36, 139-40, 167, 173-75, 199
Hegel, G. W. F., 79, 82n.15, 114, 190, 206, 208, 212
Heidegger, Martin, 1, 28, 31, 33-34, 35, 50, 89, 94, 201n.75
Heisig, James, 111n.6

I-Thou relation, 109, 111n.6, 124, 193, 215
indeterminacy, 204-5, 208, 209
individuals, composite, 136-40, 167; compound individuals, 136, 140, 167
infinite, 27, 42-43, 77, 79, 109, 118-19, 194
intersubjectivity, metaphysics of, 4, 9-11, 15-47, 53, 62, 70-71, 75, 79, 91-92, 105, 109-30, 131-55, 157, 177-78, 185, 190, 191-93, 195, 201, 207-12, 213, 216-17. *See also* subjectivity
inverse correspondence, 116-19, 122, 127, 129. *See also* absolute contradictory self-identity

Johnson, Elizabeth, 18, 20, 38-45, 157, 204n.87
Jones, Judith, 152-54

Kant, Immanuel, 17, 47, 60, 109, 190, 194
Kierkegaard, Søren, 181, 194
Kim, Jaegwon, 161-62
Komonchak, Joseph, 75n.76

LaCugna, Catherine, 17-18, 38-41, 157
Lakeland, Paul, 179-80, 213
language, 10, 49-75, 79, 86-94, 141, 143-44, 186-87, 192-93, 197, 215; icon, 26-27; idol, 26-27; metaphor, 54-56, 165, 215; narrative/story, 192-93; symbol, 55-64
Laszlo, Ervin, 2, 11, 132-37, 151, 170n.22
Levinas, Emmanuel, 77, 109, 193-94
life-world, 65-66, 138-39, 140-45
logocentrism, 1, 75, 81, 86, 94-103, 199, 201, 210
Lonergan, Bernard, 11, 17, 46n.92, 47, 68-72, 74, 105, 216

MacIntyre, Alasdair, 187, 189-90, 216
Magliola, Robert, 102n.81
Malony, Newton, 170-71
Marion, Jean-Luc, 24-31, 36, 43, 157, 195
matrix, ontogenetic, 114, 117n.21, 119n.26, 123-28, 146, 149-51, 172, 174n.32, 175, 176, 194-95, 205, 209n.110, 215. *See also* Nothingness, Absolute
McCarthy, Thomas, 64
Min, Anselm, 102n.81, 145-46
mind-brain connection, 11, 157, 159, 160, 161-63, 164, 168-71, 169n.21, 173, 177-78, 186
model/analogy, 53, 56, 165
Murphy, Nancey, 6, 145n.39, 160-61, 164n.15, 170-71, 185-91, 214, 216

Nagami, Isamu, 52-54
Neville, Robert, 8, 201-7, 213
Nietzsche, Friedrich, 28, 89-90
Nishida, Kitaro, 10, 55, 110-20,